UnPresidented

JON SOPEL

UnPresidented

Politics, pandemics and the race
that Trumped all others

2

BBC Books, an imprint of Ebury Publishing
20 Vauxhall Bridge Road,
London SW1V 2SA

BBC Books is part of the Penguin Random House group of companies
whose addresses can be found at global.penguinrandomhouse.com

First published by BBC Books in 2021
Paperback edition published by BBC Books in 2021

www.penguin.co.uk

A CIP catalogue record for this book is available from the British Library

ISBN 9781785944420

Typeset in Sabon Next by seagulls.net
Printed and bound in Great Britain by Clays Ltd, Elcograf S.p.A.

The authorised representative in the EEA is Penguin Random House Ireland,
Morrison Chambers, 32 Nassau Street, Dublin D02 YH68

Penguin Random House is committed to a sustainable future for our
business, our readers and our planet. This book is made
from Forest Stewardship Council® certified paper.

To Debby and David Horsford

And Debby Baum

People who kept me sane during Covid

Contents

Prologue

What follows is the diary I kept during probably the most tumultuous presidential election in American history, whose repercussions are still reverberating, and whose long-term consequences are still playing out. It is quite unlike the book I originally intended to write and had discussed with my publishers. I had envisaged an account full of planes, trains and automobiles; zigzagging across America from one campaign stop to the next, roadside motels and late-night greasy burgers, and pizza joints. The pandemic put paid to that. But a global pandemic claiming the lives of hundreds of thousands Americans was the least of it in political terms; what makes this the most tumultuous election in American history is that the incumbent refused to accept the verdict of the people. There would be no concession; no contrition; no acceptance of convention.

It would culminate in the dangerous events of 6 January, when the Trump-supporting mob violently stormed Congress as it was about to certify the victory of Joe Biden. It was an attempted insurrection that took American democracy to the brink; it was an attempted insurrection that, in the early stages at least, Donald Trump was cheering on.

The diary runs from well over a year before the election, when the President travelled to Florida to announce that he was running for a second term, and goes through to the Saturday after polling day when Joe Biden was declared the victor. In theory that should have marked the end of the story and my record of it, but with the President showing no sign of accepting the result it was clear that there was still some way to go – and much that could still happen. What the pandemic did rule out, however, was the option of just extending the period I kept my election diary. Production schedules at the printing works in times of Covid had no flexibility. What was agreed had to be stuck to. The book was scheduled to be printed before Christmas 2020, and that's what we had to stick to – even though the hardback would not cover the events leading up to the inauguration, or Trump's second impeachment.

When this election diary project was discussed with my publisher Yvonne Jacob and literary agent Rory Scarfe, we anticipated there would be the odd plot twist, that 2020 would throw up some very Trumpian surprises – but I have to confess that a global pandemic to rival the Spanish Flu, an economic downturn to match the Great Depression, and race riots to rival 1968 were things I hadn't foreseen.

At the start of 2020, my wife, Linda, and I moved out of our Georgetown house and into a much smaller apartment. She was moving back to the UK so that she could be of more help to her 93-year-old mother, and because I would be travelling incessantly for the election within the US, and could hop back and forth across the Atlantic whenever I chose, it all seemed to make sense.

That plan didn't work out so well. Everyone has had to face their own challenges and demons through this horrible period. With our son Max living in Australia with his wife, Kate, and now their daughter, Eliza; with Linda back in London with our daughter, Anna, the world has suddenly seemed – once again – a forbiddingly big and disconnected place. Not being able to see each other has been tough. But I know so many people have been through far worse.

As I write this I am in 'solitary confinement' in a five-star hotel in Sydney, locked in my room, a guard sitting outside, quarantining for

14 days ahead of seeing my son for the first time in 14 months, and getting to meet my granddaughter for the first time.

Thankfully I had some wonderful American friends in Washington during the early months of the pandemic. Debby and David Horsford have been absolute rock-stars – on the phone to suggest socially distanced walks, or sitting out in their garden for dinners six feet apart. And the other person is Debby Baum, my former next-door neighbour. She and her three daughters, Ann, Maddy and Mary Douglass, have let me join them on their walks, cycle rides and trips to their house out on the Chesapeake Bay. You have no idea how much it meant to me to be able to escape occasionally from being alone in my apartment. Thank you.

Finally, I have to thank the team. The bureau in Washington has been a really happy place to work, and thanks in large part to the bureau chief, Paul Danahar – a great boss, and a good friend. And then there's John Landy, who's been my cameraman since I arrived, seven years ago. He is a cerebral Australian (oxymoron jokes, anyone?). Not only does he shoot wonderful pictures, but will then say to me when I'm scripting in the edit suite, 'I think maybe you can phrase that better.' (The first time he did this I thought I might kill him.) Annoyingly, he invariably has a point. He is huge fun to be with, and though there have been a lot of tense moments I don't think we have once fallen out. And then there is our producer, Morgan Gisholt Minard. I had only worked with her a bit before this campaign, but she has been the best. Hard-working, creative, thinks of everything, likes a glass of good red wine. Also, Morgan has read over much of this to remind me of key bits I might have overlooked or overwritten. And the real joy of this little team: we all trust each other to do our jobs, and do them well. And we have a lot of laughs along the way.

This will be the third book that I've written since I have been in DC. History will come to its own verdict (probably a deeply divided one) on Donald Trump, and the legacy he has left the US and the world, but as a correspondent to be here, covering this period at this time has been sometimes exhausting, sometimes exasperating, sometimes exhilarating, but overwhelmingly it's been unforgettable: the wildest of rides, the journalistic assignment of a lifetime – the flavour of which I hope will come out in the pages that follow.

For this paperback edition the easiest thing would have been – simply – to bolt on my diary from the period after I stopped writing in November through to, say, inauguration day on 20 January. But given the convulsive, troubling, unique events that unfolded in America we need to take stock. And to ask one question: was American democracy – the shining city on the hill, to use the biblical reference that Americans are wont to use themselves about the exemplary nature of their democracy – taken to the brink of destruction just because of one man's inability to look himself in the mirror and say 'I lost' when all the available evidence indicated that he had?

Jon Sopel,
Sydney,
May 2021

What Happened Next

It is said that there are five stages of grief: denial, anger, bargaining, depression, and acceptance. But with Donald Trump it very quickly became clear in those sulky, raging, pouty weeks after the election that there is an additional phase. Between denial and anger there is litigation. And lots of it. Lawsuits here, there and everywhere. It shouldn't come as a surprise to anyone. It has been his MO throughout his business career. If at first you don't succeed, sue.

For the Biden team in the days after the election there was a singular focus. Ignore Donald Trump, his tweets, his provocations and his embryonic legal fight. In Bidenland they just wanted to get on with the mammoth task of putting together a cabinet, getting up to speed on key national security considerations, getting briefed by the Pentagon on troop dispositions, by the CIA on different perceived threat levels – and, perhaps most critically given the raging coronavirus numbers, getting briefed on where America stood with the fight against Covid and the readiness to roll out a vaccine.

From Trumpland, there were two narratives emerging. One version had it that Donald Trump in his heart knew that the game was up, that he had lost, but he needed time to process that, to come to terms with the reality that he was a one-term loser (and this narrative was the dominant view of the Republican Party). Let him rage and put up a fight, the argument went; show his base that he is not going quietly into the night. After that he will do what the constitution requires him to do – concede and organise a peaceful transfer of power. Just give him some space to let off steam in the meantime. It was as though these people were applying the Churchill quote about America to the outgoing president – Donald Trump can always be relied upon to do the right thing once he has exhausted all the other possibilities. But in the days and weeks immediately after the election the signs were not propitious.

In British politics a change of government happens with brutal swiftness: election Thursday night, and if you're the prime minister and you've lost, the removal van comes in on Friday morning to remove your personal effects, you wave goodbye to the civil servants – and off you go into the sunset. Meanwhile your successor is off to Buckingham Palace and by Friday lunchtime is inside Number 10 getting used to the new home on which they've just been given a five-year lease.

In the US system there is an elaborate and protracted transition. It has to be like this because the professional civil service is so much smaller than it is in the UK. Nearly all the key personnel in government departments serve at the pleasure of the president; nearly everyone is a 'special advisor'. It is also a national artefact, dating back to when the elected officials had to travel by horse and carriage – which from, say, Seattle is going to take some time.

What normally happens is that the day after the election, the president authorises an obscure official – the head of the General Services Administration – to release the funds so that the president-elect can start paying the salaries of the people who will be the key staff members dealing with defence, national security, immigration, the pandemic, the environment – and on and on. And they will then meet with the outgoing Trump officials to get briefed on all the key issues. But Donald Trump refused to set the transition process in train.

Eventually the head of the GSA, Emily Murphy – a Trump-appointed official, naturally – did set the wheels in motion for the transition, writing to Mr Biden as 'the apparent president-elect'. The funds were then released, but grudgingly and with a lip distinctly curled.

Maybe it was wishful thinking on that section of the Trump inner circle who thought that this was just a temporary toys-out-of-the-pram moment, because from Trump himself the language was 'no surrender'. To anyone who would listen, he was maintaining – on zero evidence, and we will explore that more – that there had been massive fraud, voting machines had been fixed. He had won; and won by a country mile.

And that was the other narrative: to misquote George H.W. Bush, 'Read my lips, I am never going to concede.'

This can be explained partly by ego and narcissism. Can you imagine what a blow it was to his sense of self – the 'very stable genius', as he described himself – that he'd had the stuffing kicked out of him by the 78-year-old, sometimes bumbling Joe Biden – Sleepy Joe, of all people? He made clear how unconscionable it was during the final weeks of the campaign. 'Running against the worst candidate in the history of presidential politics puts pressure on me,' Trump told supporters at a rally in Georgia. 'Could you imagine if I lose? My whole life – what am I going to do? I'm going to say I lost to the worst candidate in the history of politics.'

But that is what happened, and how must it have hurt that he would be soon joining that relatively short roll call of presidential one-term losers? Since the Second World War only George H.W. Bush, Jimmy Carter and Gerald Ford had failed to win re-election. This was a man who liked to compare his achievements in office to America's Civil War leader, Abraham Lincoln; and who did nothing to dispel notions that his facial features should be chiselled and carved into the towering granite at Mount Rushmore. Accepting defeat was not what the 45th president was going to do.

But it is worth reflecting on this: what was it that led to Donald Trump's first impeachment (we'll get to the second one later)? It was fear and recognition that the one person in the Democratic field of hopefuls who posed the greatest risk to him was Joe Biden, for all that Trump tried to demean and belittle him. Why on earth send his errand boy, Rudy Giuliani, on that bizarre mission to strongarm the Ukrainians into digging up dirt on Hunter Biden, and by implication his father, Joe? It was self-evident: Trump was terrified by the threat the former Vice-President posed. There were no such elaborate efforts to undermine the candidacies of Pete Buttegieg, or Kamala Harris, or Bernie Sanders, or Elizabeth Warren, or, or, or. Just Joe Biden.

Donald Trump is a zero-sum game man. It is perfectly binary. You win or you lose. And one thing you can't take away from him is that he has a visceral sense of danger – his fear of Joe Biden was entirely rational, well founded, even if the steps taken to destroy his nomination were reckless in the extreme. And there was another fear that Donald Trump had that was rational and grounded in reality. By being turfed out of office, Trump was losing the immunity from prosecution that – arguably – he felt he was entitled to as a serving president. The 45th president seemed to act with impunity because he believed he had immunity. It won't come as a surprise to read that he took a maximalist view of his powers – i.e. he could do anything he liked as president and it would be beyond the reach of the Department of Justice. But that only lasts while you're the president. Election defeat to Trump was what kryptonite was to Superman.

A number of friends of Donald Trump said that he fretted repeatedly about the legal jeopardy he could face: the Mueller report had identified a number of occasions when as president he might have obstructed justice. And one thing was certain. Were Trump quietly to pack his bags, there would be no full pardon bestowed upon him by the incoming president, as happened when Gerald Ford succeeded Richard Nixon and issued a full pardon for any crimes committed while Nixon was in office – to end 'our long national nightmare', as Ford called the whole Watergate debacle in his inaugural address.

There was much speculation that Donald Trump would do something never done before – and that is issue *himself* a pre-emptive pardon. It was considered seriously, but the President was dissuaded by the White House legal counsel from the path of self-exoneration for a number of reasons: first and foremost, to accept a pardon means acknowledging guilt of wrongdoing. And he was never going to do that. It is also legally highly questionable, and would doubtless end up before the Supreme Court.

One other crucial thing: a pardon is only relevant to offences under *federal* law. If you have broken *state* law all bets are off; you can still be prosecuted. And four months on from being out of office, Trump still is the subject of at least two investigations – one, a longstanding inquiry into the Trump Organization conducted by the District Attorney in New York City, and a similar one being carried out by the state – both of which relate to allegations of fraud over the value of properties held by the former real estate developer. There is another legal case pending in Georgia, and that is a direct consequence of his behaviour after the election – but like Trump's second impeachment we will get to that shortly.

In the post-election period, Trump kept up his barrage of tweets that the election had been stolen and had been the subject of fraud. Perhaps the most unusual aspect of these weeks was Donald Trump's own behaviour. He remained more or less hidden from view. This President has always believed he is his own best spokesman. But for over three crucial weeks he didn't answer a single question from reporters. He was scarcely seen; he made the odd desultory comment – and would then walk off without expanding.

But if he was so confident of his case, why wasn't he out there selling it? He is, after all, the great marketeer. The master manipulator. Then on the Thursday night at the end of November when American families come together to celebrate all that they have in the annual Thanksgiving he did – finally – answer a few reporters' questions. Asked if he would agree to leave the White House if the electoral college vote went against him, he said: 'Certainly I will, certainly I will and you know that.' But he gave every impression that conceding was not what he was contemplating. 'It's going to be a very hard thing to concede because we know there was massive fraud,' he said, repeating the by now familiar allegation for which still no proof had been produced.

This first Q and A session since the election was odd for other reasons too. I know: a lot of the Trump presidency hasn't conformed to what you might call conventional, but this did stand out. In the Diplomatic Reception Room on the lower ground floor of the residence someone had set up a desk and a chair that was way too small for the bulk of the President. It was as though Donald Trump was sitting in a Fisher Price toy desk and chair set. Or like those parent/teacher evenings when you occupy the chair your six-year-old normally sits in. It was almost a perfect metaphor for the reality that power was shrinking away from him. Or was it a sign that he'd lost control? For a man who cares so much about the image and the visual, this was the Thanksgiving gif that kept on giving for the wags on social media. And his mood was distinctly testy when one reporter challenged him on the grounds for his complaints about the election result. 'Don't talk to me that way,' the President erupted. 'You're just a lightweight. Don't talk to me that – don't talk to – I'm the President of the United States. Don't ever talk to the President that way.'

During this period, when he wasn't on the golf course the President remained holed up inside the White House, with whole weeks of nothing marked on the published diary, meeting an ever-diminishing number of officials who were keeping the faith with him. It became vaguely comedic – each evening the White House would issue notification of the President's schedule for the next day – and it read the same: 'President Trump will work from early in the morning until late in the evening. He will make many calls and have many meetings.' That was it.

It was striking in this period to go into the White House and to observe just how few officials were around. A lot of the grown-ups wanted nothing to do with what was unfolding. The corridors were empty, and as the building hollowed out those that were left were the most fervent, die-in-the-last-ditch Trump loyalists.

There was a twin-track strategy: a legal one, spearheaded by Rudy Giuliani – entirely constitutional, entirely proper, looking for any irregularities in the results from key swing states that could alter the result; and a less creditable one – the President getting on the phone to key election officials, or inviting them to the White House to try to 'persuade' them not to certify the results.

You would imagine that when you're the president of the United States – even the outgoing one – you would assemble the brightest and best legal minds to make your case. But the motley crew led by Giuliani was like something out of a freak show. Its apotheosis came with an eagerly awaited news conference that was going to be given from Republican HQ in Washington. The headquarters of the Republican National Committee in Washington has many grand suites. But this presser would unfold in a small, cramped room with poor ventilation and a lot of camera lights. Giuliani had a meltdown. No, not metaphorically. Literally. The hair dye he'd presumably applied that morning started to bubble and melt on his head, leaving rivulets of brown liquid running down his cheeks, his forehead, his nose. How could you possibly concentrate on a single word he was saying when you were mainly wondering whether the drip coming down from his sideburns was going to reach his chin before the one barrelling down his face from his forehead. He was having a really bad hair day.

But if the sight of Rudy's face with its mud-coloured streaks is all we remember, that is probably just as well - because his legal team were promulgating some pretty far-fetched conspiracy theories to explain away Donald Trump's election defeat. One of the lawyers, an imposing woman called Sidney Powell, advanced the theory that the President had lost in Georgia because of a conspiracy involving – and I hope I have remembered all of this correctly – the Venezuelans, the Cubans, the Chinese, George Soros (you can't have a good conspiracy theory without him being somewhere in the mix), a former mayor of Chicago and Hugo Chavez – who'd been dead for seven years. The voting machines used in the state had apparently had the software 'fixed' so that Donald Trump's votes wouldn't be counted. And all of these people were in cahoots with the people running the Georgia election, of course.

When it was pointed out that those in charge of the Georgia ballots were fervent, Trump-supporting Republicans, that was brushed aside with an allegation that they'd been bribed by the aforementioned conspirators. No evidence was provided. The next day Ms Powell went on a right-wing fringe TV channel to announce she would be wreaking biblical vengeance against the state of Georgia, that she would 'blow it up' and unleash the kraken monster.

The next Monday a press release came from the Trump campaign announcing that she'd been dropped from the legal team. Too outlandish, even for Rudy Giuliani. She (along with Giuliani and others) is now fighting a multi-million dollar lawsuit brought by Dominion, the makers of those voting machines. And her defence is truly special. Her legal team seeking to have the defamation case dismissed wrote: 'No reasonable person would conclude that the statements were truly statements of fact.' In other words when she made all these allegations any reasonable person would have concluded they were bullshit.

Other organisations that regularly parroted the President's claims would also fold quickly when faced with legal challenge. The right-wing TV network, Newsmax, issued a statement on its website, stating that it had found 'no evidence' for the conspiracy theories advanced by Mr Trump's lawyers, supporters and others, and apologised to the Dominion voting machines employee, Eric Coomer, who Newsmax had alleged was behind the 'scam'. 'Newsmax has found no evidence that Dr Coomer interfered with Dominion voting machines or voting software in any way, nor that Dr Coomer ever claimed to have done so. Nor has Newsmax found any evidence that Dr Coomer ever participated in any conversation with members of "antifa", nor that he was directly involved with any partisan political organization.'

As climb-downs go, that was pretty comprehensive. But it almost spat defiance compared to the right-wing magazine, American Thinker, which made this craven statement about their reporters' coverage: 'These pieces rely on discredited sources who have peddled debunked theories about Dominion's supposed ties to Venezuela, fraud on Dominion's machines that resulted in massive vote switching or weighted votes, and other claims falsely stating that there is credible evidence that Dominion acted fraudulently. These statements are completely false and have no basis in fact.'

The myriad court cases, launched with such gusto and fanfare, fared about as well. There were over sixty in all, and 61 of the lawsuits were thrown out; one exception was a small partial victory in a case in Pennsylvania that affected only a handful of votes in a state that Biden won by over sixty thousand. Some of the judges who heard these cases, yes, had been appointed by a Democrat president, but many had been selected by Donald Trump himself. They rejected the fraud allegations and charges of ballot rigging out of hand.

And Donald Trump had problems closer to home. The man he'd appointed to be head of election security, a lifelong Republican called Christopher Krebs, declared the result the safest in US history. The Attorney General, William Barr, who was the scourge of liberal jurists for his muscular – and some would say inappropriately partisan – interventions on the President's behalf, reached the same conclusion. No fraud had taken place that would alter the outcome of the election. Get over it, they were saying to the President: you lost. Both men were fired – and demeaned – by Trump.

What was striking in this period was not how many senior Republicans spoke out against the President; what stood out was how many of them had seemingly lost their tongues. Even though the results of the courts and the judgements of the most senior officials were the same. If America is a nation of laws, and the men and women who are charged with administering those laws – the Justice Department and the courts – come down unanimously in one direction, you would think that would be that. But no.

Which brings us to the other part of the Trump strategy: try to strongarm those in the key swing states whose job is to certify the results into not doing so. The President phoned in to a bizarre meeting of Pennsylvania lawmakers, where Rudy Giuliani – who was there in person – held his mobile phone to a microphone as the President railed against the election results. Michigan lawmakers were invited to the White House to have a private meeting about that state's results with the President. It looked dodgy as anything.

But then came Trump's tussle with the authorities in Georgia. The Secretary of State in Georgia, Brad Raffensperger, is a lifelong Republican who voted for Donald Trump and paid money towards his campaign – but whichever way he counted the results (and they were counted and recounted), the result was the same: Joe Biden had carried the state with a majority of 11,779 votes. Trump did what he does. On social media he went after Mr Raffensperger. And in one tweet at the beginning of January the President revealed that he'd been on the phone to the senior election officials in the peach state. Trump called him clueless, and said he couldn't answer any of his questions. But Raffensperger fired back with this: 'Respectfully, President Trump: What you're saying is not true. The truth will come out.'

And – boy – did the truth come out about what unfolded on that call. The hour-long audio file was leaked to the *Washington Post* in its entirety. It is astonishing as much for what Donald Trump says as what it reveals about his state of mind. The stand-out quote was Trump saying this: 'So look. All I want to do is this. I just want to find 11,780 votes, which is one more than we have. Because we won the state.' In other words find me those votes so I am declared the winner. He doesn't let it go: 'So what are we going to do here, folks? I only need 11,000 votes. Fellas, I need 11,000 votes. Give me a break.'

When he is told that he didn't win the state and that he's got his facts wrong, the President seems to become bullying. 'The people of Georgia are angry, the people of the country are angry,' he said. 'And there's nothing wrong with saying, you know, that you've recalculated.' When he doesn't get his way the President seems to threaten legal consequences for Raffensberger if he doesn't do what he's asked. Again and again, the President insists he won the election by hundreds of thousands of votes. Again and again he tells those on the call there is no way that he lost.

Donald Trump is now the subject of potential legal action in Georgia. The charge would be 'election interference', a felony crime that carries a prison sentence.

There was also an exceptional legal move instigated by several

Republican states, and backed by large numbers of Trump-supporting members of Congress. Led by Texas, they would petition the Supreme Court directly to overturn Joe Biden's victory in the electoral college. Never mind that the people behind this move are the very defenders of a state's rights to manage its own affairs. Here were the attorneys general of a number of states arguing they knew best, and that results had to be overturned in states over which they had zero jurisdiction. The Supreme Court said it would have nothing to do with it – and Trump couldn't have been more angry, particularly with the three justices whom he had appointed.

With the legal path having failed dismally, and his effort to coerce state officials to 'fix' the results in his favour coming to nought, if Donald Trump was going to upend the will of the people there was only one roll of the dice left – he would have to persuade the joint session of Congress *not* to certify the results of the electoral college, that had been signed off as safe by the Secretaries of State in all fifty states of the Union.

This is a purely ceremonial occasion at which the Vice-President, Mike Pence, presides in his role as President of the Senate. It was to happen on 6 January, just two weeks before Joe Biden's inauguration on the 20th. And even at this late stage, Trump was pressuring his doggedly loyal number two to throw away the rule book. To add to the tension and the apprehension, Trump asked his supporters to descend on Washington in a show of strength to 'stop the steal' – the Trump ultras' increasingly shrill slogan. Donald Trump told them on Twitter, 'Be there, will be wild!'

Now Donald Trump is sometimes accused of hyperbole, of reckless exaggeration, even of falsehood. Let no one say there was anything OTT about this tweet. January the 6th *was* wild. And dark. And deeply troubling. And violent. And American democracy for a while seemed on the brink.

For a start, Mike Pence, who for four years had done everything that was asked of him by Donald Trump, and displayed a loyalty that teetered on the slavish and supine, made clear in a carefully argued letter that at this critical juncture he was going to follow the constitution – not Donald Trump. It was a grievous blow to Trump and one for which there would be no forgiveness. Pence had joined the list of non-people who had dared to say 'no' to Donald Trump.

The rally, which was held on the Ellipse – the area of parkland just beyond the South Lawn of the White House that goes down to the Washington Monument – had brought tens of thousands of Trump supporters from all over America. It was a frigid, grey morning. Over the years I have lost count of how many Trump rallies I've attended. Let's just say lots. And they have invariably been great fun. A lot of fancy-dress; the atmosphere of a fiesta. Trump is a great showman and entertainer. I try to capture some of that in the first diary entry that you will read after this chapter. On 6 January in DC the atmosphere was 180 degrees removed from that day in Orlando in June 2019 when he launched his bid for a second term.

The jibes about me being fake news had no mocking element. It was aggressive. These people – every single one of them – bought totally the assertion that the election had been stolen from Donald Trump. When you asked for evidence, they said it was everywhere, but couldn't point to a single specific that would have altered the outcome of the election. These people ridiculed the idea that Joe Biden got more votes than Barack Obama, though didn't question that Donald Trump had also performed brilliantly, given his handling of the pandemic.

There was a visceral anger among these people, and the mood – as I tweeted before the rally had even started – was distinctly edgy. I met a couple of young guys who had driven across the country from Boise, Idaho to be at the rally – a distance of roughly two and a half thousand miles each way. They were dressed like extras from the *RoboCop* movie. Grey/black body armour, helmets, and carrying rucksacks with undisclosed accessories inside them. They said they hadn't come seeking out trouble . . . but if trouble came and found them, well, then they would be prepared. I would the next day see them dangling down from the gallery of the Senate about to jump down onto the Senate floor. Looked like they had gone in search of trouble after all. People in the crowd were berating me for wearing a mask and demanded that I take it off; and telling my cameraman where he could stick his tripod. It was unmistakably hostile.

Something else has changed in the years I have been covering the Trump presidency. Initially the admiration for Trump from his base was that though he wasn't perfect, might not always tell the whole truth, might be a bit 'naughty', he stood up for them; he would be their champion. The outsiders, who felt neglected by the Washington elite, had a knight in shining armour – with a bit of tarnish around the edges.

But on 6 January it was more cult-like devotion. The only truth that existed came from the lips of Donald Trump and his most loyal acolytes, so any argument you put that Joe Biden had won fair and square was met with total incredulity – and fury. And when you cited the senior Republicans from the VP downwards who weren't buying it, they were dismissed as deep state swamp creatures, or RINOs – Republicans in name only.

And after Donald Trump addressed them and told them they had to march on Congress; that they had to show strength and couldn't be weak; that they had to 'stop the steal' – they followed him to the letter. He ended his speech by saying this to his angry supporters: 'We fight. We fight like hell and if you don't fight like hell, you're not going to have a country anymore. So let's walk down Pennsylvania Avenue.'

On 6 January 2021, the Trump mob ruled. This was an attempted insurrection; a concerted effort to stop the certification of election results that the courts had deemed safe and that every one of the individual states had certified. This is – normally – a purely ceremonial rubber-stamping operation, taking around half an hour from beginning to end.

Instead, when I went on the *Ten O-Clock News* that night, the mob was still in control of Congress and Joe Biden's victory had not been certified. In my live report I said that I thought American democracy was in a precarious position – and added that I could not believe I was uttering those words. It wasn't hyperbole. It was true. This is being described as America's darkest day; the day when the beacon of democracy for the rest of the world was nearly extinguished, as rioters ran amok, defiling the most sacred sanctum of American democracy. We've all seen scenes like this in third world, tinpot regimes. But in America?

Some have sought to argue that what unfolded on 6 January and the days leading up to it was the system working. The attempts led by President Trump to have the results overturned had failed. He had bent the constitution to breaking point, but when it looked like it was going to snap, the safety mechanisms – the much-vaunted checks and balances – kicked in; the strength and durability of American democracy had prevailed.

But what is easy to forget is how close it came.

What if the VP, Mike Pence (very soon afterwards called a 'traitor' and facing death threats from Trump supporters), had gone along with the President's demands not to certify the results? Ditto the Senate majority leader, Mitch McConnell – both of whom had hitherto shown all the backbone towards Donald Trump of cooked spaghetti. What if the Secretary of State in Georgia had acceded to the President's slightly menacing demands to 'recalculate' the ballots and given him the extra 11,780 votes that he needed to win? What if a lowly Michigan official had bent to the President's will and refused to certify Joe Biden's comfortable victory in the state?

In the end 170 Republican members of the House of Representatives voted *not* to certify Biden's victory. One of them would explain to me afterwards he'd felt he had to do this because so many of his voters believed that the election had been stolen from Donald Trump. So rather than alienate his base and incur the vengeful wrath of Donald Trump he would vote against certifying Biden's victory. Leadership, anyone?

Or, to put it another way, does American democracy rely on a handful of people doing the right thing to survive – even though it is at huge personal cost to themselves, when surrender would have been easier? The Georgia election official now needs security 24/7 as a result of standing up to the President. An action that has resulted in multiple death threats.

The other thing about the 2020 election is that it wasn't even that close. Biden polled millions more votes, and won the electoral college easily. This wasn't JFK's squeaky tight win of 1960 (when there almost certainly *was* widespread fraud), or 2000 (when it all came down to a few hundred votes in Florida). But what if it had been really tight? Then the pressure on state officials from the President might have been irresistible.

What we saw on 6 January was a massive security failure. But the real fragility of American democracy had been on display in the weeks leading up to that fateful Wednesday in January. There was a coup attempt which was thwarted, thanks to a few honourable patriots acting on principle, acting to uphold the constitution. But it was a close-run thing.

Hunkered down in the White House as the events of 6 January unfolded, Donald Trump in the early stages was apparently pleased with his handiwork, and was in no mood to call off his dogs of war.

One tweet attacked Mike Pence for not having the courage to do what he should have done. Soon afterwards the mob that had violently stormed the Capitol were chanting, 'Hang Mike Pence.' And moments later CCTV captures dramatic footage of Pence's Secret Service detail bundling him down a staircase to a secure location. Congressmen and women are cowering in their offices with tables and wardrobes rammed against doors to stop the mob. It was touch and go.

Donald Trump then put out a video on Twitter that called for the protestors to go home, but he says to the mob that have sacked the Capitol and injured dozens of policeman, 'We love you, you're very special.' And he would follow that up a little later with a tweet that seemed to justify the violence; certainly it was not a repudiation of the behaviour that the world was watching with rapt and appalled fascination: 'These are the things and events that happen when a sacred landslide election victory is so unceremoniously stripped away from great patriots who have been badly treated for so long.'

It would be one of Donald Trump's last tweets. In the wake of these astonishing events the social media platforms finally lost patience and he was kicked off Twitter and Facebook. And Democrats started the process of impeaching the President – again.

In the immediate aftermath of 6 January the President did make a statement condemning the rioters and making clear that they were not acting at his behest – which is odd, because that is exactly what it looked like. And indeed, many of the rioters who were arrested in the massive FBI operation that unfolded afterwards have given witness statements making plain that they thought they were obeying the President's instructions when they invaded the Capitol.

The impeachment trial would take place after Donald Trump had left office. On 20 January the inauguration of Joe Biden took place and the peaceful transfer of power took place as the constitution prescribes, with the Democratic Party victor taking the reins of power at midday.

He took the oath of office on the West front of the Capitol; there was poetry (fabulous poetry from a prodigiously talented young African American woman, Amanda Gorman), there was music – but it was as abnormal an inauguration as you could imagine. The pandemic meant the numbers invited to attend were dramatically curtailed. And then there was the legacy of 6 January. There were no crowds on the Mall. None. The Capitol resembled a garrison town. Fencing, razor wire, armoured personnel carriers and heavily armed soldiers everywhere. At the crack of dawn I cycled along deserted streets to Congress. Only the national guard were to be seen. A celebration of Democracy? Up to a point. But it was also democracy in a defensive, fearful crouch.

And one person in particular was missing. Donald Trump announced he wouldn't be attending – the great tradition where the outgoing president metaphorically passes on the baton to his successor was dispensed with. For Trump to attend would have been public acknowledgement that he'd lost; so he stayed away. And instead demanded that he be given a red-carpet farewell from Joint Base Andrews. A stage was erected, but it was a sparcely attended affair. And as Air Force One taxied onto the runway to take him to Mar-a-Lago, Frank Sinatra's 'My Way' was belting out on the PA. Yep, no one could deny that he had done it his way.

Donald Trump stayed hidden out of view in Mar-a-Lago while his second impeachment trial unfolded. It did not lead to a 'conviction' that would have seen Donald Trump disbarred from holding public office again, but it was the most bipartisan vote to convict in American history. Seven Republicans broke with the leadership to find Trump guilty of 'incitement of insurrection'. The Republican leader of the Senate, Mitch McConnell, was not one of those who voted to convict. He argued that constitutionally you could not use the weapon of impeachment when someone has left office (someone did wryly suggest that this was the same as saying to the traffic cop when you're pulled over for speeding, yes I might have been travelling at 20 mph above the speed limit then, but now I'm stationery, so you can't convict me). Nevertheless he was unsparing in his attack on Trump's behaviour. He was practically and morally responsible for what had happened. 'They [the mob] did this because they'd been fed wild falsehoods by the most powerful man on Earth because he was angry he lost an election,' McConnell said.

Joe Biden stayed away from offering a commentary on the Trump impeachment while it was going on – he was certain the result would see Trump acquitted. And he was right. Instead Joe Biden wanted to get on with governing.

But as he notched up 100 days in office I struggled to think of a single great soundbite from the preceding three months. The daily White House briefings are a snoozefest. There are no fights, no name calling. President Biden has not called me 'another beauty', he hasn't declared the media the enemy of the people, he hasn't fired his National Security Advisor for lying to the Vice President over a call to the Russian ambassador, he hasn't sought to introduce a chaotic ban on Muslims from entering the country, resulting in mayhem at the border. No middle of the night twitter storms, no payments to porn stars, no rollicking MAGA rallies.

Dull. Dull. Dull.

With Donald Trump I was live outside the White House nearly every night. It was a TV journalist's version of a daily blow-out meal. The main nightly news running order more or less had me written into the template Trump/Sopel. With Biden? I'd be surprised if the producers in London remember how to spell my name.

So, is this the most boring president ever? Well no. Absolutely not. This is a far more interesting presidency – so far – than I think any of us could have imagined. The sad thing, from a purely selfish point of

view, is that what it isn't is a made-for-TV spectacular, which is what I
have feasted on these past four years. Donald Trump always had an eye
for the visual and outrageous. He knew how to make himself the
centre of attention; Biden seems to relish the lack of histrionics, and
seems to think it is important for people to focus on what he delivers,
rather than what he says. Most strange.

We reported that Joe Biden – all 78 years of him – would be a transitional president. He would be there to lower the political temperature;
try to heal a divided nation. Take the absurd politics out of the response
to Covid. Improve vaccine roll-out. But that aside not do too much. He
appointed a largely technocratic cabinet, presumably to perform
managerial functions. Maybe make the trains run on time a bit better,
but not change all the rolling stock, let alone alter the gauge of the
railway. A fitting ambition for Amtrak Joe.

But maybe we got that all wrong. Is it possible that far from being
transitional, he's transformational? And that word is not freighted
with a positive or negative connotation – it is merely a statement based
on the ambition of what we've seen so far. And voters will soon decide
whether it's for better or worse.

Let's start with the $1.9 trillion stimulus package. The headline
from the passing of this humungous piece of legislation was that
nearly all adult Americans would receive a cheque for $1,400 to help
them cope with the hardships brought about by the pandemic. It was
cash in hand to a lot of Americans, and won massive approval – from
Democrat and Republican voters alike – although not a single GOP
lawmaker would back the proposal.

But look beyond the headline and lift the lid on this policy a little
further. There is a lot to see. Perhaps most significant is the extension
of child tax credits. Poorer families could soon be receiving up to
$3,000 per child per annum. It is estimated this one measure will lift
literally millions of youngsters out of poverty. As things stand, this

measure is for 2021 only – but it is clear within the White House that Joe Biden wants to make it permanent. It is a major piece of social policy. It is big potatoes.

With the passing of the stimulus package – or the American Rescue Package as it is more properly called – Biden wanted to correct something he felt that Barack Obama had got wrong when he came to power and inherited the mess of the financial crisis in 2009. Yes, Obama passed a variety of measures – but with hindsight it was seen as too cautious; not ambitious enough.

He's planning something similar for America's infrastructure. Again, the price tag will be in the trillions. Again, the ambition will be immense – not just the staid repairing of bridges and roads (important and vital though that is); it is about making digital access more equitable – but it goes wider than that. Way wider. 'It is not a plan that tinkers around the edges,' the President told an audience outside Pittsburgh. 'It is a once-in-a-generation investment in America.'

The wish-list of what it will achieve goes on and on. The infrastructure plan will create millions of jobs in the short term and strengthen American competitiveness in the long. It will lead to greater racial equality. The focus on new, cleaner energy sources will help the nation fight climate change.

Now there is an element of motherhood and apple pie in this shopping list, but the statement of intent is big, and this is what makes boring old Joe Biden so interesting. Arguably the dominant idea in American politics for the past forty years has been the low taxing, economy deregulating, budget balancing, competition encouraging, union limiting small government of Ronald Reagan. The same is true of the influence of Thatcherism in the UK – yes, there have been 13 years of Labour government since Maggie's demise, just as here there have been the Clinton and Obama terms since Reagan. But arguably they operated within, and were defined by, the orthodoxy of the monetarist economists who held such intellectual sway on both sides of the Atlantic.

After the morale-sapping defeats of the 1980s – both for Labour in the UK and Democrats in the US – the head scratching was intense on what they needed to do to win, and both Bill Clinton and Tony Blair came to believe that tax raising, big government pledges would just ensure that history repeated itself and the cycle of defeat would go on.

But Biden – for better or worse – wants to use the pandemic and woeful state of America's infrastructure to say unapologetically to the American people, 'Yep, big government is back.' It is territory that Republican opponents – still trying to sort out their post-Trumpian identity– will be keen to fight on. Joe Biden, though, seems to be relishing the battle; making the case for higher taxes on corporations and the wealthiest.

This is a big break with the past and a mighty gamble. So far, his approval ratings on the ground where he has chosen to fight – handling of coronavirus, the economic stimulus, his plans for infrastructure – have been positive. Less so the chaos there has been at the Southern border; something the President now acknowledges is a crisis. And the perennial issue of gun control is going to lead to a lot of huffing and puffing, but it's hard to see what he will be able to achieve through legislation, given the fine balance of the Senate.

Around 60 days into his presidency, Biden brought together an interesting group of people at the White House. The presidential historian, Jon Meacham, was asked to assemble a number of his most eminent colleagues for a sit-down that Joe Biden was anxious to host. He is already thinking about his legacy and what he needs to do to secure it: what was the limit of presidential power; what lessons could he learn from his predecessors. At one point he turns to – perhaps – the most revered of these presidential scholars, Doris Kearns Goodwin and says 'I'm no FDR, but . . .'

Perhaps Joe Biden is eyeing this as his moment to deliver a New Deal à la Franklin Delano Roosevelt, or the Great Society, with its war on poverty and fight against racial inequality that was championed in the 1960s by Lyndon B. Johnson.

The taunt of Donald Trump during the campaign was that Biden may have been in politics for over four decades, but what did he have to show for it. Looks like in power he is trying to give a mighty clear answer to that question – even if it doesn't make for great theatre.

In the months after Donald Trump left office, he didn't leave Florida. With the Twitter and Facebook bans remaining in place we are not given that hour by hour, blow by blow update on Trump's mood swings. He's set up an office and there is a steady stream of emails updating journalists on who he wants to settle scores with. But through one relationship, we can see the power that the President still exerts. That relationship is with the House of Representatives minority Republican leader, Kevin McCarthy.

But let me spool back very quickly. McCarthy had been a cheerleader for Donald Trump when he was in the House. Always supportive; always riding to his side. But then, after the storming of the Capitol on 6 January, the most senior Republican congressman went his own way and said this: 'The President bears responsibility for Wednesday's attack on Congress by mob rioters. He should have immediately denounced the mob when he saw what was unfolding.'

So far so brave. But then McCarthy feels the icy blowback from the Trump base, and from the former President himself, who was enraged. McCarthy then says Donald Trump can't be blamed, and his fast-changing analysis settles on the slightly ludicrous take – *all* Americans were responsible for the riot that left five dead. Which is pretty much the same, if you think about it, as saying no one was responsible.

And to heal this breech, Congressman McCarthy flew to Mar-a-

Lago to kiss the ring, seeking forgiveness and absolution for the momentary lapse. But more importantly, if you read the statement put out by Donald Trump's office afterwards it shows that the former President still believes he is the Republican Party's kingmaker; the powerhouse that ambitious GOP wannabes need to bend the knee to. And it feels reassuringly familiar in tone. The first paragraph of the statement issued by Trump's office says this:

> The meeting between President Donald J. Trump and House Republican Leader Kevin McCarthy at Mar-a-Lago in Palm Beach, Florida, was a very good and cordial one. They discussed many topics, number one of which was taking back the House in 2022. President Trump's popularity has never been stronger than it is today, and his endorsement means more than perhaps any endorsement at any time.

Do you see what I mean about the tone being reassuringly familiar? I mean, close your eyes and you could almost imagine it was written by Mr Trump himself – even though it is in the third person singular. And as for the claim that his popularity has never been stronger – can anyone point me to the polling evidence that substantiates that?

The ex-President may have lost power, but he is determined to maintain his grip on the Republican Party. In essence he's saying, if you want to win back the House from Democratic control in November 2022, you need me on side. Because I can create hell if I'm not. And the defenestration of the third most senior Republican in the House, Liz Cheney, is proof of that. She voted to impeach Trump and has been unsparing in her criticism of the President's repeated election fraud claims. Trump called on McCarthy to move against her. And he did. She's been removed from office.

For the past few months Donald Trump has not been seen much.

There have been occasional TV appearances. But do not think he has gone away. His grip on the American public may have loosened, and the political temperature may have dropped a few degrees, but his hold on the Republican Party is vice-like. Donald Trump is casting a long shadow, and will continue to do so for a long time to come.

18 June 2019, Orlando, Florida.
503 days until polling

Yes, I know it is more than five hundred days out from the 2020 election, but this is where Donald Trump's bid for a second term begins, and a campaign diary has to start somewhere. His campaign launch at the Amway Center is this evening. And it's no accident he's chosen Florida. It's the bellwether state where the weather today is anything but belle. It is steamy hot, pouring with rain, thunder, lightning and no air that is worth breathing. My suit and shirt are clinging to my skin like damp rags after repeated soakings. Outside thousands – literally thousands – are queuing to get in. Excited, dressed up, indefatigable, enthusiastic. Forget the storms, they're here to see Donald. The faithful are really faithful. Devoted.

I ask one man – on camera – what he likes about the President, and he tells me he is Jesus-like. He has been sent here to do God's work. I have thought of Donald Trump in many ways in the past three years that I have been reporting on his doings on a daily basis, but I struggle to see this particular similarity. Anyway, I smile benignly, thinking this bit of *vox pop* is definitely going to be on the news. One woman I speak to has travelled the breadth of America to be at the rally. She's come from California. The crowd, when they become listless after waiting in line for hours to get through layer upon layer of security, start chanting 'Four more years', then 'Lock her up' – one of the unexpected hits of the 2016 campaign – and 'Build the wall', still a firm favourite. One man – he must have been six feet six inches tall – is a dead ringer for Abraham Lincoln, and dressed like him too. We all want our photo next to him.

MAGA hats (Make America Great Again) are selling like hot cakes; people have improvised and designed their own Donald Trump costumes. During the arduous 2016 campaign I never saw once this level of enthusiasm, adoration even, for Hillary Clinton. Two and a half years into his presidency he still has a big section of the American public eating out of the palm of his hand.

Eventually, I make it through security into the Amway arena. And inside the air conditioning has been put on Arctic tundra setting. In a moment you feel as though you have crossed from the jungles of Borneo to the Siberian wastes. I'm convinced I am going to contract pneumonia. I'm convinced my soggy Savile Row suit is going to transform into an icy crisp. This cannot be good for you.

First it's the warm-ups: Don junior comes on and does his dad impression; the Vice-President, Mike Pence, comes on and does his utterly besotted impression (who knows, he might well be – or maybe just positioning himself); and then it's the top of the bill: Donald and Melania come out to whoops and hollering like a boy band might get from an audience of adolescent girls – and while this audience is decidedly older, the decibels aren't any lower.

The speech, full of unfinished sentences, is a meandering, scatter-gun rehash of all the things he said in 2016 – with some big boasts (fair enough) about the state of the economy. What struck me in '16 was that he was at his best when attacking the enemy – Hillary, the deep state, Obama, the Washington swamp, America's economic rivals over-seas. But who does he attack now that he is the incumbent – and the only record to go after is his own? On this performance, that is going to need some working on. It has to be more than Robert Mueller and the witch hunt, and the Speaker of the House, Nancy Pelosi, and the do-nothing Democrats. That feels a bit anaemic.

What I had forgotten, though, having not been to many Trump rallies since the last election, is how well he feeds off the audience. At one point he has been reading off autocue for 15 minutes – and it is dull. Lists of things we've done; lists of crimes committed by the Democrats. The audience is quiet and fidgety, so he starts riffing on whether Make America Great Again was the greatest political campaign slogan of all time. Spoiler alert – he thinks it was. And he gets the audience involved. Hands up if you think this; hands up if you think that. And then he starts road-testing the slogan for 2020: Keep America Great. Yes, the audience cries. Yes, Donald Trump cries. No one does politics as entertainment better. And so it shall be. MAGA is out. KAG is in.

Momentarily I feel sorry for all the traders out on the street with their stalls full of MAGA merchandise. But it's a passing concern. KAG hats are a whole new marketing and merchandising opportunity.

None of this, however, will be my stand-out memory of the evening. It's what we find out earlier about the arrangements for the media. The press pen is cordoned off at the back of the arena. We have special passes that give us access. There is steeply raked tribune, where all the TV crews can film the rally from. Behind this makeshift grand-stand, and without a view of the stage, are rows of tables and chairs where the scribblers can work – those who toil for the newspapers and agencies. Secret service officers are posted at each of the two access points to the media area. After physical attacks on some of us on previous occasions from fired-up Trump supporters who've taken to heart the President's verbal attacks on us as enemies of the people, this has become sadly necessary.

At 6pm, two hours before Donald Trump is due on stage – and an hour before he even arrives in Orlando – I make my way out towards the exit of the press pen to go to the toilet. A scrupulously polite secret service officer tells me I am not allowed to leave. Not only that: I won't be able to go from our confined area until the crowd has completely dispersed at the end of his speech. I am doing the mental maths: assuming he's half an hour late on stage, speaks for an hour and 15 minutes (par for the course), the crowd takes half an hour to disperse … well that means I am going to have to keep my legs crossed for four hours and 15 minutes.

I remonstrate with the officer, who tells me I will have to speak to the White House 'wrangler' who is in charge of enforcing the rules. The woman in question is young (in her early twenties), in a red dress, thick set and unsmiling. No, I would go further than that. Having tried charm, humour, outrage and anger, I am going to say she has never smiled in her life. There was a downward turn of her lips, an indifference in her eyes and a demeanour that just screamed 'Don't mess with me.' There is no chance of Stockholm Syndrome if she is to become our jailer for the next 17 months. If she were to audition for the part of Rosa Klebb in the Bond movie, *From Russia With Love*, the casting director would be telling her to lighten up a bit. Hatchet faced doesn't begin to describe it.

She doesn't give an inch. We are not allowed to go to the bathroom. I momentarily contemplate what the reaction would be if I go in for an involuntary one-man dirty protest and pee on the floor of the press pen. Can you imagine the fun Donald Trump would have with that? No, it's going to be sit tight and hang on.

But then my mind goes back to a Japanese TV game show made famous by Clive James in the 1980s. He had a series called *On Television*, in which he took us around the world with his wry humour and beautiful writing to watch some of the bizarre programmes that were made in cultures very different from our own. In one episode a Japanese TV show was highlighted that I remember distinctly. Men stood in barrels of icy water in their underpants. It is freezing outside too. They then had to drink pints and pints of ice-cold lager – and the winner was the last one who had to rush out of the barrel to go and urinate – a sort of Iron Man for bladders. The programme was called *Endurance* (look it up on YouTube … I promise I'm not making this up).

Endurance indeed. Welcome to the 2020 campaign. I think I might need to have additional supplies of it airlifted in. Still, after tonight, only 502 days to go.

27 July, US–Mexican border, New Mexico

I am here to do a stocktake on the Trump presidency for the *Today* programme, and to interview the architect – and many would say the intellect – behind Trump's 2016 election victory, Steve Bannon. He was the campaign manager who transitioned to one of the most senior roles in the White House. He is the fight-picking, take-no-hostages, burn-it-all-down, disruptor-in-chief. Bannon was the leader of the 'build the wall', anti-immigration, pro-tariff brigade. He would describe himself as an economic nationalist; his many opponents would prefer to use the epithet 'racist'.

Miles off the highway, you had to drive past an amusement park (some of the characters we would subsequently meet looked like they may well have lived their lives there), and then go in a four-wheel-drive vehicle on unmarked, scorched, dry-as-dust tracks, through the sprawling land belonging to the American Eagle brick company, that lead you eventually to the border with Mexico. Roadrunners scuttle out of the way as we drive, under clear blue skies and a sun rising over the valley.

The first thing we see is a marquee and a couple of tents. Welcome to the 'Symposium at the Wall: Cartels, Trafficking and Asylum'. In the marquee, with fans whirring, struggling against the odds to keep the stiflingly hot air circulating, an unusual bunch of right-wing politicians, misfits and supporters have gathered. You know the scene in the first *Star Wars* film where Luke Skywalker goes into the bar and there are all those crazy creatures...

What they look out on is a new stretch of border wall that has been privately funded. 'Build the wall' was a slogan that got Donald Trump elected, but to this day very little construction has actually taken place – although a Supreme Court ruling a week ago should help the President in that endeavour.

Bannon has the unkempt, shambolic look of one who has spent the night sleeping on a park bench. He has rheumy blue eyes and bags under them that are so big and heavy that if you were flying Ryanair and tried to check them in, you would be subject to a hefty additional charge. The dark blue shirt he was wearing looked as though it hadn't seen a washing machine in a good while – and certainly had never been introduced to an iron. At one point, an aide wearing Chanel pumps (bet you don't see many shoes like that on this piece of desert scrub) fusses about a stain on the shirt. Why just the one? There were so many she could have pointed to.

He revels in the furious reactions he provokes. I had doubted the interview would take place – past experience has suggested he's not 100 per cent reliable. I hadn't met him one-to-one before, and wasn't quite sure what to expect. He is charming – and off camera very gossipy. He is well read, and has a sense of history. Since getting booted out of the White House and falling out with Trump (something that I suspect still hurts) he has tried to evangelise his message of right-wing populism across Europe. But I am not here to talk to him about that; I am here as the North America Editor to talk about Trump.

Before we sit down for the interview he offers criticism of the Trump campaign, and jokes about Trump's shortcomings; he is candid too about the strength of some of the Democratic Party opponents.

I also thought it interesting that this scourge of liberal opinion is clearly a big consumer of BBC News and the *Guardian* newspaper. But once the cameras are rolling the candour is – frustratingly – jettisoned for a straight down the line defence of the President. I push him hard on racist comments that Trump has recently made about four Democratic congresswomen from minority backgrounds – how they should go back to where they came from. He is evasive. At the end of the interview he says to me, 'You're a tough hombre.' I reply that I bet he says that to everyone. He makes a persuasive case about the need for a wall – framing it as a way to stop the cartels from engaging in human trafficking, as well as drugs.

It was said of Peter Mandelson, the éminence grise of New Labour in the 1990s, that he was a Blairite before Blair. You feel the same about Bannon. He was Trumpian before Trump, and did a lot to shape the isolationist, nationalist, protectionist message that was the hallmark of the Trump campaign in 2016 and will doubtless be the spine of 2020 too.

POSTSCRIPT: I knew interviewing Bannon would be controversial, but I didn't realise the utter venom it would provoke. Twitter went to war with him – and me. I stood accused of being a fellow traveller, an enabler of fascism, a racist lickspittle. I was told I had betrayed my Jewish heritage – because Bannon was a Nazi by any other name. We stood accused of giving him a platform. (A platform is where you allow someone to say whatever they like unchallenged – actually I thought it was an interview where we pushed back forcibly.) Weren't we making his views respectable and bringing them into the mainstream?

Well, his views were what Donald Trump fought an election on, and having won it, he pursued those policies in office, so I guess they are what some would now say *is* the mainstream. They were what enough Americans voted for in the election to secure the 270 votes needed to win the electoral college. Also, Bannon was at the very heart of the 'hostile takeover' of the Republican Party.

He is not a crank or an outsider, and he certainly isn't a nobody. He has been at the heart of government and remains very well connected to key decision makers in Washington. In our increasingly polarised politics, are we to say we are going to ignore people we don't like, and ban them from the media? That, to me, is a very odd notion of free speech. It also shows a distinct lack of self-confidence. Surely our job is to hear different opinions – but at the same time challenge and scrutinise the arguments they are putting forward. Yes, maybe in the airing of the interview we should have made more effort to contextualise Bannon's views; and am sure there are other things I could – and should – have done differently. But banning him from the airwaves, as many were advocating? The logical extension of banning Bannon is to ban Trump too. No?

This interview was done for the *Today* programme, who had set the whole thing up. The last time I had presented the *Today* programme at Broadcasting House was more than 20 years earlier, and one of the guests in the studio that morning was Radovan Karadžić, then leader of the Bosnian Serbs, and held responsible for the terror inflicted on, and the grotesque ethnic cleansing of, the Muslim population in Bosnia. He was in London for the ill-fated Bosnia peace talks; today he is a convicted war criminal after his trial at The Hague, and will spend the rest of his life behind bars. He was interviewed then because he mattered. In the course of my career I have sat down with people whose views I find utterly repellent and obnoxious. And I will try to do those interviews with rigour and courtesy. If the BBC – or any of the other great news outlets in Britain – decide that they are going to censor unpopular opinions from the airwaves, then I think that far from defeating extremist views, we are creating a fertile breeding ground for populism to grow and spread; where the 'banished' become quasi-martyred souls who have been cast out by a fearful establishment – and their videos will spread like a virus on the internet. We are then succumbing to a 'yes I agree totally' world, where all we can tolerate listening to are our own views being played back to us, echoing satisfyingly our world view, our heads nodding approvingly. That does not serve democracy well.

After the extreme discomfort of being subject to such Twitter rage I become aware of an irony – that apparently not only *shouldn't* I have interviewed Bannon, but I *should* have interviewed him for longer. Why hadn't I covered Cambridge Analytica; why hadn't I asked about Viktor Orban; what had he been doing with Marine le Pen, and why has he bought this monastery in Italy?

I am reminded of one of my favourite jokes, in which two elderly Jewish women are eating lunch at a kosher restaurant and one complains to the waiter, 'The food is disgusting and inedible.' And the other woman chimes in, 'And such small portions.'

29 July, New York

In New York to meet Gary Cohn. He spent the first year of the Trump administration as the Chairman of the National Economic Council. In other words, the chief economic advisor to the President. And if this White House has been riven by two competing factions with Steve Bannon at one pole, then Gary Cohn is at the other. While Bannon represents the tear-it-all-down, isolationist tendency, Cohn led the globalist, anti-tariff, free-trader brigade – and he was one of the few who had the courage to publicly call out the President for his remarks after neo-Nazis clashed with anti-racism protestors in Charlottesville during the first few months of the Trump presidency.

I meet Cohn on Wall Street (where else) – and he is everything that Bannon is not. He is immaculately turned out. He glows with health, has a firm handshake and is physically imposing. His crisp, white shirt is monogrammed, his dark blue suit is hand-tailored and hangs beautifully. You could easily cut your finger running your hand down the crease of his trousers. And the point of the crease seems to fall perfectly to the neat turn-up, bisecting what appear to be alligator skin loafers. Yes, snappy dresser.

But in certain other respects the two have similarities – both seem to have a preternatural intellectual self-confidence and belief. Both are convinced of their rightness; both sure that their path is the only route for America to travel. In our interview with Cohn he makes clear his disagreement with Trump on his stewardship of the economy: he rubbishes Trump's claim that the administration is bringing back manufacturing jobs to the US, and he says that the trade war that the President launched against China is hurting the US far more than it is the Asian behemoth. But despite his earlier outspokenness after Charlottesville he – like Bannon – refuses to go near questions about whether the President is a racist.

And as with Bannon, some of his off-camera comments are gold. As I sit down to commence the interview he tells me – only half-jokingly – that the three pages of notes that I have on my lap are more briefing material than Donald Trump has read in the entire time he has been in the White House. Cohn later tells me that while Trump will read newspaper articles (particularly those that are about him), he has a profound allergy to briefing documents that seek to tutor him – an allergy that teeters on the edge of anaphylaxis.

At the end of the interview and we are filming what we call 'the reverse' shots – i.e. pictures of me listening intently, which we use as a means of editing sound. (Whenever you see a very short clip of the reporter nodding sagely, be sure that has been done to link two bits of what an interviewee has been saying. With radio you can just splice the sound together, but obviously if you do that for TV the interviewee's head will jump from one position to another. Thus, the reverse shot of me.)

Anyway, we are filming the reverse and Cohn then does start opining on whether the President had been racist, and whether Trump knew exactly what he was doing in saying those things, and whether it had all been done to gin up his base. As I momentarily wonder whether this sound might be usable, his aide – who looks like she might have been a super-model in a previous career – moves in like a hawk to tell me and the production team that this is all off the record and CANNOT be used. She leaves no one in much doubt. This is one of the most frustrating parts of the job. The interview had ended – which was all on the record. Now everything was off the record.

30 July, Detroit, Michigan

We have come here for the Democratic Party debate of presidential hopefuls. There are so many candidates that the debate takes place over two nights. Detroit I really love as a city. It has grit, and it has history – and in recent years it has been to hell and back. This is Motown – motor city. This is where the automotive industry became one of the great engines of the US economy, but where, when the financial crash took place in 2008, the great car companies flirted dangerously with going bankrupt.

In the aftermath of the crash, the city of Detroit itself had to file for bankruptcy – the largest municipal bankruptcy filing in American history. About a quarter of a million people just vanished; left the city, abandoning their homes, their streets. Whole districts became a ghost town, and property prices collapsed as businesses closed down or moved out. There was no money to pay the police; there were hardly any ambulances working. It was total municipal collapse. At one stage it looked as though the city's wonderful art gallery, the Detroit Institute of Art, was going to have to sell some of its most precious paintings to help pay off some of the debt.

But Detroit is coming back, and the downtown area where the debate is to be held is humming. The great art deco buildings have got occupants again, and the restaurants are doing a good trade. Go to the suburbs and the evidence of urban depopulation is still easy to find – whole streets more or less empty. But the city's mayor, Mike Duggan, in partnership with the private sector is bringing investors back. We met him at a jobs fare in the suburbs where young black men and women (and they were nearly all black) had come to find out about what they would have to do to get jobs. It was unbelievably impressive. Detroit may not be back to its 1960s heyday, but it feels like one of America's great cities is very much on the rise.

And – just like Donald Trump launching his campaign in Florida – it is no accident that the Democrats are here in Michigan. In 2016 this was meant to be part of the Blue firewall – the Democratic Party, blue collar, rustbelt citadel which would be impervious to Donald Trump's allure. So confident was Hillary Clinton of its safeness that she didn't bother to campaign here, until it was too late. Trump took Michigan with the slenderest margin of 11,000 votes – out of four and a half million votes cast in the state. That is nothing. And the Democrats want it back in 2020.

The TV debate format is unwieldy to say the least. The frontrunners are the former Vice-President, Joe Biden; the Massachusetts senator, Elizabeth Warren; and Bernie Sanders, the irrepressible senator from Vermont whose speaking style seems permanently set to shout.

Meanwhile the person way behind everyone else but making most waves is someone called Pete Buttigieg. He is the mayor of South Bend Indiana, a rustbelt town that has seen better days – a smaller version of Detroit, if you like – and I think we in the media find him the most engaging of the characters running for the Democratic nomination. He is white, gay, an Afghanistan military veteran, absurdly multi-lingual, charming and clever. I meet him in the bar after the debate, and he lives up to the superstar billing in a quiet and understated way. He has an easy, unaffected charm. His staffers are young and bright eyed – but smart. He seems to me the one to watch. But just because we in the media might fall in love with him, that's no guarantee that middle America will do the same. Indeed, there is good reason to believe that our love can be an absolute killer curse. His polling in South Carolina – one of the early voting states in the Primary process – with its large African American population is disastrous. I met a black off-duty firefighter who very calmly explained to me why a young, white gay guy, who was married, was not going to find it easy to win over a conservative, black population. He also tells me that he would vote Democrat 'so long as they don't come after my AR'. The AR15 is the assault rifle that has been used in any number of the recent mass shootings in the United States.

Beto O'Rourke, the former congressman from Texas who ran a very good Senate race against the Republican incumbent, Ted Cruz – but came up short – is also a bit of a media darling. But I think he is one of these politicians that the more you get to see, the less there is to know. I'm just not convinced how much substance there is. Like a very fine soufflé – there is a lot of air.

One other name to throw into my favourites mix: Kamala Harris – a senator from California, who seems to be making all the early running. She's impressive. She was a former prosecutor, but like a lot of prosecutors seems better at attack than defence. Am not really sure what she stands for – or where she stands on the defining issues. But boy, is she good at giving poor old Joe Biden a kicking. Hmm. Interesting that I find myself using the phrase 'poor old' – that's not an ageist thing. I wouldn't use that against Bernie Sanders, even though he is senior to

Biden; nor against Donald Trump, who is also in his seventies – and, whatever else his shortcomings may be, doesn't lack energy. Joe Biden just seems like an old boxer who has got back into the ring for one last payday, even though his management and trainers know in their hearts it's a lousy idea. He just seems off the pace, a bit forgetful – and he is certainly not floating like a butterfly nor stinging like a bee. Punch drunk. Maybe I'm being unfair. The polls have him as the out-and-out favourite, and the Democrat who would win with the biggest margin over Trump. That has to count for something. Certainly, as long as that remains the case he won't lack for big money donors.

Electability is the bit of the piece that a lot of Democrat activists seem to be ignoring. History shows that in the Democratic Party primaries you start out to win over your activists – who tend to be a lot further to the left than the bulk of the population – only to tack to the centre as the presidential election draws near and you need to garner the greatest number of votes. But in 2019 it feels different. There is a bit of a bidding war going on to see who can be the most anti-establishment radical. By planting his flag as the more centrist, the heir to Obama is drawing a lot of heat.

31 July, Detroit. A hotel room just before 01.00

So the plan for me in Detroit is to present the *Today* programme – and that means being on air from 01.00 to 04.00. An engineer has come up from Washington, and two brilliant producers have come over from London to mastermind the programme. Imogen Walford and Dan MacAdam – Imogen was with me when I interviewed Bannon; Dan joined us in New York. We've also spoken to the mayor of Detroit, the president of Ford at their sensational 1950s HQ, one of Michigan's two senators and a whole pile of wonderful voices from Republican and

Democrat areas. We have great material to feed into the programme. Martha Kearney is presenting at the London end. I am a little nervous. Yes, I'm an experienced broadcaster, but *Today* is the biggest news programme there is – and it is very seldom that I present it.

The plan is to anchor the programme from the hotel bedroom of our engineer, Nick. It doesn't go well. No. Let me go further. It's a bloody catastrophe. At 06.00 (London time) I say hello and welcome to *Today*. At 06.01 we fall off the air. Crash. I am only aware of this when, in my headphones, I hear Martha saying, 'I'm sorry, there seems to be a problem with Jon's line in Detroit.' Yes, the problem was that the room's Wi-Fi had been tested in the middle of the afternoon when only the engineer was there. At 01.00, when there was me and two producers as well, and all of us were trying to download running orders and print scripts, the router overloaded and promptly fell over. If it were an old-fashioned car, steam would have been rising in dense clouds from the radiator.

Thankfully I have this ingenious little app on my phone called Luci Live, which means once I establish communication with London I am able to broadcast in studio quality. For the next hour I present the BBC's flagship news programme on the phone. All the Outside Broadcast equipment so elaborately set up in the room is staring back at me redundant. The one really knotty problem comes when I have to speak to my BBC colleague Anthony Zurcher, who has come to the room for the interview. Because the OB is kaput, he will have to use Luci Live on his phone. But this creates feedback and howlround because we can hear each other both in real time and through the delay on the line. It is unusable. Cacophonous. Without a second's hesitation Imogen, who is tiny and petite, throws Anthony, who is very tall and thin, into the broom closet, rips the duvet off the bed and drapes it over his body, then slams the door shut. He is in there for ten suffocating, breathless minutes. It works. He gives me his insights on the debate. Martha picks up in London on my thankyou to him. Anthony emerges a deep shade of purple and wet, looking as though he has lost several kilos in the process. Maybe we could market this as the *Today* programme fitness plan.

19 September, Winfield House, Regent's Park, Central London

The residence of the US ambassador has to be one of the finest mansions in London. It is on the northern edge of Regent's Park, a mere banana's throw from the gorilla enclosure at London Zoo. I have been invited to breakfast with the ambassador, Woody Johnson, philanthropist, billionaire member of the Johnson & Johnson family, owner of the New York Jets and, after 2016, Donald Trump's appointee as ambassador. We had never met before.

I got to know the house a little when his predecessor, Matthew Barzun, was the occupant. He was Obama's man in London, and Winfield House during his tenure at the Court of St James rocked to a funkier beat. Barzun installed a turntable in the grand entrance hall, along with his extensive collection of vinyl. As a guest you would have to choose what record you wanted to listen to, and the music would pump out. When I arrived, the first thing I noticed was that the turntable and the vinyl had gone. Indeed, on this crisp autumn morning when I walked in, so had the ambassador. The house was empty. He was out on the terrace with one of the long-standing foreign service officials.

Woody Johnson is small and dapper. But there is a sheen about him. Glossy almost. And he talks in a way that I have found common (and slightly grating) among exceptionally rich and successful business people. He has an air of supreme confidence, and expresses contentious views as though they are unquestionable, self-evident facts. And as America's chief diplomat in London I would quickly discover that his views are – well – not always that diplomatic.

I had been in London that week for the launch of my book *A Year at the Circus*, charting the goings on at the Trump White House. That immediately posed me a dilemma: if I didn't take him a copy, that might appear rude; but I felt sure he was not going to like the title – or, frankly, that much of the content. I gave it to him and he was very gracious about it.

The lovingly manicured gardens of Winfield House seem to go on forever. After surveying the scene from his terrace looking south towards central London we moved inside to the dining room and a table laid up for the three of us.

The conversation quickly turned to Brexit – and far from sounding like a typical diplomat and saying, 'I'm sure the politicians will find a way through this that is in the best interests of the UK,' he had very definite views. And they were more Farage than Farage. Britain would be better off just walking away without a deal … it would be the start of a new Victorian age of greatness, a golden era, he opined.

But what about the Northern Ireland border, I asked? A theatrical wave of the hand arced skywards, as if to say 'don't bore me with tedious details'. What about manufacturing, the union with Scotland (which had voted decisively to remain), supply chains? Any query I raised was immediately batted away as being barely worthy of discussion or consideration. It was all going to be a renaissance period for the UK, and a trade deal with the US would be the crowning glory.

There was also a fascinating glimpse into the binary way of thinking that is something the ambassador shares with the President. He started talking about Theresa May – she was a loser. Simple as that. That is why the President didn't respect her. But the Queen? Well, she was a winner. And Donald Trump loves a winner. I see the Queen as many different things – public servant, inscrutable, selfless, dutiful, maybe austere – but have never ever thought of her in those terms: winner/loser. I suspect neither has she. It's a slightly odd, but telling way – and dare I say a billionaire's way – to look at the world.

We spent a bit of time discussing a future trade deal, what the parameters might be – there are the hardy perennials such as chlorine washed chicken and hormone treated beef – and how any trade deal would be contingent on what the UK agrees when eventually it leaves the EU. We also discussed what it might mean for the National Health Service – Donald Trump had got himself into hot water when he opined that 'everything would be on the table' in a future free trade agreement. I offered the view that the NHS in British politics is akin to gun law in the US context. They are the live rail in each nation's politics and must be handled with extraordinary care – or better still from a survival point of view, not touched at all.

Ambassador Johnson concurred. The President had misspoken. Of course, US pharmaceutical companies might want greater access to the NHS, and other American health service providers too. But that was it.

Then something extraordinary happened as the three of us sat round the breakfast table. To my astonishment the ambassador started rolling up his trouser leg and asked me to inspect his calf. I really didn't know where this was going – other than in a surprising direction. 'Do you see that?' he asks, pointed to an area of his leg. I am now truly outside my comfort zone. 'No, I'm not sure what I am looking at,' I reply lamely. Exactly, he tells me – that is where he had some medical intervention performed, and his New York surgeons had been so brilliant they hadn't left a mark. He now rolled his trouser leg up even higher and asked me to inspect again – this time I could see something. There was a raised purple scar. 'And that's what your National Health Service did to me when I had treatment in London.'

Like the ambassador's leg, I suspect the NHS will be on the table in future trade talks.

24 September, New York, the UN General Assembly

Bloody hell. Hadn't seen this coming. Here we are in New York for the annual meeting of UNGA. It is a time when the East Side of New York becomes a parking lot as black sedans and police motorcades take over this part of Manhattan, ferrying foreign leaders to and from the UN building on the East River to their delegation's hotels. Donald Trump is here to participate, and no doubt provoke a lot of his fellow leaders with his now familiar America First rhetoric.

But stone the crows, in Washington Nancy Pelosi has just announced a formal impeachment inquiry against Donald Trump. For some time Democrats have been trying to get to the bottom of a story about Ukraine, and why Congressionally-approved military aid was held up by the White House. That there was a whistle-blower. That the President made the aid contingent on his Ukrainian counterpart launching an investigation into an energy company of which the son of former Vice-President Joe Biden had been a director.

But equally for months she's been resisting pressure from some of her firebrand caucus to impeach him in the wake of the Mueller report – the House Speaker has held the line that the place to defeat Donald Trump is at the ballot box, not through the divisive mechanism of impeachment.

That's changed today. 'The actions taken to date by the President have seriously violated the Constitution,' the Speaker said, reading rather falteringly off autocue. She invoked the nation's founding principles. Mr Trump, she said, 'must be held accountable — no one is above the law.' I am guessing that Nancy Pelosi must know an awful lot more about the whistle-blower's complaint for her to press the nuclear button.

This is moving fast. We hear the White House is to release a transcript of the call with President Volodymyr Zelensky that took place back in July. This isn't normal. Transcripts between two world leaders don't get released. In our UN office there is now an exercise in speed reading. Can't help feeling that one of the great defences that Donald Trump has is that a lot of what he says comes out as an anagram of a properly constructed sentence. They are all words. Proper words. Just in a slightly random order. But immediately a number of things stand out:

He asks for a 'favour'.

He asks Zelensky to launch an investigation into Hunter Biden, son of the former VP Joe Biden, and now a contender in the 2020 race. To demonstrate what I mean about the 'anagram' nature of his speech, this is the key sentence: 'The other thing, there's a lot of talk about Biden's son, that Biden stopped the prosecution and a lot of people want to find out about that, so whatever you can do with the Attorney General would be great. Biden went around bragging that he stopped the prosecution, so if you can look into it … It sounds horrible to me.'

He tells Zelensky that he wants him to talk to Rudy Giuliani about all this. Giuliani is the President's personal lawyer and Mr Fixit – nothing to do with the State Department. Why is he taking a central role?

The President asks Zelensky to look into a company called Crowdstrike. It turns out this is a wholly debunked conspiracy theory that Donald Trump wants pursued. And it goes something like this: far from it being the Russians who were trying to interfere in the 2016 presidential election by hacking into the DNC computer, it was actually a Ukrainian company, and they were trying to disguise it so that Russia would get the blame.

On the call he goes after the former US ambassador, Marie Yovanovitch, saying she was bad news – and she's 'going to go through some things'.

OK. The call is pretty bad – it asks for a favour, and it asks for an investigation into Biden. But there is no threat or menace (except in the remarks related to Yovanovitch), which would make it much more difficult for Trump to defend – at least not in the partial transcript.

Also the WH document makes it clear it is not in fact a transcript. There is a caution note attached to it, explaining this has been built on other participants' notes and memories of the conversation – and is not a verbatim account.

Fasten seat belts, stow away your tray table, seats in the upright position – brace, brace, brace. This is going to be interesting.

25 September

Wouldn't you know it, as luck (?) would have it Trump is having a bilateral with Zelensky at the UN. Well this is going to be box-office.

No, it's bonkers. Teetering on surreal. This moment of high drama has Donald Trump revealing why he is so knowledgeable about Ukraine and its people: 'They're great people and I owned something called the Miss Universe Pageant years ago, and sold it to IMG, and when I ran for president I thought maybe it wouldn't be the greatest thing, going to Miss Universe and Miss USA pageants, but it's a great thing and we had a winner from Ukraine and really got to know the country very well in a lot of different ways, but it's a country I think with tremendous potential.'

There was no winner from Ukraine, but maybe that is a petty, small-minded detail. And then after a bit of awkward mutual back-slapping came the reporters' questions: had the Ukrainian president felt pressured into giving the US president a corruption investigation into the Bidens?

'Sure, we had – I think good phone call. It was normal. We spoke about many things, and I – so I think and you read it that nobody pushed me,' Zelensky concluded.

Trump had the quote he wanted, and leaped in: 'In other words, no pressure.'

Up to a point. Is the president of Ukraine – with Russian backed forces waging war on his eastern border, and totally dependent on US military aid – really going to say, 'Donald Trump tried to blackmail me?' Not a cat's chance in hell. This is a man in a horribly tight spot.

9 October, Washington

The Bernie Sanders campaign has just announced that their man has suffered a heart attack. He was admitted to hospital in Las Vegas last week – and since then we've been none the wiser. Now the admission it was a heart attack.

I wonder whether that's Bernie done. There are so many septua-genarians in this race (Elizabeth Warren, Joe Biden, Donald Trump – and potentially Michael Bloomberg is eyeing a run), you kind of forget that statistically it's almost inevitable that one of them will fall ill at some point in this gruelling process.

24 November

Mike Bloomberg is in. In the past he's always ruled himself out on the grounds that he is Jewish, pro-choice, pro-gun control, and a hugely wealthy New Yorker. Clearly that last obstacle is no longer relevant.

Trump will hate it that on the Democratic side there is going to be someone way wealthier than him. It's commonly argued that the main reason why Donald Trump has not released his tax returns is because they will reveal he is nothing like as wealthy as he claims – and may show that he's not even a billionaire. Bloomberg's entirely self-made wealth is estimated at around $52 billion, which in anyone's book (well maybe not Jeff Bezos's) is a lot of money.

If Trump likes to depict himself as smart and rich, Bloomberg could have as his bumper sticker 'smarter and richer'.

15 January 2020

Another Democratic Party candidates' debate. It seems that everyone has a curious sub-plot. This one is about the two progressives in the field – Bernie Sanders and Elizabeth Warren – who seem to be engaged in a most uncomradely spat. Warren is accusing Sanders of having said to her before Christmas that a woman couldn't win the presidency. He has furiously denied this. And does so on the debate stage. The debate ends and there is a distinct froideur between the two of them. If I'm not mistaken she refuses to shake his hand. And the conversation appears tense.

POSTSCRIPT: It was way, way better than that. They've been caught on a 'hot mic' – in other words the microphones were still picking up what they were saying in the sound gallery – even though none of it was transmitted. Warren tells Sanders, 'I think you called me a liar on national TV.' He responds, 'Let's not do it right now.'

Well, it's out now. This has brightened the day.

16 January

Have just returned from a fascinating evening at the EU ambassador's residence, and the utterly benign winter of beguilingly mild days feels as though it is about to adopt a more brutal, familiar face. There is an icy wind blowing. Today has felt like a moment. On Capitol Hill the Articles of Impeachment were carried across to the Senate by the seven Democrat congressmen and women who will be the prosecution counsel against Donald Trump.

On the floor of the Senate the sergeant-at-arms, after three calls of 'hear ye', told the senators to be quiet 'on pain of imprisonment'. The language was of a different age, and although I suspect the impeachment process will follow a familiar partisan script, it really did feel as though the senators were caught up in the history and, dare I say, majesty of the moment.

Normally while business is getting underway, these kings of the universe, these hundred men and women, soon to be sworn in as jurors in the trial of Donald John Trump, would be sitting at their desks chattering among themselves: about where they'd been over the Christmas holidays, where they were going to eat this evening, what the latest gossip was on this one or that one. On this auspicious day, however, they fell pin-drop silent as instructed.

The Chief Justice of the Supreme Court, John Roberts, in his functional black court robes will preside over the trial, and after swearing an oath to conduct the trial fairly he called upon every senator to stand. 'Do you solemnly swear that in all things appertaining to the trial of the impeachment of Donald John Trump, President of the United States, now pending, you will do impartial justice according to the Constitution and laws, so help you God?' With right arms raised, they said in unison 'I do.'

It was reverential. It was dignified. One by one, and in alphabetical order, the senators were called up to sign the 'oath book', putting in writing their pledge to uphold impartial justice. You could almost allow yourself to start thinking this is a judicial process, but for all the language of trials, juries, witnesses and evidence – and with America's most senior judge presiding – don't be gulled: this is still unmistakably a political fight. And it will be ugly.

Down the road at the White House the President was raging about the whole process being a hoax. He tweeted (with the cap lock on – always a sign of anger): 'I JUST GOT IMPEACHED FOR MAKING A PERFECT PHONE CALL,' a reference to the President's conversation with his Ukrainian counterpart – that few apart from Donald Trump himself think was perfect.

In the evening I went to a private dinner being given by the new EU ambassador for a dozen senior journalists at his residence in Kalorama, Washington's leafiest area. Stavros Lambrinidis is a loquacious Greek and a fine storyteller. His predecessor, David O'Sullivan, I had known well, and he was an occasional tennis partner. But when he and Agnes O'Sullivan left, they took their fine art collection with them. When the new ambassador arrived, the walls were bare.

Initially he asked for a donation/loan of a piece of art from each of the EU countries in Washington to showcase. Nothing was forthcoming, apart from a small, dusty piece found in the basement of the Slovenian embassy. I joked that he could have asked for something from the British Embassy, but he would have had to give it back by the end of the month when the UK pulled out of the EU. But Ambassador Lambrinidis had met a wealthy neighbour who was the chairman of the board of a famous art gallery in Texas. The gallery would offer to lend him the finest ceramics and paintings from their collection. An immensely generous offer. But there was a central concern – what would be the cost of insuring so much highly valuable artwork in a private residence? As it turns out, nothing. The EU ambassador's residence is two doors away from where Barack and Michelle Obama live, and just around the corner from Jared Kushner and Ivanka Trump's home. The place is crawling with security. The road outside is blocked off permanently, and there is a secret service detail 24/7. When I arrived at the checkpoint the USSS guy in his black sedan checked my credentials before I was allowed to proceed onto the street where the ambassador's house is situated. Art theft is not going to be a problem at this address.

The conversation round the table was largely focused on problems in EU/US relations, but at the end of the evening everyone had to make a prediction on the outcome of 2020. I was struck that no one thought it was a slam dunk for Donald Trump – even though the economy is doing so well and America is at peace, and he seems to have such a solid, iron-like grip on his base. A lot of talk that Biden would likely emerge as the candidate – although this group was divided on the likely pros and cons of Biden. Two important points were made that I mustn't forget.

First is about paying attention: although we in the media consume endless amounts of politics, we are deeply abnormal and mustn't kid ourselves otherwise. Most Americans will see Biden in 10- or 15-second soundbites on the news – and there he comes across as plausible, seasoned, a grown-up – and a powerful alternative to Donald Trump. They will not see a man who appears to be struggling to grasp detail and express his thoughts clearly as the ageing process takes more of a toll on him than it seems to be on Donald Trump (or Elizabeth Warren or Bernie Sanders or Michael Bloomberg).

The other point made by my colleague from Fox News was attention span. Right now, he said, on 16 January, we are all obsessing about impeachment and the forthcoming trial. But on 16 July? It will be gone. Superseded by a thousand different news cycles, dramas, scandals and dust-ups.

In other words, I consume too much news and my concentration is too short. For an old guy I can sometimes be really millennial.

23 January. Day two of the
Impeachment Trial of Donald Trump

The security in and around the Senate is unbelievable. Normal press credentials to get into the building aren't enough. Even in a city where I am used to tight security, this is something else. Underneath the Capitol complex, there is a subway linking the House and the Senate, and the myriad imposing buildings which house the senators and congressmen and women and their staffs. One pass is not enough. You need a special overlay issued by the Capitol police – the Capitol has its own police force. I get on Washington's version of the underground railroad (fitting really as so much of Washington was built by slaves) at the Russell Building. Before I'm allowed to board, my pass is checked, I have to produce my driving licence. My bag is searched. I am good to go, and allowed through the ring of steel security.

I get off at the Senate building and the phalanx of police say the ID round my neck isn't good enough. The pass does not pass muster. I have visions of Tom Hanks in the film *The Terminal*. I can't go forward. I can't go back. I am destined to spend the rest of my life in a permanent limbo 100 feet underneath the Capitol. Eventually I am rescued by an official employed in the Senate TV and Radio Office, who comes down to the basement, swears the affidavit that I am who I say I am. Documents are signed, photos taken, and I am now told all is OK. Except there has been a row over access to the trial. There is limited space, so we are being rotated in and out every half-hour.

Instructions are strict. No phones. No talking. No standing. Go where you are told. One journalist who wants – no, needs – to take in an inhaler causes some umming and erring. He is told it will be allowed, but he will be delayed access. Capitol police will need assurances that it is medically necessary. Maybe he should just wheeze very loudly.

Thirty-odd years ago I was a very young political correspondent at Westminster. In those days much more attention was paid to events in the Commons chamber than is the case today. Every newspaper had parliamentary gallery reporters whose sole job was to provide reports on what has happened on the Commons floor. None has them today. When I arrived in the Commons we still covered debates, and I remember looking down on the proceedings below.

As I went into the gallery of the Senate, and peered down, it all felt very familiar in terms of atmosphere, if not in layout. The mid-nineteenth-century chamber fans out in a wide arced semi-circle. The 100 senators sit in leather upholstered chairs and at what look like posh school desks – complete with ink well and a groove cut out where you can keep your pen and pencil. Now there was an innovation for the purpose of the impeachment trial. A Republican senator, feeling his colleagues would become easily bored, bought everyone a fidget spinner: essentially a tiny propeller with a ball bearing at the centre on a plastic mount that you can spin multiple times with minimum effort. As I sat and watched proceedings, the Republican senator from Arkansas, Tom Cotton, was making full use of it.

For the period I was in the chamber the Republican members paid close attention to the arguments being set out by the House managers from the Democratic Party. There had been reports that they were like fidgety schoolchildren with a supply teacher in charge. I saw nothing to support that. Whether minds were being changed, though, is a different question.

There are a handful of Republican senators who the Democrats hope they might be able to win over – centrists like Susan Collins from Maine and Lisa Murkowski from Alaska; Lamar Alexander, the 79-year-old senator from Tennessee, who is standing down in November; and Mitt Romney from Utah, who has never been frightened to show his antipathy towards Donald Trump. But, for the moment, the Republican

Party looks like a solid wall, a wall that is going to defend the President. Unless something new emerges to alter that.

26 January

I realise I am off to Iowa next week for the caucus, and when I was there in 2008 I was broadcasting in temperatures of -27 degrees centigrade. I thought my jaw was literally going to seize up. After being on for about 30 seconds I was barely able to move the muscles in my face. Twelve years on, the super-warm boots that accompanied me on that trip have fallen apart. Time to buy new ones. There's a fantastic camping, hiking, mountaineering and equipment store called REI, just by Union Station, which stocks everything and anything that you might need on a great outdoors adventure. While I am trying on my thermal lined pair I overhear two other customers being asked by the knowledgeable staff: 'So what will you be using your boots for?' 'Iowa,' they both reply. One can only imagine the spike in sales the Iowa Caucus is giving this outdoor store in Washington as journalists and politicos step out on their great quadrennial adventure beyond the nation's capital.

News is dominated by Iowa and what's coming next in the impeachment trial – but then there's something totally shocking. News of the death in a helicopter crash of Kobe Bryant. And at once all the cable channels have forgotten about impeachment – it is the life of the basketball legend that concerns them, and in fact everyone you speak to on the street.

It is getting wall-to-wall coverage. But there is something I've just seen on the *New York Times* website – reports of a manuscript of a new book by John Bolton, the President's former National Security Advisor, which flatly contradicts Donald Trump's account of what happened in his dealings with Ukraine. And Bolton ain't no junior clerical officer reporting something he heard from someone else who'd met a bloke in the pub. The title of his book is a line borrowed from the rap musical about the Founding Fathers, *Hamilton* – 'The Room Where It Happened'. Bolton was in the room where nearly everything happened. The Trump defence looks to be badly compromised by this. Surely if Republicans continue to resist calls for witnesses – like John Bolton – to give evidence, it will look like they don't want to get to the bottom of the impeachment charges. Or are frightened about what else might emerge to complicate the President's path to exoneration.

Even with the nation – rightly – wrapped up in the loss of a sporting icon, this Bolton story feels important – but I've been here before. That moment when you think something is a game changer for Donald Trump, only to re-remember that Donald Trump has changed the game.

29 January

Maybe cracks are appearing in Republican unity. Mitt Romney, the senator from Utah who was the Republican standard bearer in the 2012 presidential election against Obama, says he wants to hear from Bolton. The White House is scrambling. Republicans on the Hill don't seem to know what to say. Even the Senate leader Mitch McConnell has been blindsided.

The President denies Bolton's devastating account. But here is the question that I have been mulling for weeks: why, when the White House knew that Bolton was fed up and that he thought the 'shakedown' of Ukraine was unacceptable, knew that he kept a detailed diary of everything that happened – and had advised his staff to lawyer up and register their discontent – did the President go for the absolutist defence that his behaviour over Ukraine was perfect and nothing untoward happened, when it could so easily unravel?

The Bolton revelations are irking the White House, and fully triggering the President. You have to give it to Trump – when it comes to invective on Twitter, boy, can he deliver. Bolton has always been the hawk's hawk. He wanted confrontation with North Korea; he advocated military action against Iran. Trump in an early morning tweet says that if he'd taken Bolton's advice 'we would be in World War 6 by now'. Suspect that one had Dems and Republicans chortling in equal measure. Rudy Giuliani, the President's lawyer, calls Bolton a classic backstabber.

In politics it has always been the case that you can be flavour of the month but then very quickly discarded. But has anyone gone from hero to zero as quickly as John Bolton?

On the BBC's *Ten O'Clock News* I say the Bolton allegations have left a torpedo sized hole in Trump's defence. My former producer Lynsea, who now works for the *New York Times* as a senior producer on their brilliant podcast *The Daily*, messages me approvingly over my use of language. 'I love your torpedo sized hole,' she writes. Only to message me again immediately afterwards to say, 'That text reads awfully. I'm so sorry.'

At this stage, I'll take laughs wherever I can get them. I giggle most of the way home.

30 January. British Embassy New Year reception

Each year the ambassador hosts a New Year reception for the journalists and broadcasters. It's a great event. All the leading broadcasters from the American networks and the stars of print turn up for champagne and canapés, while the ambassador normally gives a light-hearted, self-mocking speech in the ballroom, on the lectern set up underneath the Andy Warhol portrait of the Queen.

But this year it is much more sparsely attended. Sure, some of my colleagues are already in Iowa, and maybe the social secretary has sent out fewer invitations this year. There is an acting ambassador after the Trump-inspired firing of Sir Kim Darroch. But more than one person came up to me and wondered whether this was also down to Brexit, now just 24 hours away, and a president not overly concerned about British sensibilities. Maybe the British embassy is not the hot ticket it once was; maybe the Americans don't care as much about the UK as they once did. I hope that is not right. Maybe the Warhol portrait spoke of a more swinging, joyous time in US/UK relations.

I go home with less than the usual number of canapés inside me (perhaps some of the kitchen staff had been given the night off), probably the same quantity of champagne, but a slight feeling of emptiness that I am struggling to identify.

Meanwhile, back at the impeachment drama, I am in bed and ready to turn out the light when news the White House wants to hear comes through: one of the Republican waverers, Lamar Alexander from Tennessee, has made up his mind: he's not going to vote for witnesses to be called. But not for the reasons Donald Trump would want to hear. He says the Democrats *have* made a compelling case:

> There is no need for more evidence to conclude that the president withheld United States aid, at least in part, to pressure Ukraine to investigate the Bidens; the House managers have proved this with what they call a 'mountain of overwhelming evidence' ... It was inappropriate for the president to ask a foreign leader to investigate his political opponent and to withhold United States aid to encourage that investigation. When elected officials inappropriately interfere with such investigations, it undermines the principle of equal justice under the law. But the Constitution does not give the Senate the power to

remove the president from office and ban him from this year's
ballot simply for actions that are inappropriate.

So, guilty as charged – but of the lesser offence of acting inappropriately, rather than criminally. Donald Trump will hate that bit. But it
clears the path to his acquittal.

31 January

Sure enough, the Senate vote about calling witnesses goes Donald
Trump's way. Only two Republicans break ranks – Mitt Romney and
Susan Collins. All that's left to talk about is when the vote to acquit
comes – or as one Republican senator put it, how we land the plane.
Procedural wrangles and the like mean that will have to wait until
next week. It is quite a moment.

One of the central arguments against impeachment from the
President's counsel was that the Democrats hadn't been able to
produce any witnesses with direct experience of what went on in the
White House over Ukraine and the holding up of military aid. They
hadn't been able to prove there had been a quid pro quo. But in John
Bolton here was such a witness. He was in the room. He saw what
happened. He has written up the events in a soon to be published
book. But would the Republicans call him? No.

For all the talk of a trial, and senators as jury, and witnesses, and
oath swearing, and a judge presiding – this only looks like a judicial
process. This is politics. Partisan politics.

It is instructive in one other way too. It shows the complete and
total grip that this president has on the Republicans in the House and
the Senate. The reason that Richard Nixon was never impeached was
that when the process started, a Republican delegation led by Barry

Goldwater went to see him to tell him that almost all his remaining support in Congress had gone. The next day he resigned. It was the men in the grey suits offering the tumbler of whisky and the pearl-handled revolver. But no one did that with Donald Trump – even though, as Senator Alexander said in his statement, it is clear that Donald Trump did what he was accused of doing. The GOP members of Congress are terrified of him, of how he might punish disloyalty – of how he has dealt with other senators who've made life uncomfortable for him. There are a number of grandees who had the temerity to criticise and were either forced out, or jumped before they were pushed (Bob Corker, Jeff Flake) – and they have been replaced by much more pliant creatures. A Senate that would once, proudly, act as a check on the over-mighty ambitions of a president – would see it as its duty, no less – today gave up the ghost.

President Harry Truman had a sign on his office desk saying 'The buck stops here'. Clinton, lived by the phrase 'It's the economy stupid'. Obama had as his leitmotif 'Don't do stupid shit'. Trump should have this – even though it is a bit long, and could only just squeeze onto a tweet: 'It is much safer to be feared than loved because … love is preserved by the link of obligation which, owing to the baseness of men, is broken at every opportunity for their advantage; but fear preserves you by a dread of punishment that never fails.' Maybe he could just have the shorthand version – better to be feared than loved.

Yes, Niccolo Machiavelli in his practical political handbook, *The Prince*, could be Donald Trump's spiritual guide. He probably hadn't envisaged in the Florence of the Medicis the pain that could be inflicted by a Twitter storm; thumbscrews and the rack were more the thing then. But never has a party been so cowed – so owned – by its president. The Republican party is now a wholly owned subsidiary of Trump enterprises. It's a formidable achievement.

Three co-equal branches of government, the traditional description of the checks and balances envisaged by the founding fathers?

Not so much now. Executive power is redefined and widened significantly, and that will have ramifications long after Donald Trump has left the White House. What the President can do without sanction has been broadened – and I suspect future presidents will like what this means for future battles with the legislative branch.

1 February, Des Moines, Iowa

And so it begins. The opening act of the election drama. Iowa. The small midwestern state that has an oversized importance in every election cycle. Its 'first in the nation' status has conferred an almost kingmaking power on a state that is rural, conservative, religious and overwhelmingly white. And as we fly into Des Moines, that is the predominant impression – from a few thousand feet the snow lies thick on the ground. Whiteness is all you can see.

Everyone on the plane is either a journalist or camera operator or diplomat being deployed to this 'flyover' state to take the temperature of the people who live beyond Washington. I really like Des Moines as a city. The people are warm and friendly – try and find someone rude in midwestern towns like this.

And you really do bump into people who say things like 'I've met Bernie Sanders three times and Elizabeth Warren four, but I just can't decide between them.' This is both the absurdity and the charm of the Iowa Caucus. In a country of 350 million people the idea that you have to meet every candidate several times in person before you make up your mind who you're going to vote for is palpably preposterous. But in this state of corn and soybean farmers, that's how they roll. The charm, though, is that this is old-fashioned retail politics. Anyone can fashion a slick 30-second TV commercial that will make them look good. But having to go door to door, pop in at a diner, speak at an old people's home – while cameras are never far away – is a sure way to expose those who aren't clear about their message; or only speak human as a second language.

We go out to the Hope Lutheran church as they gather for their Saturday evening service, to speak to worshippers about the Caucus. There are 2,500 people inside the chapel by the time the service begins. I speak to the pastor. He tells me – almost apologetically – there will be a higher turnout for the Sunday morning services. The place is more like an out of town mall. And it's a pretty joyous atmosphere. A rock band is singing songs about Jesus – and on the TV feed relayed outside the chapel it is clear there are multiple cameras filming the whole 'show'. The production is slick beyond belief. And the preacher is I would guess six foot four, with chiselled good looks and blond hair and is wearing jeans, plaid lumberjack shirt and Converse trainers.

He stresses to me that the teachings of Christ bring everyone together. But the parishioners are as divided as anywhere else in America. The one thing I do find, though – even among the Trump voters – is a certain distaste for the incessant tweeting, the endless fights, the hurling of insults. These people like what Trump is doing for America, but you sense they don't much like him. I ask one Trump supporter if she thinks he is godly. Her mouth makes a series of contorted shapes as she tries to figure out how to answer that. Eventually she says, 'He's a guy.' And leaves it at that.

We get a taxi from the church back to downtown Des Moines. Our Uber driver is tuned into the Elvis Presley channel on the car radio, which should ensure that she won't be lonesome tonight. 'You from around here?' she asks – knowing full well the answer is no. 'No,' we reply. 'Are you from England or Australia?' she asks. And so the conversation goes on. She wants to know if I have met the Royal Family. She is anti Charles and pro Diana. Sympathises with Meghan and Harry wanting to step back. I ask whether she will be caucusing on Monday.

She says she will have to work, so won't be, but is torn between the principle and idealism of Sanders and the electability of Biden. Aah, the central dilemma that the Democratic Party is wrestling with.

Our journey is ending as we pull up to the Residence Inn hotel, and she tells us she would sure as hell love to go to London. I tell her she ought to, and that it is a fabulous city. She mulls the suggestion for half a second. And this very polite woman unwittingly reveals an attitude that I have come across over the six years I have lived in the US about how Americans see 'abroad'. Sometimes it is born of arrogance and sometimes the result of ignorance, but you get the impression there are many people who think that everywhere that is *not* America is the third world.

'Naah,' she says. 'I can't face getting all the jabs you'd need.'

2 February, Des Moines

I am pacing myself. I am presenting *Today* from here – so going on air at midnight and coming off at 03.00. At lunchtime we head to a Pete Buttigieg rally. There are big crowds lining up on the snow-cleared paths that lead from the school gymnasium. He's incredibly fluent, charming, compelling. He takes us through his stump speech without seeming rehearsed – which is quite an achievement, seeing as this is probably the one thousandth time he's delivered it.

He seems to have the easy manner of the clever boy who lives next door – but his story is of course more interesting than that. Multilingual, a Rhodes scholar, a naval reservist who served in Afghanistan, he's also a married gay man in a conservative, religious state. Something that is drawing almost zero attention.

He talks up how Iowa has had a penchant for going for the young man (he's 38) with a slightly unpronounceable name, a clear attempt to tie himself into the Barack Obama story. But 12 years ago I vividly remember my first experience of seeing Obama up close. I went along to Keene High School, not unlike this one, to see Barack Obama – then a young Illinois senator – going through the motions. He was engaged in what then looked like it would be a hopeless battle against Hillary Clinton. It was a pinch yourself moment. Obama was a rock star speaker. Funny, with killer comic timing, he could do the soaring, aspirational rhetoric. He could do the fiery, preacher in the pulpit sermon – and he could pick out a member of the audience and talk directly to them. To watch him then was revelatory. Buttigieg is good. Very good. But he's not Obama. That said, this audience seems to love him.

From there we drive across the surprisingly sprawling city of Des Moines to another high school – this time for a Biden rally. It is a slightly smaller auditorium. The audience is a bit older – but not massively so. There is a handful of warm-up speakers who are OK. In the audience I see John Kerry, the man who fought George W. Bush for the presidency in 2004. There are a few other notables.

From years of cutting two-minute-long TV reports, I tend to listen to speeches with my ear fixed on what will make the perfect soundbite – 15 to 20 seconds ideally, without the voice ending on an upward inflection, neatly making a key point – ideally with audience erupting in spontaneous applause or laughter at the end of it. I would have struggled today. The Trump jibe that stung Jeb Bush so badly four years ago was that he was 'low energy'. Joe Biden had all of that and more. There was just something rather unconvincing, faltering, going through the motions about it. He seemed to be laboured. He went through an interminable list of people to thank. There is an audience which has come to be convinced. They don't want to hear you thanking a whole bunch of people they've never heard of – particularly as, by now, the gymnasium where he's speaking is becoming hot and sweaty. I find my mind starting to wander; thinking about the things I need to do after we leave.

The speech ends and there is, I think, a warmer reaction to it than the quality of it really justified. But as I've said before, Midwesterners are scrupulously polite.

But then I see something different. He is off stage for longer than he was on. Biden waits to speak to anyone and everyone, poses for every selfie that is asked of him. A Chinese kid in a three-piece suit asks him to sign some document. He obliges. There is a woman with a baby, a little old lady wedged against the crush barriers. Everyone is the beneficiary of having a little bit of Biden gold-dust sprinkled on them. He shakes hands, he hugs, he puts his arm round you, he looks people directly in the eye. He loves humanity. This is not an act. This is who he is. And when he shows a hint of vulnerability – as he did when he spoke on stage about the battle he has had to conquer his stammer – the people love him more.

After he eventually leaves, I run into a couple of Democratic party veterans – who served Obama and who worked on the Hillary campaign. And they are in despair. They tell me the Biden campaign is an utter shambles. They do not believe the polls that suggest it is Biden and Bernie Sanders slugging it out for top spot. The key to Iowa and its odd system of caucuses is having a brilliant ground game. A disciplined organisation. You need wily precinct captains in each of the 1600-plus locations where caucuses will be held. The Biden team have years of experience, tens of thousands of miles on the clock – but according to the two women I speak to the machine is spluttering dangerously.

We'll see.

3 February

The *Today* programme goes well. We had recorded some very strong interviews, thanks to the hard work of my producer Dan. I hadn't slept at all well the night before, and I know I have a very long day ahead of me. I discover that wherever enough Iowans can gather there can be a caucus – so there is to be a caucus in Glasgow. And another in Paris. But then I discover a gem of a fact – there is to be another in Tbilisi. It would almost be negligent not to make the obvious joke on *Today*, which I do with relish. 'And there'll be caucuses in the Caucasus.' That makes me happy.

As we have a debrief and kickback in the engineer's bedroom where we've broadcast the programme from, I go for a stupidly aggressive solution to my fear of not sleeping. I take half an Ambien sleeping tablet washed down by a cup of Jack Daniels. Not good. Really not good. Outside the window of the hotel we have a train line where these never-ending freight trains snake past. I wake up feeling as though I have been hit by one. Note to self: if you must, occasionally resort to a sleep aid; and if you are going to succumb to a little nightcap – do one. Or the other. Not both. Never.

Caucusing needs a bit of a description. There are no ballot boxes, polling booths or voting cards. You gather at a caucus venue. You sit and chat, and you go and sit in different parts of the room depending on who you are supporting – and attempts are made to persuade you to come over to someone else's side. This process goes on for an hour, at the end of which the numbers are added up. Often there is a tie, and a coin-toss will decide the winner of that precinct. There is a bit more jiggery-pokery than that. The Iowa Democratic Party have devised a new app on which the numbers are passed over to a central counting area – from which the final results will be declared. The process starts at 7pm, ends at 8, with results by 9. Happy days. Or at least that's the theory.

I'm at Bernie's victory rally at the Holiday Inn, just out by the airport. I am feeling pretty lousy – not just because of my sleeping tablet/bourbon indiscretion. I have a sore throat and feel rough as sandpaper. But though we wait, results come there none. Nothing. Zip. Nada.

All the TV networks are getting testy. Schedules have been cleared to deliver the Iowa results – except there aren't any. The tone of coverage is quickly changing. Why the hell is Iowa the first state in the country to vote, when it is so unrepresentative of the rest of the country? It is mostly rural and overwhelmingly white. How come this midwestern state has so much power? Caucuses, which have until now been depicted as a charming, old world throwback to a bygone era of up close personal politics, are now being depicted as shambolic anachronisms that should be abolished.

But ultimately, how the hell has the Democratic Party managed to screw up quite so royally, as it is doing right now? That is a question to which there is no answer. This was to be the Democratic Party's night; a night when almost whatever the President did or said wouldn't matter, because all attention would be on the candidates fighting it out in Iowa. And they absolutely blew it.

And that left every sane commentator declaring the result as follows: the unofficial winner was Donald Trump, whose sides must have been hurting from laughing so much. Second place goes to Michael Bloomberg, who hasn't bothered to run in Iowa. His calculation was to sit out the two small states of Iowa and New Hampshire – in the hope that no clear runaway winner would emerge – and in the ensuing confusion he would insert himself into the race. It's looking like the billionaire has made another smart bet.

Eventually Bernie Sanders comes on stage to talk to his – by now – well lubricated supporters. All the other candidates do the same. History will record this was an election night when no candidate would make a victory speech or a concession speech. The only address to make is a total confusion speech.

What a lamentable advert for democracy this has turned out to be.

4 February, Des Moines to Washington

Am on the 07.30 flight back to Washington, which means leaving the hotel at 05.45 after a late finish the night before. Urggh. On the tarmac Emily Maitlis and I record a trail for a new podcast called *Americast* which we are going to do this evening. It is not an impressive display of technical prowess as we struggle to work out how to record on our phones and send to London. But then I remember I have an app that does this (which works considerably more efficiently than the Democratic Party's election app). The plane is packed with film crews and disgruntled, tired journalists who've travelled a long way to report on an election with no result.

It's also going to be a very late night tonight, with Trump giving his State of the Nation address – which will, undoubtedly, attract his biggest TV audience between now and the election. All the networks as well as the cable channels will be carrying it live.

SOTU (as we in the know refer to the State of the Union) is easy to play for laughs. The visuals are spectacular. The Speaker Nancy Pelosi reaching out to shake Donald Trump's hand before he speaks; him refusing to take it. She, sitting behind him while he makes his speech, becomes a one-woman meme factory, with exaggerated eye rolls, raised eyebrows, mouthing 'That is not true.' And then her finale, which can be seen either as a *coup de grâce* or a display of childish petulance, when she picks up her copy of the State of the Union address and very exaggeratedly tears it in two, while Donald Trump stands before her. Him milking the applause from the Republican side of the chamber. Her playing to the Democrat gallery.

It is also SOTU as a reality TV show. The Presidential Medal of Freedom, the highest civilian award that can be bestowed, is given to Rush Limbaugh (the syndicated right-wing radio show host is a divisive spear carrier in America's culture wars); a serviceman's wife and her children are asked to stand up – her husband is away serving in Iraq, and the President salutes the sacrifice and privations of America's service families. But tonight – surprise! – in a *This Is Your Life* moment, in walks the husband in his uniform to the astonishment of wife and children. She puts her hands in front of her mouth and gasps. The cameras zoom in to capture the first tear falling down a cheek. It is schmaltzy. Then there is a scholarship given to a young African American girl from Philadelphia so that she can escape being 'trapped in failing government schools' to attend a better school. Cue more gasps, more tears. Except this fourth grader isn't at a failing government school, it would later turn out, but at a highly sought-after Charter School. And so it went on.

Television is a slave to images, and of course I include all these things in my report for that evening's bulletin. But the most important thing about the speech is none of this. The psychodrama with Nancy and the gurning reality TV interludes are all a distraction. There is a serious political and electoral purpose to this speech that a lot of commentators overlooked.

Yes, there was plenty of red meat that he threw his base – the award to Limbaugh, tough talk on gun rights and clamping down on abortion. Strong words on immigration, promises to defeat socialism. That was to be expected. But there was a striking number of shout-outs to the African American community in a very positive way, from saluting those who fought in the Civil War, through to the civil rights movement. He made a point of talking about how unemployment among the African American community has never been lower, and he set out plans to assist black colleges. He talked about criminal justice reform and the efforts he has made to have released from prison those facing long prison sentences for non-violent drug offences.

It is true the President's standing among the African American community is pitiful. Only around 3 per cent of the black community voted for Trump at the last election. And sure, he would like more of them to vote for him.

But this was not the real target for this love-bombing by the President. No, what it seemed to me a lot of commentators missed was that this was *all* about white, college-educated women. Let me explain. This was about winning back a demographic who abandoned the Republican party in the 2018 midterm elections, and were the key determinant in allowing the Democrats to take back control of the House of Representatives, where this speech was taking place. These women from the suburbs had voted – by a clear majority – for Donald Trump in 2016, even after the *Access Hollywood*, 'grab them by the pussy' tape. But by the midterms – and after the disclosures about the hush payments to Stormy Daniels and a *Playboy* model, and the comments he made after neo-Nazi rioting in Charlottesville – they had taken against him. They thought he was a racist, a misogynist. This SOTU speech was an attempt to broaden his base: say nothing to alienate your fiercely protective core support, but try to tempt back some of those who abandoned you. It was clever.

5 February, feeling poorly in Georgetown

This is turning into what will be Donald Trump's best week since moving into the White House. Monday: the Democrats' Iowa shambles; Tuesday: the State of the Union success; and now today his certain acquittal on the impeachment charges as the Senate prepares to vote. This place moves at a dizzying pace, with vertiginous highs and lows.

It's time to drag myself into the office to watch the inevitable denouement. But what have I learned in my time doing this? Nothing is ever straightforward; nothing is ever linear. I have said it often enough in my two-ways from the White House: always expect the unexpected.

And an hour or two before the vote is due in the Senate, up pops the last Republican to run for the presidency before Donald Trump. Senator Mitt Romney from Utah, who ran against Obama in 2012, is on his feet. Romney has the looks of an ageing Hollywood leading man. Chiselled features, dark hair that is now greying, baritone voice – but the 72-year old still cuts an elegant dash. And his speech is one that will be replayed down the ages. It is delivered slowly and purposefully. This devout Mormon, who has always wanted to shy away from talking about his faith, is emotional, his voice occasionally cracking at the enormity of what he is saying, and maybe the burden he's been carrying. It is scorching; a searing indictment of Donald Trump. He started by talking about his faith and his responsibility as a 'juror' in this trial:

> As a senator-juror, I swore an oath before God to exercise impartial justice. I am profoundly religious. My faith is at the heart of who I am. I take an oath before God as enormously consequential. I knew from the outset that being tasked with judging the President, the leader of my own party, would be the most difficult decision I have ever faced. I was not wrong.

But then to the meat of it:

> The verdict is ours to render under our Constitution. The people will judge us for how well and faithfully we fulfil our duty. The grave question the Constitution tasked senators to answer is whether the President committed an act so extreme and egregious that it rises to the level of a high crime and misdemeanour. Yes, he did.
>
> The President asked a foreign government to investigate his political rival. The President withheld vital military funds

from that government to press it to do so. The President delayed
funds for an American ally at war with Russian invaders. The
President's purpose was personal and political. Accordingly,
the President is guilty of an appalling abuse of public trust.

What he did was not perfect. No, it was a flagrant assault
on our electoral rights, our national security and our fundamental values. Corrupting an election to keep oneself in office
is perhaps the most abusive and destructive violation of one's
oath of office that I can imagine.

This was dramatic enough in its own right, but it had a wider signif-
icance even if it wouldn't affect the outcome. There was no way two
thirds of the Senate was going to convict and remove Donald Trump
from office. But what it did was rob the President of one of his central
claims: that the Republican party was entirely united, and no one
supported what he called the election hoax. It would also mean that
that night's headlines (and never underestimate the extent to which
this president is driven by how he is reported) would not be the
straightforward, hands-down victory he craved. Romney had written
his way into the story with this excoriating address.

The vote when it came was what everyone had predicted it would
be. On the first article of impeachment – the abuse of power charge
that Romney referenced – they voted 48 in favour, 52 against conviction; on the second charge of obstructing Congress it was 47–53.

Who knows how long this will live in the memory – there will be
a thousand mind-blowing events, I'm sure, between now and election
day. But I suspect what Mitt Romney has said won't be forgotten –
and will be weaponised by Democrats as they seek to build their case
about why Donald Trump shouldn't be elected for a second term.

6 February, Georgetown

Now feeling so poorly that I am spending the day under a duvet. I want to sleep, but I can't take my eyes off the television. First up, Donald Trump is at the National Prayer Breakfast – it is multi-faith, and non-partisan. Not that you would have known it. He piled into his political opponents, accusing them of being 'very dishonest and corrupt people'. They were trying to destroy the country.

Moments before he took to the lectern there was a message of tolerance from one of the preachers. Not for the first time, Donald Trump showed no interest in Jesus's teaching in the New Testament about turning the other cheek. The President on the morning after his acquittal was more driven by the Old Testament principle of taking an eye for an eye. Without naming them, he went after the Speaker, Nancy Pelosi, who was sitting just a few feet away at the head table, and Mitt Romney, who had voted to convict him. He accused them of hypocrisy for citing their faith while supporting his impeachment.

This was breakfast. His real feast – with starters, *amuse-bouches*, main course and dessert – would come at lunchtime. In the East Room of the White House the cameras were invited in – but this wasn't a news conference with the press asking questions. And it could not have been further away from Bill Clinton's contrite performance after he had been acquitted from his impeachment ordeal. Whether it was *faux* or real, he was the very picture of contrition back in 1999. 'Now that the Senate has fulfilled its constitutional responsibility, bringing this process to a conclusion,' he intoned, 'I want to say again to the American people how profoundly sorry I am for what I said and did to trigger these events, and the great burden they have imposed on the Congress and on the American people.'

That was not Donald Trump's text. He declared this day a day of celebration. The rows of seats in front of him were filled by his most ardent supporters – from the Senate and the House, as well as key members of his administration, and the defence team who had argued the President's case at the trial – and they smiled and clapped excitedly. For an hour the President singled out for praise those who had stood most closely to him, while those who had sought his conviction were variously evil, corrupt, vicious and mean. It was alternately rambling and mesmerising.

But what it showed above all else was the extent to which the President had total control of all the levers of the Republican Party. This was now his party. They now march to Donald Trump's raucous and unconventional tune. Only Mitt Romney had really dared to question the President; a couple of others went in for a bit of mild, self-serving and unconvincing hand-wringing. But the rest just fell meekly into line. The Republicans – once the party of Lincoln, the party of Reagan – are now the servants of Trump.

And the much-vaunted separation of powers has never looked so enfeebled. As the President introduced his legal team, one man seemed to be as enthusiastic in his applause as anyone else in the room – it was the Attorney General, William Barr. The man who is meant to be the neutral arbiter of justice, the man who is meant to oversee the justice system in a way that is colour-blind, seemed as caught up in the occasion as everyone else. As my brilliant colleague, Nick Bryant, put it: 'William Barr got up from his seat at the event to clap and salute Trump's legal team, suggesting the wall that should exist between prosecutors at the Justice Department and political operatives at the White House has been flattened.'

And the one thing that was absolutely clear from this and the National Prayer Breakfast: those who had 'crossed' the Donald were going to pay a price. A hefty one.

7 February

I'm still sick, thanks for asking.

If Wednesday's acquittal was Trump vindicated, and Thursday was Trump vindictive, Friday would turn out to be all about Vindman (who knew things could be so pleasingly alliterative). Lieutenant Colonel Alexander Vindman was the Ukraine specialist on the National Security Council at the White House, who testified to the House Intelligence committee, having first flagged his concerns to his superiors about the President's call with Volodymyr Zelensky, and the 'favour' the President asked for. He had fled the Soviet Union as a child with his father and brother. He joined the US army, was injured in combat, became a Purple Heart recipient and had risen to the rank of Lieutenant Colonel.

On the face of it, his story sounds like the classic embodiment of the American Dream. An immigrant family embracing the Stars and Stripes; Vindman and his brother both doing so well that they end up working in the White House. At the end of the soldier's testimony to the impeachment inquiry, he had a message for his father. He told him not to worry, and that in America no one is punished for telling the truth.

But no one calls the President's integrity into question without facing the most brutal backlash from the attack dogs on sympathetic cable news channels. Could Vindman be trusted? Maybe he wasn't really a loyal American after all. Maybe he was working for the other side; perhaps still feeling loyal to Ukraine, the part of the Soviet Union he left as a three-year-old. For a nation built on the toil of successive waves of immigrants, it's unmistakably nationalist stuff.

Two days after Donald Trump's acquittal, Vindman is escorted off the White House grounds, and is to be 're-assigned' by the Pentagon. His brother, a lawyer, is also forced out, even though he had played no part in the impeachment inquiry.

Revenge would also be taken on Donald Trump's handpicked ambassador to the European Union, Gordon Sondland. The money he had pumped into the Trump inauguration committee had bought him a plum ambassadorship, but it was no insurance against the President's wrath. He had after all told the impeachment inquiry that there was a quid pro quo in the President's dealings with his Ukrainian counterpart. Some senior Republicans who had been the beneficiaries of Sondland's munificence pleaded with the White House to give the wealthy hotelier the option to resign and spare him the humiliation of being summarily fired.

Not a chance. The President had scores to settle, and lessons to teach – and the order of the day was rubbing noses in the dirt. And with as much public shaming as it was possible to muster. Sondland and Vindman would serve as both a lesson and a warning to anyone else who might decide at some point in the future to put conscience and public duty before fealty to the President. No doubt Tony Soprano would approve.

This has been, to my mind, the runaway best week of Donald Trump's presidency: the Dems are in hopeless disarray, he's been exonerated from the latest existential threat to the presidency, his enemies have been slain, those around him will have become even more quiescent, he has given a tactically smart State of the Union address with his eyes firmly fixed on the November election. And he has shown who is unquestionably in charge. Chaotic and noisy it maybe, but he's bloody formidable.

11 February. Polling day, New Hampshire

You can sense that anxiety levels among senior Democrats are high. Not over who should win, but that there should be a winner; that the chaotic incompetence of Iowa should be an aberration, not part of a pattern. We go to a polling station in Nashua in the south of the state, in a strongly blue-collar area. Representatives of each candidate are standing on the road, waving forlornly as voters drive straight past them to park in the school playground. Turn-out is brisk, according to the polling station manager – and up on four years ago.

In the evening we go to the Bernie Sanders results party, which is being held in a college gymnasium at Southern New Hampshire University. We have filled in all the correct forms and have been allocated a space on the back of the riser, with a view of the lectern where Sanders will come and address his enthusiastic, young supporters. And *young* is an important part of it. This is Bernie's core. Just like Jeremy Corbyn, another septuagenarian who went for politics' biggest prize, his strongest support was from young people.

The space on the riser is so tight that the tip of my nose is virtually touching the camera lens. And – typically – someone who hadn't filled in the necessary accreditation is trying to muscle in on our position. He is from a French network, and doesn't seem much bothered by our protests about him encroaching. *Je m'en fou*s seems to be his general attitude. He and I are heading for a no-deal Brexit.

In the auditorium on the big screen they are showing CNN. When Pete Buttigieg takes to the stage the crowd start chanting 'Wall Street Pete, Wall Street Pete' – a reference to the fact that Buttigieg has raised money from wealthy donors as well as so-called ordinary Joes. This may seem like normal political knockabout. But these are people from the same party. And there is plenty of evidence of the nastiness of a lot of the people in Sanders's campaign.

At a small Biden event some arrived carrying a coffin, a macho attempt to show what they would do to the former Vice-President and his presidential bid. But Biden is someone whose wife and daughter were killed in a car crash many years ago; and his beloved son, Beau, died of cancer four years ago. Carrying a coffin to an event he was hosting is at its most benign crass insensitivity, at its worst cruel beyond belief. The campaign trail is full of stories of 'Bernie's people' and how unpleasant they can be; but also how little he does to rein them in.

Just before 11pm comes confirmation that Bernie has won. He takes to the stage with wife Jane and assorted children and grandchildren. Sanders's style of public oratory has one setting: full throttle. There are no quiet, pastoral passages where you have to lean in to hear what he's saying – the volume is set to 11. For our *Americast* podcast that I do with Emily Maitlis I try to imitate Sanders at the breakfast table, barking out his needs in that thick Brooklyn accent: 'PASS ME THE BRAN FLAKES, JANE. BRAN FLAKES ARE NOT JUST FOR THE BILLIONAIRES AND WALL STREET AND THE 1 PER CENT. WHEN I'M PRESIDENT BRAN FLAKES WILL BE FOR EVERYONE.'

20 February, London

Am back in the UK to present the *Today* programme for a few days. My alarm has gone off at 03.15. And it is brutal. The reason it feels as if you are getting up in the middle of the night is that you *are* getting up in the middle of the night. As my eyes finally decide they do remember how to focus, I look at my phone to see what is happening in Las Vegas, where the TV debate is still going on. Holy moly. It sounds like an absolute bloodbath. Vegas, the scene of so many heavyweight prize fights down the years, seems to have hosted a contest where one trainer should have thrown the towel into the ring.

I momentarily berate myself for not having got up an hour earlier to witness it for myself, but very quickly come to my senses. Chief knife-wielder was Elizabeth Warren. I catch up with some neat CNN commentary. 'Bloomberg went in as the *Titanic* – billion-dollar machine *Titanic*. *Titanic*, meet iceberg Elizabeth Warren.' She was scathing: especially over his treatment of women, the non-disclosure agreements they were made to sign. For Bloomberg it was two hours of pure torture and humiliation.

The killer blow, which would get played and replayed *ad infinitum* by the cable channels, was this from Senator Warren: 'I'd like to talk about who we're running against,' she said. 'A billionaire who calls women "fat broads" and "horse-faced lesbians". And no, I'm not talking about Donald Trump. I'm talking about Mayor Bloomberg.' Booof. It was a punch to the gut that left him gasping for breath. Later he would tout the number of women he had appointed to senior leadership positions within the Bloomberg foundation, noting, 'I have no tolerance for the kind of behaviour that the #MeToo movement has exposed.' But if that was the Bloomberg jab, Warren was waiting with a swinging left hook that nearly detached his head from the rest of his body. 'I hope you've heard what his defence was: I've been nice to some women,' she said to audience applause. 'That just doesn't cut it.'

23 February, Geneva

Before I fly back to the US, we go to Switzerland to see our dearest American friends, Aaron and Helene, who are now living in this wonderful *belle époque* apartment, looking directly onto the lake. He is (broadly) a moderate Republican; she is (unswervingly) a Democrat. We start talking about the race, and money. As a foreigner I am legally not allowed to donate money to a campaign even if I wanted to. But that doesn't stop me getting at least half a dozen begging emails a day from assorted Dems and the Trump campaign: chip in here, why not donate this. 'You pitching in could really help our campaign, Jon.' But Helene laughs when I tell her this. She shows me her email inbox. She is receiving on average 100 emails per day from Democrats begging for money; from presidential candidates to congressional contests to – I don't know – the local dog-catcher. It is relentless, off-putting, intrusive – but I guess it's the price you pay for the ruling from the Supreme Court in the Citizens United case, which holds there are no limits to the amount that a candidate can spend in an election. The most important part of a US politician's job is not policy; it is rattling a collecting tin.

25 February, Washington

The Dem circus has now moved to South Carolina, ahead of this weekend's primary. I am watching from my apartment, which is not the same as being there and going to the spin room afterwards. But sometimes distance is a good thing. It is being screened by CBS, and watching the two anchors handle the debate reminds me of those long-gone schooldays when a dippy, well-meaning supply teacher would be thrown into the lion's den, to wrestle with 30 14-year-old boys doing their adolescent worst. Unruly doesn't begin to describe it.

But it seems to me – and maybe this is simply because the bar is so low – that the best night is had by Joe Biden. There is much more aggression, more bite, more focus to his attacks. It feels as though this is an all-or-nothing strategy. His team have long made clear to us that South Carolina is his firewall.

At the end of the debate each of the candidates is asked what is a common misconception about them. Biden replies, 'The biggest misconception is that I have more hair than I think I do.' It is hard not to warm to the sheer humanity and decency of Biden. It is a life that has been well lived, and consistently marked by the most testing and awful personal tragedy. He has overcome so much. But here at the age of 77, has he got the energy, the 'smarts', the hunger for it?

26 February, White House Briefing Room

The coronavirus feels like it is changing everything. This is a torrid week, and share prices are in freefall. The administration's messaging on what individuals should do, how to protect yourself, what its impact will be, who will be tested, has been chaotic and mixed – and that is being kind. The President's claims that it is no worse than the seasonal flu, that there could soon be no cases in the US, that it will disappear as fast as it arrived, were designed to reassure consumers and companies. But the evidence from around the world is pointing in the opposite direction. Concern is well founded, and the markets are reacting accordingly. Coronavirus is suddenly not just a public health emergency; it has the potential to upend the Trump campaign's 2020 calculations of going to the country on a record of economic success and a booming stock market.

And, sure enough, there is evidence of the urgency in the form of a stunning op note (a sort of press release that also doubles as a heads up on the day ahead) put out by the White House press shop. The President is going to hold a news conference in the Briefing Room. The Briefing Room! In the three and a bit years that he's been president he's only come to the Briefing Room once, and that was to make a statement – and not answer any questions. The room has fallen into total disuse under this administration. The daily briefing has been abandoned – there hasn't been one of those since March 2019. If the President wants to speak he will do so when he is seated in the Oval Office with another world leader sitting beside him – normally looking on slightly bemused. Or he will answer reporters' questions on the South Lawn as the rotor blades of Marine One are turning about 20 paces away. Neither is ideal for a measured conversation.

So the Briefing Room, which was opened in 1970 during the Nixon administration, and was built on top of the now drained indoor swimming pool, has become a place where reporters do their lives from if it is hammering with rain outside; and a storage area for camera crews' tripods and lights, for photographers' ladders – while the seven rows of seven blue seats which are assigned to the different news organisations have become rather dust covered.

But tonight they will be dusted down. The President is coming by. And one of the first things he says is that this is going to become a daily event. (Soon after, I get an email from a woman called Tamara Keith who works for National Public Radio – the nearest the US has to BBC radio – telling us that while it is good news that the Briefing Room is coming back to life, 'The bad news is that during this period of fallow, many of us started using the briefing room for storage, stand-ups and as work space. With the resumption of briefings, we need to clean house. It isn't safe to have gear, step ladders, cables, boxes of batteries, coats and backpacks all over the briefing room,' she wrote, 'and we would all appreciate your cooperation in tidying up.')

There are many things that stand out from the news conference, perhaps the main one being that the President isn't going to be taking the lead as coronavirus supremo – that role is going to fall to Mike Pence. When has the President ever taken a back seat? It leads to the obvious explanation that for all his apparent blasé demeanour, that coronavirus is no biggy, the President knows all too well this is going to be difficult – so if anyone is going to get it in the neck if things go wrong, better Pence than him.

Even if the President has put himself in the back seat, that hasn't stopped him being a back-seat driver – and trying to drive the car in a different direction from the path set by the public health experts advising Mike Pence.

Is this going to be one of those rare occasions when Donald Trump's freewheeling style of saying whatever he likes is going to come back to bite him on the bottom? When it comes to claims about how many miles of new border wall you've built, or how many manufacturing jobs you've brought back, no one is paying that much attention. But this is a health emergency, and a time when facts and accurate information do matter. We'll see.

But there is one quote from him that is either going to show that the US is totally bucking the global trend, defying the epidemiologists and a miracle is happening, or it is going to be a remark that will hang very heavily around the President's neck – and will be replayed again and again.

This is the comment: 'When you have 15 [coronavirus cases], and the 15 within a couple of days is going to be down to close to zero, that's a pretty good job we've done.'

One other thing today: a man called Jim Clyburn has come out and backed Joe Biden for South Carolina. He is the most senior African American in the House of Representatives, and his electoral district is in the state. His is the endorsement that all the candidates wanted. Biden's got it. And he needs it. Although polls suggest he is in the lead, it is tightening, with Bernie Sanders resurgent after Nevada, and Tom Steyer the Californian tech billionaire spending a small fortune in the state – and clearly hoping to do well at the weekend.

28 February

An odd follow-up to the Trump news conference. The White House is almost blaming us (the media) and the Democrats for coronavirus, or at least people's concern about it. The President said that CNN were 'doing everything they can to instil fear in people', while some Democrats were 'trying to gain political favour by saying a lot of untruths'. The acting White House chief of staff, Mick Mulvaney, ramped it up still further, telling a conference of conservative activists that journalists were hyping the coronavirus because 'they think this will bring down the President; that's what this is all about'. Really? You sure, Mick?

But maybe this was all handy deflection. Because if there was one thing spreading faster than this mystery new virus, it was Wall Street jitters. Its famous index is the thing dearest to Donald Trump's heart. The Dow Jones on Friday closed down over 10 per cent on the week – the biggest fall since the financial crisis of 2008. A deadly combination. A lot of Americans don't know which to worry about more – their health or their wealth. Both seeming far more precarious than those halcyon pre-virus days a few weeks ago.

29 February, Spartanburg, South Carolina

A diner. Seems as if all US journalism depends on a diner: it is so quintessentially American, and the views expressed there are so far from those you will hear when you are stuck inside the tight, enlightened, *bien pensant* confines of the nation's capital. A black guy with a face that has a mouth with a handful of widely dispersed teeth, and a face where a number of warts seem to have embedded themselves, is calling out the orders from the long queues lining up to eat at one of Spartanburg's most famous eateries, the Beacon Drive-In. 'Half pounder, extra fries, Rueben and fries, chicken and fries' (are you starting to see the common denominator?). Here at the self-service counter you don't just get a plate of food. Every person seems to collect a food mountain. A gargantuan portion of deep fried anything and everything. The fries are piled so improbably high that you could turn it into a game of Jenga. You are more likely to find bacon in a mosque than a side of quinoa. I think if the owner had a real entrepreneurial flair he would have opened a pharmacy next door selling anti-cholesterol and heart pressure drugs – not to mention indigestion tablets. Or maybe a funeral home. We film behind the serving counter and it looks like a skating rink there is so much grease and fat on the floor. I notice that lemonade is priced by the gallon. Plates of food should be measured by the ton.

I am doing cheesy (melted, natch, and served with fried onions) vox pops along the line. It is the Democratic Party primary and I want to know who they're voting for, and why. It's fascinating. And just a bit scary.

This is the South after all. South Carolina is where the first slave ship arrived from Africa in 1619. Virtually every black person that I speak to in this line for their burgers and fries says they are voting Biden. Why? Because he was Barack Obama's vice-president, and as the wingman to the US's first African American president, he has a hold on their affections. I am not particularly surprised. But this did strike me – *every* white person I speak to tells me they're not voting in the Dem primary. They're Republicans, they tell me. Actually that's not quite right. What they say is they're Trump supporters. They're MAGA. And they proclaim it boldly. Not scientific, I know (in fact wholly unscientific) – vox pops never are – but it's an insight that's hard to shrug off. It's said that race is America's original sin. The impression here in the South – or at least from this one diner – is that black people vote Democrat; white people for Trump.

We go to film at a college baseball game. Wofford are hosting Merrimack, a college near Boston. Like all US college sport, the standard is unbelievably high. We've come here to tap into the support from young people for Bernie Sanders. But this is a private college, and this, we discover quickly, is not a Bernie crowd. A few hundred people are watching. I fall into conversation with some parents who have made the journey down from Massachusetts. One of the fathers asks where I am from, and when I say the BBC, he's off. 'What's your country going to do about all the no-go areas?' I am not sure what he means, so I ask. Big mistake. 'All the places where white people like you can't go. You know the towns where the Muslims have taken over.' I say there are no such places. He laughs at me as if I am an idiot. 'They've even got their own policing,' he insists. I try reasoning, but it is, I realise, a waste of time.

Easy to be defeatist about this, and just think what is the point of continuing with conventional journalism when so many people don't want to entertain views that challenge their way of looking at the world; their own 'truths'. But it spurs me on. Even though there are bits of BBC bureaucracy that drive me mad, broadly our mission is the right one: to educate, entertain and inform. And the job has never been more challenging and never more important. This encounter reminds me of that. If we are not in the business of challenging falsehood, then we might as well pack up and go home.

Anyway, back to the South Carolina primary ... The polls close and the networks waste no time in declaring Biden the winner. The exit polls are that strong. Biden is back ... he was only biden his time (I always really want to be a sub-editor on the *Sun*). Support given to Biden by the black community is decisive. The former Veep wins in every county of the state, and sweeps to a much needed victory – like Mark Twain, reports of his death are greatly exaggerated. And that would form a central tenet of his victory speech: 'Just days ago, the press and the pundits had declared this candidacy dead,' Biden told supporters. 'Now, thanks to all of you, the heart of the Democratic Party, we've just won and we've won big because of you. We are very much alive!'

It also sets off a much-needed chain reaction – the money is starting to flow back in, as centrists start to believe that it might well be Biden who will emerge as the standard bearer for moderate Dems. And boy does he need the cash. He is being outspent and outgunned by Bernie Sanders. And this, of course, is as nothing compared to the bottomless funds of Mike Bloomberg. His latest announcement is that he is going to buy a three-minute long advertisement in key markets, setting out how he believes the coronavirus outbreak should be dealt with. A three-minute ad? Who's ever heard of such a thing? Who's ever been able to afford such a thing?

Steyer is out. He hasn't performed as well as he had thought he would and announces to his supporters that he is ending his campaign.

2 March, Vermont

I am presenting the *Today* programme tonight ahead of Super Tuesday. Howard Dean, the former trailblazing candidate for the Democratic nomination 20 years ago and one-time governor of Vermont, comes to meet me at our hotel in Burlington to record an interview. What I had forgotten was that he used to be a physician. He refuses to shake my hand and elbow bumps me instead. I do wonder how this is going to affect our behaviour in this globalised world.

I am in bed by 7pm, and manage three hours' sleep before getting up to prepare for *Today*. Nick Robinson is in London. Not surprisingly, the programme is dominated by the coronavirus, and an excellent interview he does with the Health Secretary, Matt Hancock. The central question I try to answer in our coverage from Vermont is whether Bernie Sanders will build up an unstoppable momentum on Super Tuesday. Well, it's just become a whole lot more complicated. Amy Klobuchar, the formidable senator from Minnesota, has also withdrawn, and both she and Pete Buttigieg have come out – in what looks like an exquisitely coordinated move – to throw their weight behind Biden. If you are a centrist Democrat, the fear is that the division over who should be the candidate will inadvertently hand it to Sanders – the longer there is a multitude of moderates, the more they give Sanders the space to build up an uncatchable lead. But now Buttigieg and Klobuchar are out. Tonight that fear has dissipated. If Obama is playing this violin, he's playing it like a Stradivarius.

3 March. Super Tuesday

Polling day is invariably dull for a journalist. All you are really doing is waiting for the last voters to cast their ballot – and then preparing for an exciting night. Maitlis is presenting *Newsnight* from Washington. I tune in to see what and who she has got on the programme. And I can't believe my eyes. One of her guests (introduced deadpan by Maitlis) is Krystal Ball, a Democrat strategist. As you start to speculate on what the results might be, you have someone alongside you who can look into her …

Anyway Twitter lights up in the best way possible. Mikey Smith, a journalist on the *Mirror*, furnishes me with some other gems. There was an Idaho governor called Butch Otter – he was a noted opponent of gay marriage – and married someone called Gay. There was the Colorado State Senator, Randy Baumgardner, an Alabama State Treasurer called Young Boozer – and not forgetting the New Hampshire congressman, Dick Swett. Others chime in with other memorable names. I recall that when I first worked in local radio, and we had to read the news off what was called the 'rip and read' from London, delivered by a chuntering Telex machine in the office, there was a South Korean foreign minister called Lo Bum Suk. That took some saying out loud.

But now the polls close. And immediately there seem to be the makings of a memorable night. The race in Virginia is called immediately for Biden. This is big. Virginia is what is called an 'open primary' – meaning you don't have to be a member of the Democratic Party to vote. It looks like a lot of disaffected Republicans have come out to back him – along with the African American population, just like in South Carolina a few days earlier.

Biden is surging. I mean, wipe your eyes with disbelief, surging. If over the course of the previous few weeks of diary entries I have given the inadvertent impression that I think he is dead in the water, a lost cause, lacklustre, off the pace and enfeebled – of course dear reader, you have just misread and misinterpreted what I was saying (thankfully book publishing hasn't yet gone in for emojis, as I think I might have earned a Pinocchio for that). This is Lazarus-like. Or that phoenix. Or Tottenham last season when they were about to be knocked out of the semi-finals of the Champions League by Ajax, only for Lucas Moura to score that memorable hat-trick (we Spurs fans have very little to celebrate at the moment).

Over the course of the night, Biden is notching up win after win. This is so wildly exceeding expectations. And there are so many quick observations to make. First of all – and who can't feel a slight sense of schadenfreude about this – money can't buy you love, and it can't buy you votes either. Bloomberg has spent five hundred million bucks, and all he has to show for it is a win in the US Pacific territory, American Samoa. Our Washington bureau chief, Paul Danahar, tweets it would have been cheaper for him to have gone to American Samoa and built every resident who voted for him a new house. I add that he could have thrown in a nice yacht too. Yes, he has the money to carry on – but surely he can't. Surely he's done?

Elizabeth Warren – who I've thought over the whole thing has been the single most impressive candidate: strong on policy, sharp debater, good with people – has done poorly. And what must have rubbed salt in the wound was to come third in her home state of

Massachusetts behind Biden and Sanders. There is surely no path forward for her.

At the Sanders rally in a convention centre on the edge of Burlington there is a persistent, drizzly rain falling that wouldn't feel out of place in London in November. It kind of fits the mood in the auditorium, where Sanders will soon take the stage. I find a mix of defiance and defeatism, paranoia and disappointment. These people want to believe that Sanders will be the candidate – but a number of people say they fear he will somehow be 'robbed' of a crown that should be rightly his. That the Democratic establishment will conspire against him. That skulduggery will force him from the race. But as we watch on big screens the results coming in from around the country, it seems that it is Democratic voters who are determining this. Sanders has won Vermont; he seems on course to win California; he's tied up Utah. But this is Biden's night. A student I speak to tells me he's not going to vote for any other Democrat in the field; it's Sanders or nobody. When I suggest to him that if all Sanders supporters took that view it might result in Donald Trump winning a second term, he seems momentarily flummoxed, as though that thought had never occurred to him. And then shrugs.

Bloomberg and Warren have to make their decisions – but Super Tuesday has sorted something out: it's now a two-horse race for the Democratic nomination. It is now between a 77-year-old white man – Joe Biden – and a 78-year-old white man – Bernie Sanders – fighting for the privilege to take on in November a 73-year-old white man (with a light tinge of orange). A Democrat race that started with so much diversity in terms of race, gender and sexuality has come down to this. No worries about the glass ceiling this election cycle.

4 March

A colleague passes on this priceless *aperçu*. Pete Buttigieg, who is 38, could sit out the next seven presidential elections and decide to offer himself up as a candidate for the 2052 contest – and he would still be younger than the three people left in the race now. Wow.

Super Tuesday has become winning Wednesday for Joe Biden. The transformation in his fortunes just gets more remarkable. The big boon today to his campaign is the decision of the multibillionaire Mike Bloomberg to get out of the race, and throw his lot in with the former Vice-President. Rarely can $500 million have bought so little. But in this abortive bid, Bloomberg – with his infinite resources – built a nationwide campaign infrastructure with a team of 2,000 staffers. If the former New York mayor bequeaths this machine to Mr Biden, and it looks like he might – that is a game changer.

Joe Biden has responded on Twitter, saying, 'I can't thank you enough for your support ... this race is bigger than candidates and bigger than politics. It's about defeating Donald Trump.' Bernie Sanders after disappointing results last night is trying to figure out how to respond. It looks as though he is going to go after Joe Biden in uncompromising terms, something he's been reluctant to do until now. This could become an ugly brawl between two men in their late seventies.

Someone else wants to stick his oar in on what is happening in the Democratic Party – and that is Donald Trump. His tweets read as though he has become a staff member on the Bernie Sanders campaign. 'So selfish for Elizabeth Warren to stay in the race,' he writes. 'She has Zero chance of even coming close to winning, but hurts Bernie badly.'

So let's try and unpack this, because there is deliberate strategy here. The simple explanation is that Trump wants to face Sanders in the presidential election – because he believes he will be able to throw the kitchen sink at him: Crazy Bernie is a socialist, married in the Soviet Union. Friend of the commies in Venezuela – and can be trusted to crash the US economy just like Chávez and Maduro have done in a once wealthy oil-rich state. It is every Republican's dream to fight the election on those terms. But it also prepares the ground for if Bernie doesn't win the nomination. With repeated tweets about how the Democratic establishment is trying to steal the nomination from Sanders, the President is trying to sow discontent and disaffection among Bernie's young supporters. Obama may be able to make a violin sing – but no one trolls like Trump.

5 March

And now Warren makes her emotional exit from the presidential stage. It's on her doorstep in Massachusetts. Her husband Bruce and golden retriever Bailey at her side. She tackles the issue of gender head on. One of her hallmarks was to talk to young girls and make a 'pinkie promise' with them. She would get down to their level, so she could make direct eye contact. And she would interlock her little finger with theirs, and would say, 'I'm running for president because that's what girls do.'

Clearly upset, she says, 'One of the hardest parts is all those pinkie promises.' And she spoke of the 'trap' of gender for women running for the highest office. 'If you say, "Yeah, there was sexism in the race," everyone says "Whiner!" If you say, "No, there was no sexism," about a bazillion women think, "What planet are you on?"'

But who does she back? Well, she's not saying. In terms of simple policy alignment she is much, much closer to Bernie than Biden: she and Bernie are both on the left, progressive wing. But as we all know, politics is more complicated than that. There is clearly personal animus between Sanders and Warren. And she has made clear that a candidate is responsible for the behaviour of their supporters. That was a broadside at Sanders, if ever I heard one.

Also, if she believes that Biden is now the unstoppable force in this race, why waste leverage getting behind Bernie. I bet if Biden wants her support – and it would be a big prize for him – she could put a hefty price tag on that. Treasury Secretary? VP? Suspect she's not going to rush this decision.

9 March, Washington

Am kind of startled by the response – or should I say lack of it – to the coronavirus outbreak in the US. I was at a dinner on Saturday night, and there was from a number of smart people a kind of 'whatever' response – as if it is all a fuss about nothing. No worse than the seasonal flu. I come into work, feeling there is something I need to get off my chest. So I do what journalists do. I write a blog about it, which I hope you'll forgive if I summarise here.

There are two numbers that Donald Trump has consistently cared about and watched like a hawk. And they are inextricably linked in his mind. The first is his approval ratings. The second is the stock market. While other presidents have seen that as a barometer to keep a watch on, none has obsessed about Wall Street like Donald Trump. His calculation is that if the stock market is soaring, then his approval ratings will go up and QED – he will be re-elected in November this year. So every time the Dow Jones or the S and P 500 hits a new high, he tweets to celebrate it. 280 times to be exact. In other words, roughly once every four days of his presidency he has exalted the markets.

But with the arrival of the coronavirus, the markets have taken fright – and have been plunging vertiginously over the past couple of weeks. Today the steepness of the decline was such that it set off a circuit-breaker alarm on Wall Street. It fell by more than 7 per cent, and so trading was suspended for 15 minutes.

President Trump is used to fighting from his bunker when a crisis arrives – and let's face it, the past three and a bit years haven't lacked drama. But the coronavirus is quantitatively and qualitatively different from anything he has faced. How do you hit a virus? Who's to blame? Who's the guilty party? Who do you tweet at? Covid-19 doesn't have a Twitter account.

And in the midst of a health emergency, what is sacrosanct for anxious citizens – and frankly investors on Wall Street – is reliable information, a consistency of message from the government about the risks and how they can be mitigated – and that information flow will be based on the best available scientific evidence. No other factors should intrude.

In the United States as the administration has scrambled to mount an effective response the messages have been mixed, and not for the first time the president has been contradicting his own advisors and medical experts. From the outset of the coronavirus, Donald Trump has sought to play down its seriousness, and overestimate America's preparedness. He said the spread was under control. It isn't. He's said that the number of cases may soon go down to zero. They haven't, and it was not the advice he'd been given. He suggested that people with symptoms should go to work if they felt well enough. They shouldn't.

The critique is that the reason the president is contradicting his vice president (who has been put in charge of the nationwide response), and the public health professionals reporting to Mr Pence, is that the president needs the markets to remain buoyant; they are vital to his re-election strategy. The kinder explanation is that he doesn't want to engender panic, leading to the ludicrous scenes that we saw from the UK at the weekend with people filling their baskets with toilet rolls (how long are people planning to self-quarantine for?).

Soon after I wrote it, as if to underline my point the President tweets this: 'The Fake News Media and their partner, the Democratic Party, is doing everything within its semi-considerable power (it used to be greater!) to inflame the CoronaVirus situation, far beyond what the facts would warrant. Surgeon General "the risk is low to the average American".'

Confession: this evening I went home and I had been told that my 24/7 pharmacy, CVS, would be getting in a fresh delivery tonight of hand sanitiser. So at 9pm I wander up Wisconsin Avenue, and sure enough there's been a delivery. I am told that I should come back in 45 minutes when they will have unpacked. While I'm waiting outside, a former UK cabinet minister rings me to say how much he likes my blog. We enter into a long conversation. But I realise that inside the pharmacy the hand sanitiser is on the shelves and is fast disappearing. I cut him short, and buy two small pocket-sized packets. I don't feel proud, but I equally feel relieved.

10 March

Mississippi, Michigan, Missouri, North Dakota, Idaho and Washington State are voting today.

For the first time – amazingly – Covid-19 has affected political behaviour. First Bernie Sanders and then Joe Biden have cancelled events they were due to be holding tonight. A belated acknowledgement that bringing crowds of people together might not be such a smart idea. Donald Trump, though, is still planning his rallies across the country.

Fascinating, but I'm getting the impression there's an 'Anyone but Sanders' sentiment developing among Democrat voters. Seems those in the Dem/independent camp are more fixated on who can beat

Trump, than who has the purest political ideas. African American voters are staying solidly with Biden. Six more states are voting today – and as the polls close the exit data is fascinating. Yes, he is crushing it with African American voters. But Sanders is doing far worse than he was four years ago. And white voters – and particularly white working-class male voters – who propelled him to a famous victory in Michigan four years ago against Hillary Clinton are not turning out for him tonight. And what is the difference from four years ago? Hillary Clinton isn't on the ballot. Hard to overstate the antipathy there was towards her – and Bernie Sanders capitalised on it.

Now that she's gone he's struggling. Blue-collar America it seems didn't embrace Sanders four years ago so much as reject Hillary. And this time it's born-again-Biden mopping it up. Within a short time of the polls closing, Mississippi, Michigan and Missouri were called for Biden. He is building up a big lead in the delegate count.

This is a dismal night for Sanders, and he has gone home to Vermont to await the results – or sulk. Maybe both. An unusual move? You bet it is. What's more, word comes late in the evening that he intends to say nothing tonight. He is such a gargantuan voice on these occasions that it is hard to imagine him just staying schtoom. That's not Bernie. Unless of course he is considering his position in the race. In truth, unless something extraordinary happens, I cannot see a path to him winning the nomination. This is Biden's. It feels the race is over. To all intents and purposes Joe Biden is the Democratic Party nominee for 2020.

Nature, and politics in particular, abhors a vacuum. And the silence from Vermont is filled by a raucous yet calculating Joe Biden. Yes, he takes a victory lap on notching up another set of impressive wins. But he also talks admiringly of the campaign fought by Bernie Sanders, the tenacity of his supporters, the moral purpose that he has injected into the race. It is as if the race in Biden's mind is over, and it is now time to set about putting back together the Democratic Party and corralling its warring factions into one fighting unit.

But oh how Joe Biden has lulled his Democratic rivals into a false sense of security. There we were mistakenly believing that the man was utterly useless and that his campaign was going down the toilet. What a strategy: come fourth in Iowa, a wayward fifth in New Hampshire, way behind Bernie Sanders in Nevada – and then proceed to mop up. Well, that's rewritten the rule book.

11 March

I am flying today to see my son, Max, and his wife, Kate, who live in Australia. I would like to say that I have woken up excited at the prospect, tingling with anticipation. I am desperate to see them. Linda and my daughter, Anna, are flying from the UK. But instead, I have woken up with a stomach that is knotted with tension – it feels as though someone with very large hands has grabbed my intestines and attempted to give them a Chinese burn. I feel anxious. What is happening with the coronavirus I feel is a slow-moving tsunami that is about to take over all our lives. I worry could there be a worse time to travel. I have done a bit of reporting from dangerous places – and I have the same feeling as I do when I am about to board a flight that will end up with me being somewhere that we call in the business a 'hostile environment'. It is the time when all your inner demons come out to play; and park themselves on your shoulder, taunting you. There is a serious feeling of trepidation, and you look in the mirror and ask yourself 'What the f*** am I doing here?' And why. This was the distinct feeling I had after 9/11 when I boarded an Air France flight to Delhi before connecting to Tajikistan, before crossing the demilitarised zone to go into Afghanistan. It is a bit how I'm feeling this morning.

I spend a bit of the day recording *Americast*, where we go over the results from the night before – but also the impact of coronavirus, and I expand on some of the territory I covered in the blog. At the same pharmacy where I picked up the hand sanitiser the other night I have witnessed someone in the queue in front of me being told that they had a 'copay' of hundreds of dollars (i.e. their insurance only covered so much, and to collect their prescription they would have to pay the rest – the copay). Only for the prescribee to say they can't afford it, and walk out of the store without the drugs the doctor has prescribed for them. I was in New York, just over a year ago, when I realised I had run out of my preventative asthma inhaler. I went to a doctor who wrote me out a prescription for the equivalent drug that I had used in the UK. The pharmacist across the street checked whether they had it in stock. They did. She tells me apologetically that the inhaler would cost $375. It has 80 'pumps' – and you are meant to take it twice a day. In other words, it would last 40 days. The pharmacist asks whether I still want it. I give her my health card – and she comes back with a smile on her face and tells me there will be nothing to pay. Seems I have great insurance.

We finish the podcast recording and then word comes that Sanders is to make a statement from Vermont. There is a frisson of excitement, a little static energy, around the newsroom. Is he calling it a day? Throwing in the towel? It turns out to be an odd statement – he talks about how the Democrats want this resolved, and accepts that Joe Biden is seen – at the moment – as the best man to defeat Donald Trump. He accepts that his performance has been disappointing, and that he was roundly beaten last night, and the week before on Super Tuesday. And – just like those essays you wrote as an undergraduate with that portentous final paragraph 'so therefore I conclude that …' I expected the senator to say that he was packing up his tent. But he didn't. He said that he would carry on for the time being – but you sense that he is not going to be sticking around until the bitter end.

I have a few hours to kill before I head off to the airport. And decide that a smart use of my time would be to go to the supermarket, and stock up with some essentials that I can put in the freezer in case things have changed by the time I get back from Oz. The Trader Joe's on Wisconsin Avenue is quiet. I breeze round, fill a small basket – no lines at the check-out – and head home. Only the liberally scattered hand sanitiser giving a clue that things have changed a tad.

Donald Trump is to make a primetime address from the Oval Office when I will be about an hour into my flight, and I debate whether to hook up to the plane's Wi-Fi to see if his breezy, nothing much to see here tone has changed. I succumb. And it has. People living in the Schengen Zone are going to be banned from entering the US. Although, somewhat bizarrely, the UK and Ireland are to be exempted. Won't that just lead to French and Germans etc jumping onto a flight into Heathrow, or onto the Eurostar, and then heading to America that way? I see there's a lot of comment that whilst the President has yet to find a way to punch at the Covid-19, the way he's framed his remarks conveniently blames Europe, the European Union and China for the outbreak. Always good to have someone to scapegoat.

But given the importance of this White House set-piece, and that this was an address delivered via teleprompter – so the President was sticking to a text – there were nevertheless astonishingly sloppy mistakes. He said he was 'suspending all travel from Europe to the United States', when in fact it would affect only non-US citizens, and he said it would 'apply to the tremendous amount of trade and cargo' across the Atlantic, when in fact trade would be untouched. There then followed a series of clarifications and corrections from the White House. If the goal is to show you are on top of this, to reassure the American – and global – audience, maybe a little bit of fact-checking could had been done before the President went live.

One other milestone that the President won't have liked is this: we are now in a bear market. The Dow Jones industrial average closed today 20 per cent down from its peak – and that means the bull market that began after the financial crash of 2008 is now officially over.

If this didn't grab America's attention, a separate announcement certainly did. 'March Madness', the massively popular college basketball tournament, is off. For the weeks that it is on Americans talk of little else. It fills the TV schedules. And everyone in offices up and down the land tries to fill out their 'bracket' – their guess of which colleges will get through the early stages of the knockout tournament and win through to the finals. That is off. And so too is The Masters, the iconic golfing 'grand slam' event that takes place each year at Augusta National in Georgia. The rest of the NBA season is to be suspended. And one other thing that will have caught the public's attention is a post on Instagram from America's most loved actor, Tom Hanks, and his opera singer wife. They have both contracted coronavirus in … Australia.

None of this eases my anxiety.

18 March, Sydney

Another really restless, fitful, sleep-disrupted night. It is just impossible to switch off from what is happening on the other side of the world. The news just seems to be getting worse and worse. On a totally inconsequential personal note, I wake to the news that the BBC is canning *Americast* and some other podcasts and news programmes so that resources can be channelled into one that will focus on coronavirus.

Seems that staffing is down 25 per cent because of illness and people self-quarantining. But after the destructive divisiveness of Brexit, when so many people seemed to take against the BBC (sometimes with justification), I feel immense pride to see how we are responding. The BBC is not known for its deftness, but the speed with which it is responding to this emerging crisis – not just in news – is truly impressive. The director-general Tony Hall reaffirms the Reithian mission statement which is now nearly a hundred years old – to educate, entertain and inform. The BBC irrelevant in the age of Netflix, Hulu, Amazon et al? It's never seemed more important at this time of peril, and by all accounts, audiences are responding accordingly. A public service broadcaster has rediscovered its voice and its *raison d'être*.

I'm loving my time being with Linda and the kids, but this all adds to my sense that it is more and more untenable to stay put. If none of us had anything to go back for it would be tempting – and wonderful – just to go and rent a place on a beach somewhere far from the madding crowd for a few months and ride out the storm. But this is impractical. We all have differing commitments. We have our regular conversation about the pros and cons of staying or going. Our mind is made up when Max sends a link to a *Times* story suggesting that the Foreign Secretary, Dominic Raab, may be about to order the closing of Britain's borders. But we can't seem to change our flights on line, and I hold on for over an hour to get through to speak to someone at BA – to no avail. So we pack our bags and head straight to Sydney Airport.

On the way to the airport I email a BA contact in Washington who connects me with the person who runs the Sydney operation for BA. I track him down in the airport, and he is fantastic. Says we are right to get out ASAP. Who knows what will be running in a few days' time. But there is no way Linda and Anna can get on the flight leaving today. After much tapping at a computer keyboard, he tells us with a flourish that they are on the flight tomorrow via Singapore. That's one part of the jigsaw completed. I need to find a flight back to the US – and the best option is to go via Honolulu.

We all feel a sense of relief that a decision has been made and that a plan is in place. That evening we have a farewell dinner at Catalina, one of Sydney's most beautiful and finest restaurants. It overlooks Rose Bay, where the seaplanes come and go from. It is a lovely evening, and the sky is changing colour every 15 minutes from orange, to a shade of purple, to a dark blue as the sun sets over the Pacific. The evening is wonderful, though it is tinged with all the uncertainty that coronavirus has brought. When will we all be together again? When will I next see Max and Kate? When will I next see Linda and Anna? I try to shake off these thoughts and just be 'in the moment'. Bloody difficult. And tomorrow is going to be draining, I know.

19 March, Sydney to Honolulu

This is my longest day. Ever. And that is not a piece of self-indulgent, soppy Sopel melodrama, it is a fact. The nine-hour flight to Hawaii departs Sydney Airport at 6pm on Thursday evening. And arrives into Honolulu at 05.30 (roll of drums) on … Thursday morning, having crossed the international dateline. In other words, it has taken me minus-12 hours to get here. You see what I mean about it being a long day. My Thursday is going to last 45 hours, because of the minus-21-hour time difference. I'm sorry this is like the kind of confounded maths puzzle that always made my head hurt when I was at school. If Jonny leaves Sydney on a plane at x and he travels at a speed of y, then etc, etc.

But it has been trying. The coronavirus is affecting everyone and everything. I go to get a trim (I do this in Sydney because I think the mayor in DC has ordered the closure of all shops except the grocery stores), and the guy who owns the salon and is cutting my hair says that he has had loads of cancellations, and is worried about how he'll meet his overheads if this goes on. He says he borrowed heavily to set up the business, but it could all disappear. The hotel we check out of is more or less empty. Our Uber driver to the airport is in her fifties, I would guess, she has her elderly mother living with her, who is very unwell. But she has her kids too running in and out of the house and she's worried that they could inadvertently bring the virus with them back into the house. She had been driving all morning, but had only made $20AUS. And at the airport itself, 20,000 Qantas workers have just learned they are going to be laid off. The woman who tries to check me in is just waiting for the email from the company to drop. She is a former police officer and tells me she has commitments that mean she has to work. It is devastating.

It would be wrong to say the airport has the air of the US embassy, just before the fall of Saigon, when people are on the roof trying to clamber aboard the last Huey out of the city – but there is a good deal of anxiety around. A young woman is distraught at the check-in counter next to mine, tears running down her face. She can't get on the flight she needs to. There is a problem with my ticket, too. The head of Qantas ticketing is eventually called and he has to ring the Department of Homeland Security in the US. I am questioned about when I was last in the UK (24 February), and had I been anywhere else? Why could they see on their computer records that I had a ticket from Sydney to London? Because I was due to go back in a few days to present *Today*, but have cancelled because I would be unable to leave London. Eventually I am cleared.

Linda and Anna's plane back to London leaves an hour and a half before mine. I feel distinctly moist-eyed as they disappear onto the jet-bridge. I try to board my flight a little later, and the computer has said no. My boarding card has caused something to flash red on the computer. I have to wait to one side as a supervisor is called. I really don't think America wants me back! Am trying not to take it person-ally. Eventually he comes to the judgement that if there was a real problem, then the airline would have never been able to print a boarding pass for me in the first place, and he tells me that I am good to go.

The plane is pretty empty, although one of the cabin crew tells me all the flights will be rammed coming back, as the Australian prime-minister has ordered all Australians to return home before the borders are closed. A man in the row behind me starts coughing just before we take off. Once we are airborne, I move seats. I take a little tablet, and sleep most of the way.

At Honolulu Airport (where I needn't remind you it is not yet dawn on Thursday morning) my long day is going to get longer. The brilliant Global Entry process doesn't like me. I do not pass go and do not collect $200. The photo receipt has a big cross on it, so I have to wait to see a Customs and Border Patrol officer. He fingerprints me and asks various questions. I am told that I will then have to see a CDC representative. The CDC is the Center for Disease Control, and the body in charge of the battle against coronavirus. Another man in uniform escorts me over to it and hands my passport over to the CDC officer.

Seeing my UK passport, he immediately puts on a mask, goggles and – ominously – latex gloves before approaching me. This is not good. I feel myself starting to perspire with worry about what is going to happen next. My mind starts performing somersaults – surely I am not going to have to undergo a medical examination? I've never liked the snap of latex gloves for fear of what might happen next. 'If you'd bend over, Mr Sopel …' Perspiring at this point is probably the worst thing I can do and will be the fastest route to getting myself banned from entering the country. But he wants to know nothing more than whether I have been to Iran, China or Europe in the past 14 days. I tell him I haven't, and I am sent on my way. He goes next to a Slovakian who *has* been in Europe in the past fortnight. I think his stay with the CDC will be rather longer.

The hotel I have booked into is a few miles down the coast from Waikiki beach. It is on the ocean, and has an air of faded 1960s grandeur – all fairly brutal, boxy steel and glass. Along one corridor are the photos and the letters of thanks from all the celebs, royals and presidents who've stayed there. It's impressive: Charles and Diana, Presidents Obama, Carter, Bush, Reagan and Clinton; Elton John, Sammy Davis Jr, Elizabeth Taylor, and on and on and on. The hotel is huge. I realise my mental picture of Hawaii derives from the original TV show from that era, *Hawaii Five-O*, with Jack Lord playing Steve McGarrett. I remember we used to charge around the playground singing the theme tune and shouting, 'Book him, Danno, Murder One.' The Kahala hotel conforms exactly to expectation.

Inside it is like a vast mausoleum. No one is around. A hotel which would normally expect to be nearly full – it is spring break – has only 20 per cent occupancy. I have a beach front room, and to get to it I have to walk past a lagoon in which a few dolphins are enclosed to entertain the young children – except nearly all the families have gone. I think, like the dolphins, everyone in the hotel is feeling slightly trapped, too. Most people are on a layover, en route to somewhere else.

I have dinner by myself in the restaurant, but am told that from tomorrow it will be takeaway only at all the hotels' restaurants and bars.

21 March, Washington

Dulles Airport is my least favourite on earth. It is the total triumph of theory over practice. The main terminal is attractive, the architectural brainchild of a famous Finnish/American called Eero Saarinen. But everything else about it is awful. It was designed so that there would be no need for satellite terminals. Buses would collect you directly from the plane, doing away with the need for jet-bridges etc. They would be on telescopic legs that would pull alongside the aircraft, and once the passengers had alighted the legs would concertina to drive you to the main terminal, where you would clear customs etc. These awful buses are still there, but you still wait for the jet-bridge, then you walk through the satellite terminal to catch the bus that takes you to the main terminal. Or the interminable as it should be more accurately called.

The flight from Honolulu takes nine hours – and I heard every cough and snort and sniffle from the people sitting around me. And call me paranoid, but it seems that's all these people did: cough, snort and sniffle a lot. My hand sanitiser and Clorox wipes are exhausted by the end of the flight. The plane was rammed, but the cabin crew thought this would be the last time they would be flying for months.

The Washington Flyer taxi driver who takes me into the centre of DC is gloomy. He spent all day at the airport yesterday and only got one ride. I tip him generously, and he thrusts a card into my hand imploring me that if I need anything, he is there for me. My apartment, which overlooks the Potomac River, feels like an oasis of calm, away from the ever-changing landscape. After a couple of hours' sleep I go for a walk. Washington is dead. I live off Wisconsin Avenue, one block south of M Street, one block north of the Potomac river. Saturday lunchtime and M Street in Georgetown is normally heaving. Today it is dead. Nearly all the shops are shut. But I am able to go to the local grocery store and pick up the few bits and pieces I need. Now I am self-isolating.

And one thing I realise very quickly: if I am to stay sane I am going to have to ration how much news I ingest – which is an odd thing for someone to say whose whole livelihood depends on people binge-eating our content.

22 March

A tale of two tweets. Each the President posted on Sunday night, and each in its own way emblematic of Donald Trump and his response to this crisis. The first demonstrated an impatience with the severe measures the US was taking to tackle coronavirus. It said: WE CANNOT LET THE CURE BE WORSE THAN THE PROBLEM ITSELF. AT THE END OF THE 15 DAY PERIOD, WE WILL MAKE A DECISION AS TO WHICH WAY WE WANT TO GO.

In other words, lift restrictions and raise the shutters on the US economy as soon as possible. Donald Trump's messaging has been consistently erratic, and sometimes what the President has said has been starkly at odds with what his experts have recommended. There are endless examples of things he's said that either the Vice-President or the White House coronavirus task force have had to correct. But the policy – critically – until now has followed doctors' orders: social separation, self-quarantining, ramping up testing – and responding as the leader of a nation at war with this hidden enemy.

There was just one occasion in today's briefing when the mask slipped and the war leader morphed back to being the street fighter. When he was told in the Briefing Room that Mitt Romney – the only Republican senator to vote for Donald Trump's impeachment – was self-isolating for fear of coronavirus, he said in a voice heavy with sarcasm, 'Oh gee. Mitt Romney's isolating. That's too bad.'

But this emerging policy of lifting the shutters on the US economy is a sign that the President wants to break with his public health professionals, and go with his gut. Why? Well, because the President's whole re-election strategy for November was built on going to the country with a stock market soaring, and unemployment at a record low. And this is a president who has always backed his gut over experts.

Except Covid-19 is likely to result in the exact reverse – record highs for joblessness, the stock market in a slump, and the US economy in the toilet. A far cry from the Keep America Great playbook. And there are many business leaders who similarly feel that the remedy is worse than the disease; that an economy is being sacrificed for a small percentage of very vulnerable people – and many of those voices have the President's ear.

If he does change course, which he seems determined to do, and say to people infected with coronavirus that it's OK for them to return to work, providing they wear a mask, it would be a life and death gamble. Potentially many lives and many deaths.

If he doesn't, then he is going have to go to the country as the leader who took America through its darkest hour, as Churchill described that period after the fall of France, and claim that he, Donald J. Trump, is best placed to lead them into the light. This isn't what he planned. And that brings us to the second tweet from Sunday night. He railed at the media – even his beloved Fox News. 'All I see is hatred of me at any cost,' he said. This president craves praise, and at the moment it's decidedly thin on the ground – even from normally reliable ciphers.

23 March

Where's Dr Fauci? Anthony Fauci is the diminutive director of the National Institute of Allergy and Infectious Diseases, but has an outsize importance in reassuring Americans and the nation's health professionals that the administration's fightback against coronavirus is being guided by the science and not by whim. Today, though, in the White House Briefing Room Dr Fauci is absent. It is hard not to go back to Cold War Kremlinology and the intent study of who is sitting next to whom at Moscow's Mayday parade to guide you on who is up and who down in the Kremlin. Does Fauci's absence suggest he has become a non-person? Is he now labouring in Washington's equivalent of a Siberian salt mine? Certainly, at times, very delicately, he has corrected what the President has said. And has given a clue as to how frustrating it must be to work with a president who plays fast and loose with the facts. He told *Science* magazine (in a probably too candid interview), 'I can't jump in front of the microphone and push him down,' referring to Trump. 'OK, he said it. Let's try and get it corrected for the next time.' I'm guessing the President won't have liked that.

Across the US, things are worst in New York. It is the first city to feel the strain; it won't be the last. Nearly half the Covid-19 cases in America are now concentrated in the East Coast state. And the city's public hospitals are buckling. The city's mayor, Bill de Blasio, and the governor of the state, Andrew Cuomo, are issuing increasingly dire warnings about the impending cataclysmic crunch point.

There are shortages of ventilators and personal protective equipment. Some private companies are switching production effort to meet the demand for additional ventilators – but Donald Trump has resisted calls to use powers under the Defense Production Act to force companies to produce scarce goods. Although the federal government is offering some help, there is a serious structural problem – and it's mad. Bonkers. At this time of national crisis in the US, individual states are competing against each other for masks and gowns and face shields – and that is driving up the price, with vendors selling to the highest bidder. This too would be addressed by using the Defense Production Act, but the President is resisting on ideological grounds. He says it's akin to mass nationalisation, adding, 'Call a person in Venezuela, ask them how did nationalisation of their businesses work out.'

On a personal level, the Foreign Office has just issued revised advice to British nationals, telling travellers to come back to the UK.

That doesn't worry me – but there is also an accompanying warning that flights could soon stop across the Atlantic. I had spoken to an FCO contact about precisely this last night. Time to go back to London, methinks. The two BA flights a day from Washington are now down to one a week. I book a seat on it, to the immense relief of my family in London.

So, it looks like just four days after arriving back, I will be returning to Britain. Note to fellow travellers: Sydney to London via Honolulu and Washington DC is not the fastest way to get from Australia to the UK. Just thought I'd mention it.

28 March

The President is escaping his own social distancing today. For the first time in weeks he's leaving the White House grounds. He's flying down to Virginia Beach, the huge US naval base, where the hospital ship, the *Comfort*, is setting sail to New York City harbour to help alleviate an over-burdened health system. He is going along with the Defence Secretary to wave it off.

But before boarding Marine One, he lets off a little hand grenade. He says he is considering quarantining New York, New Jersey and Connecticut. You what? No one I speak to has a clue what that means. No one has an idea how you would possibly enforce such an order. And, perhaps more saliently, it is very unclear whether the President has the authority to order such a thing.

Our initial judgement is that this is a throwaway remark, and not to be taken seriously. But then he confirms it by tweet. Yes, he is serious. The New York governor, Andrew Cuomo, just looks perplexed when it is put to him. White House officials aren't able to shed much light either.

It later emerges that the Republican governor of Florida, Ron DeSantis, has been on the phone to the President asking him to impose the quarantine, to stop all those New Yorkers from flying down and bringing their coronavirus with them. And rather than quietly reflecting on whether this is something that might be feasible, the President has just come out and said it out loud, setting a million hares running.

The coronavirus is playing into one of Donald Trump's great strengths and loves. He is his own reality TV show director. Need a new storyline? I know, we'll give them quarantining for the tri-state area around New York. It's an instant hit. It's leading all the news shows. Guests are hurriedly booked by the cable channels to fill the airtime, all pontificating on the various aspects of how this could be enforced and by whom. And pondering the question of whether this is presidential overreach.

And wouldn't you know it – at 8.30 on Saturday evening, just as I am preparing to write a piece for the Sunday morning bulletins on the practicalities of this, Donald Trump tweets that having considered it, he's decided that a quarantine of those three states won't be necessary after all. End of story. But it had filled airtime, with him centre-stage – or am I being harsh?

29 March

Oh, my word. No, I am not being harsh at all. Remember we are in the midst of a global pandemic. Remember that the numbers of those infected and dying are skyrocketing. So what does the President tweet about today? Let me give you a sample of a few of his tweets:

President Trump is a ratings hit. Since reviving the daily White House briefing Mr. Trump and his coronavirus updates have attracted an average audience of 8.5 million on cable news, roughly the viewership of the season finale of 'The Bachelor.' Numbers are continuing to rise ...

... On Monday, nearly 12.2 million people watched Mr. Trump's briefing on CNN, Fox News and MSNBC, according to Nielsen – 'Monday Night Football' numbers. Millions more are watching on ABC, CBS, NBC and online streaming sites, and the audience is expanding. On Monday, Fox News ...

... alone attracted 6.2 million viewers for the president's briefing – an astounding number for a 6 p.m. cable broadcast, more akin to the viewership for a popular prime-time sitcom ...

Because the 'Ratings' of my News Conferences etc. are so high, 'Bachelor finale, Monday Night Football type numbers' according to the New York Times the Lamestream Media is going CRAZY. 'Trump is reaching too many people, we must stop him,' said one lunatic. See you at 5:00 P.M.!

30 March

Cometh the hour, cometh the governor of New York. Andrew Cuomo is becoming the alternative voice of the coronavirus crisis. He has been holding a daily briefing, and it has become required viewing. Over the weekend, in my splendid isolation, and spending too much time scrolling through Twitter, I saw this from a well-known Republican commentator. She wrote: 'My life is divided in two parts. 1. Andrew Cuomo's daily press conference. 2. The rest of the day.'

Every day millions of Americans – from across the US – are tuning in to hear from the Democrat governor of New York. In many ways he has become the voice of the crisis. And all the cable news channels – yes, Fox News included – are taking his daily press briefings live. From beginning to end. Whatever you think of his politics he is a superb communicator. He sits alone and talks seemingly effortlessly to graphs and charts, figures and tables. It is calm, but it is firm. If Donald Trump has given a series of over-optimistic assessments of the outbreak that he's then had to walk back from, Governor Cuomo has been the counterpoint.

His approval ratings, like the coronavirus outbreak itself, are soaring. But with him there's no sign of the curve flattening. The latest poll I've looked at suggests that 87 per cent of registered voters in New York State think he's doing a good job. And in this divided country 70 per cent of Republicans approve of the job he's doing. That's unbelievable.

He does folksy – at Sunday's briefing it was his Italian family lunches, all meatballs, pasta and sausage – and yesterday he did presidential. His deep voice, with an unmistakable New York accent, called for the country to come together; that the virus doesn't discriminate between Republican and Democrat.

This Italian American from New York City is political royalty – his father Mario was also governor of New York; he married a Kennedy; his brother is a top CNN anchor. So he's not a nobody who's emerged from nowhere. But this outbreak has propelled him to superstardom. And that is leading a lot of Democrats to mutter, why isn't he our candidate for the presidential election? At the moment the lesser-spotted Joe Biden is in a state of seemingly never-ending limbo. Bernie Sanders hasn't thrown in the towel, but all future primaries have been postponed. Yes, Biden is the frontrunner to win the nomination, but the 77-year-old is socially distancing at home. And that means he's struggling to have his voice heard. Worse still, he is virtually invisible.

At the weekend Biden issued a proclamation. He tried to throw down the gauntlet to Donald Trump on the handling of the crisis, but it got scant attention. Andrew Cuomo on the other hand is front and

centre – all day, every day. And Donald Trump – the other voice of
this crisis – has not been slow to stir the pot, commenting that Cuomo
would be a better candidate than 'Sleepy Joe'.

Trump and Cuomo have known each other for decades. They grew
up in the same New York City borough of Queens. They have been
friends. They have fallen out. What is clear is that the President has
a grudging respect for him. When Cuomo was about to marry into
the Kennedy clan in 1990, Trump was in the throes of his made-for-
tabloid, crash, bang, wallop of a divorce from Ivana. He sent Cuomo a
jokey video for his stag night. 'Whatever you do, Andrew,' Mr Trump
advised, 'don't ever, ever fool around.'

Happier times. Cuomo has shown himself in this crisis to be
deadly serious.

31 March

It took the best part of a month from the first coronavirus death for
the toll to reach a thousand in the US. In under a week, that figure has
trebled – and America has now overtaken China in declared fatalities.
The epicentre of the outbreak is New York, and there the state governor, Andrew Cuomo, has presented figures showing the number of
people being admitted into intensive care is still rising. He says all effort
is focused on preparing for when the number of outbreaks reaches its
peak. Then he says New York will need twice the number of hospital
beds it currently has. Meanwhile the President's leading health advisor,
Dr Anthony Fauci, says the federal government is considering advising
people to wear masks when they are out in public. If the policy does
change, that will be just the latest example of the administration shifting position. But it will be a difficult announcement to make, and one
that could sow confusion and anger. Because it raises two important

questions – one, why wasn't this said earlier? and two, more practically – where on earth can you buy one?

The White House briefing

What an astonishing difference a week makes. Gone is the talk of America re-opening for business at Easter, with churches packed; gone too is the talk of this being like a flu season. Instead the President's tone was sombre and urgent. America was in the midst of a great national trial unlike any it had faced before. Social distancing is a matter of life and death – and he delivers this message to Americans: 'This is going to be a rough two-week period. As a nation we're going to have a really rough two weeks. Our strength will be tested and our endurance will be tried.'

The sugar-coater supreme was now marketing a pretty bleak product. This was stark. A return to normality has been put on hold, and not for the first time the President's upbeat assessments have been defeated by Covid-19's pervasiveness.

What brought this dramatic change of tone is modelling which suggests a best-case scenario of a hundred thousand American deaths; and possibly a quarter of a million. The President said that if there had been no mitigation the numbers could have been ten times that. And that led him to chide the British government – for its consideration of a 'herd immunity' policy.

2 April

Unemployment is off the charts, more or less literally. Pre-coronavirus the record one-week growth in unemployment was around 750,000 during the recession in the early 1980s, and there was a smaller spike during the financial crisis in 2008. Last week 3.2 million signed on. This week it is 6.7 million more. Nearly 10 million Americans have lost their jobs in two weeks.

3 April

I am getting used to my own company. Though, worryingly, I found myself talking to the TV today. That's really not a good sign. If coronavirus doesn't get me, insanity probably will. A presenter on MSNBC kept on putting a question to a guest who was on Skype, when it was clear there was a comms problem. So I found myself alone in the apartment shouting at the presenter, 'She can't hear you. Move on.' Oh dear.

Actually I'm fine being home alone. Although I have told the cleaner that she can't come into the apartment for the next few weeks, so I've paid her what she would have earned. It must be so tough for casual workers like Lucy, who are at the margins, and whose income has suddenly evaporated.

I also went this morning to Whole Foods at 7am to take advantage of the 'seniors only' hour. I was desperately hoping that the nice lady with the face mask at the entrance would say, 'I'm sorry sir, you have to be over 60 to qualify to come in at this time,' but she just waved me through with all the other old farts. When I'd finished, I joined a socially distanced line at the check-out (there is tape laid out on floor to show how far you need to stand apart), and went to get one other thing that I'd forgotten, only to find an old woman in a mask now standing at my shopping cart when I got back. I had to explain this was my shopping not hers. Oi vey. An uncomfortable glimpse into the future. The woman who mislays her shopping cart, meet the guy who is shouting at the television.

Anyway the woman this morning at the entrance to Whole Foods was ahead of the curve. At this evening's briefing, the main story to emerge was the recommendation from the White House Coronavirus task force that people should now wear some kind of face covering. There is rising concern that asymptomatic people could be spreading the virus. In his introductory remarks Donald Trump explained the thinking behind the proposal. And then came questions – would he wear a face mask, as the American people were being recommended to? The answer was a version of 'You must be bloody joking'. What he actually said was 'I just don't want to wear one myself … Somehow, sitting in the Oval Office, behind that beautiful Resolute Desk, the great Resolute Desk, wearing a face mask … I don't see it for myself.' What sort of leadership is that? Isn't that a classic case of 'Do as I say, not as I do'?

5 April

God bless the Queen. She is fabulous. You would never describe her as feely/touchy – she is of her era and her aristocratic background. But making the connection in her address between what Britons are going through now and what happened in 1940 (when she first made a nationwide address), when children were evacuated for their own safety – my mother who was growing up in Essex ended up in Carnarvon – is brilliant. And so well judged.

For the first time in over two weeks we hear there is going to be no briefing at the White House this afternoon. A 'lid' is called. That is when the pool reporters are told there will be no more events today, and they can go home and get on with the rest of their lives. I go out with a couple of friends for a socially distanced walk in the rural Maryland boondocks.

By the time I come back into Washington I hear there has been a change of mind. Donald Trump will be holding a briefing after all. It is set for seven o'clock. Why the change of mind? Was there some new breakthrough? An important message that urgently needed to be communicated with the American people that wouldn't wait? Oh. Joe Biden was due to be holding an online town hall at exactly the same time. Funny that. Poor old Joe. He can't get a word in edgeways. In a way you do have to marvel at the sheer brutality of the Trump machine.

The briefing is dominated by one thing: hydroxychloroquine. Again and again the President touts its merits in fighting coronavirus. It is an anti-malarial drug that has been around for decades. Seems that two medical panellists on a Fox News show have come to see him, along with the programme's presenter, to pitch this drug as a key weapon in the fight. There is only anecdotal evidence about its worth. There have been no tests with a control group. But Donald Trump, who has no medical training, is selling it like a timeshare at one of his properties. He believes it is so good, he might take it himself (even though he doesn't have coronavirus); there isn't time to wait for tests. And even if it doesn't do any good, it's a safe drug – so worth a try. When one of the reporters tries to ask Dr Fauci what he thinks, the President prevents the top medical guy in the room from answering

I am reminded of the old Jewish joke. The leading actor at a play at the National Theatre keels over mid-performance. A doctor in the audience rushes up to help. While he is giving the stricken actor assistance, a little old Jewish lady in the dress circle shouts out, 'Give him some chicken soup.' The doctor ignores her, so she calls out again, 'Chicken soup. Give him some chicken soup.' The doctor, incredulous at this, turns to the old woman and shouts at her, 'It won't do him any good.' Quick as a flash she replies, 'But it von't do him any harm.'

6 April

Have been meaning all day to sit down and write but totally distracted and destabilised by the news that Boris Johnson has been admitted to intensive care at St Thomas's, just across Westminster Bridge from the Palace of Westminster. The glib messaging from Downing Street that he was broadly fine and just running a bit of a temperature was gone.

It's not just that the statistics for me now have a human face, it is the sheer unbelievability about everything. A world pandemic. A British prime minister at this critical time for our nation now in ICU. And at the White House briefing, the President revealing (or maybe that should be claiming) that US therapeutics companies with which the administration had been dealing had been ordered to 'contact London immediately' and ride to the rescue. 'We've contacted all of Boris's doctors,' the President said, 'and we'll see what takes place – they are ready to go.'

I can only imagine how that has gone down with the brilliant NHS staff treating him. I speak to a good friend at the embassy. He professes to know absolutely nothing about it – but doesn't dismiss it as a possibility. He says it is precisely the sort of thing that the President might have ordered – with his chief of staff, Mark Meadows, talking directly to his Downing Street counterpart.

I rang the desk in London to see if they wanted me to file overnight on what the President had said about the PM at his briefing. No, I was told by the overnight editor – they would just run a clip of Trump speaking. But she was pleased that I had rung because one of the big cheeses had called saying I should be on standby overnight. Rumours were swirling in political circles that he was on a ventilator, and if he didn't make it through the night they would want a piece from me. This destabilises me even more.

I hate the lazy use of the word 'surreal' to describe something that might be slightly out of the ordinary. But this all *does* feel surreal – and actually quite upsetting. For the first time in the two and a half weeks that I've been back in DC and living this life of isolation and social distancing I feel really homesick – probably compounded by the sense of extreme vulnerability that I suspect we are all feeling right now. I was going to have a non-alcoholic Monday. Screw that.

From my days at Westminster I have interviewed Boris Johnson many times. I would not lay any claim to friendship. But he is infectiously (not a great word in the circumstances) good company. I remember being with him in Beijing at the Olympics in 2008 – he was there as mayor of London, the next city to host the games – when he came to a news conference and started talking about table-tennis as 'wiff-waff', and none of the translators had the faintest clue what he was on about. Whatever charisma is, Boris has got it. I thought as a politician he could be a rogue and opportunistic (not unique character flaws among elected representatives, or broadcasters for that matter), but he won the election decisively, he does seem to have a plan – whatever you may think of it – and he is *our* prime minister.

Insofar as this lapsed, slightly agnostic Jew prays, I do pray that he gets through this quickly and can resume his position to guide the country through these terrible times.

8 April

What we have learned is that coronavirus is totally indiscriminate in who it infects. But, in the US, not who it kills. What's emerging from early figures being collated is that the African American community is dying in much higher numbers than white Americans. It's not a story of the virus being racist; it's an uncomfortable story about inequality – the black community tends to be way poorer and has been for generations. The consequence of which is that if you're black you're much more likely to suffer from diabetes, obesity, heart disease and hypertension. The very things that make coronavirus lethal. The US Surgeon General, Jerome Adams, who is black, spoke powerfully about how he too suffered from heart disease and asthma and was pre-diabetic – and that this was a legacy of poverty.

The figures are startling. In Milwaukee, Wisconsin – so far – nearly three-quarters of those who've died are black, but they represent just a quarter of the residents in the city. Across in Illinois 42 per cent of those who've lost their lives are African American – but are only 14 per cent of the population. And it's the same in the Deep South – in Louisiana the black community accounts for 70 per cent of the deaths, but only around 30 per cent of the people who live there.

And another aspect of this is that if you're poorer you are likely to live in more densely populated areas in higher occupancy housing. So where you live leaves you more susceptible to catching the disease, and being black leaves you more likely to die from it. A terrible double whammy.

Race has been the great – and scarring – dividing line in America since slavery. The coronavirus, unexpectedly and unimaginably, is shining a new light on its reverberations nearly two centuries on. There's nothing new in recognising the health disparities between black and white America – but Covid-19 is showing how deadly they are.

I was in the middle of preparing a report on this when another piece of news dropped: Bernie Sanders is dropping out of the race for the Democratic Party nomination. In 'normal' times such a piece of news would have led, but these are not normal times.

10 April

It is somehow unimaginable, unbelievable that in the most famous city of the richest country in the world they are digging mass graves for those who can't afford a funeral, and for those who died of coronavirus with no next of kin. Hart Island is a faded, run-down piece of land just off the Bronx in New York City. The buildings look abandoned. All that looks modern are the mechanical digger, the men in white overalls with shovels and the stacked rows of plain, wooden coffins.

Nearly 8,000 people have died in this state alone, and they are struggling to deal with all the burials.

Outside New York hospitals stand refrigerated lorries, acting as makeshift morgues. The whole healthcare system is creaking. There is an important glimmer of good news, though – which is that the number of people being admitted to hospital is falling sharply … allowing Donald Trump to claim, 'We are at the top of the hill.'

The President had originally wanted America to reopen in time for Easter, with churches packed. But in the Oval Office today this was the reality. No crowded pews. Just a blessing from a bishop – and for nearly all other Christians this unique Easter will be online, virtual and socially distanced. One church that will be open is the Cathedral of St John the Divine in Manhattan, the biggest Anglican cathedral in the US – but this New York landmark won't be available for worshippers. It is being readied as an additional field hospital.

12 April, Easter Sunday

Trump raging on Twitter. Really seems to be rattled, or angered (maybe both), by extensive *New York Times* reporting on the decision making and failure of the administration to act quickly enough

... and charting in detail the failure of the President to heed the warnings of his senior health officials and close advisors. It's one of those classic *NYT* long reads – incredibly well sourced with a lot of granular detail.

Trump is lashing out at the media – but also shifting blame wherever he can. The President retweets someone who had used the hashtag #firefauci – this is an ongoing psychodrama. It seems there are many on the right who want to shoot the messenger.

13 April

This morning I had a delivery to my house from the nearby off licence – or liquor store, as they say over here. And I put a jokey picture on Twitter of a bottle of gin and eight bottles of tonic, with the caption that at least I had the next week sorted. After leaving the White House Briefing Room tonight following a marathon two-hour twenty-minute press conference (a record), I felt I could have knocked off the whole lot in one sitting.

This has been the most dizzying, jaw dropping, eyeball popping, head spinning occasionally buttock clenching (and as it dragged on, pelvic floor testing) news conference I have ever attended. And I was at Bill Clinton's news conference in 1998, when he faced the press for the first time after his relationship with Monica Lewinsky. I was at this president's first White House gathering, when he called me 'another beauty'. I was in Helsinki when he had his first news conference with Vladimir Putin, and seemed to prefer to believe the Russian leader over his own security and intelligence chiefs on interference in the 2016 election. I was in Vietnam when Trump gave a news conference after his talks with Kim Jong Un had unceremoniously collapsed. So I've sat in on some corkers.

What made tonight's encounter unique was the context. And secondly, this was, if you like, a distillation (all the talk of gin I think forced me to use that word) in one news conference of what three and a half years of Donald Trump has been like to cover.

There are more than 22,000 Americans dead because of coronavirus; more than half a million infected – and remember in late February Donald Trump was saying there were a handful of cases, but that would soon be down to zero.

Yet Donald Trump walked into the Briefing Room with scores to settle with the media. This wasn't about the dead, the desperately sick, the people fearful of catching the coronavirus. This wasn't about those who had lost their job, or feared losing it. It wasn't about the people now lining up at food banks to get sustenance. This was about *him*. And more particularly his profound sense of grievance that the media has been critical of his handling of Covid-19.

If you think that is an unfair exaggeration, after a few moments he said he was going to play a video. It had been produced by White House staff, even though it bore all the hallmarks of a campaign video. If it was a movie it would have been called 'Coronavirus: Why Donald Trump is Great; and the Media Awful.' Because it was a White House production, this had been paid for by US taxpayer dollars.

One of the reporters quoted in the film would complain immediately afterwards that her words had been taken out of context. If you were watching the news conference on TV, you would have seen the film. But in the Briefing Room, where I had my vantage point, Donald Trump was alternately scowling at us, then pointing and smiling derisively – and then smirking, as if to say, 'Look at all you losers – I've nailed you with this.'

Contempt seemed to ooze out of every pore. Central to the President's argument is that at the end of January he stopped a lot of flights coming from China, and that had saved countless thousands of American lives. One reporter from CBS pushed back forcefully, arguing that bold move though that was, it wasn't followed through with any meaningful action in February, when testing was minimal, and precious time was lost. The President was enraged. You could see the fury coursing through him as he replied to her extremely rudely (while not answering the detail of her arguments). He called her a 'fake' and 'disgraceful'.

So here we have a president who apparently hates us. But. But. But. He stuck around and answered questions for a full hour and a half. It was like a band on their farewell tour wanting to do one more encore. He loves it. He is in his element. And he hates us too.

Going back to my previous experience of news conferences, I always think you are lucky if you get to ask one question. Most often you don't get to ask one – particularly if you are from a foreign news organisation. Tonight I think I asked the President five questions (and one of them got a 'that's a very good question' – ten points for me). He loves to engage.

This president is more accessible than any senior politician I have ever known. And who can complain about that? He stood there and took all questions for an age, knowing full well this was playing out across all the US networks – and around the world, given the range of messages I got from all and sundry. But it is also confounding. You feel he wants people's love, and can't understand it when it is not forthcoming.

Then there is power. Coronavirus is unlike any enemy he has faced before. It's unlike any enemy that any of us have come up against, as it doesn't have a face. And Donald Trump is great when there's a name and a face. Lyin' Ted, Sleepy Joe, Crooked Hillary, Little Marco – and on and on and on. But there really isn't much point insulting a virus. It doesn't really respond and seems utterly indifferent to what names it is called.

Before becoming president, Donald Trump ran a family business where everyone answered to him. At tonight's news conference he gave every impression of wanting to run America like that.

He has said he wants to reopen the US for business as quickly as possible – if you're interested, my Q and A with him concerned the feasibility of that. A laudable ambition, but is that his prerogative, or that of the 50 state governors? Remember the US has a federal constitution.

Donald Trump was in no doubt tonight that it was up to him to decide when America lifted the shutters and changed the sign on the door from 'closed' to 'open'. But if it was down to the individual states to decide on when it was appropriate to issue 'shelter in place' orders – and the President said he couldn't order six states controlled by Republican governors to enforce social distancing – how can it be his prerogative to order the reverse?

Andrew Cuomo, the Democratic governor of New York State, said this after listening to the President: 'The Constitution says we don't have a king. To say I have total authority over the country because I'm the President, it's absolute, that is a king. We didn't have a king, we didn't have King George Washington, we had President George Washington.' That is not how the guy who ran the family firm sees it.

As I left the White House at the end of this rollercoaster ride of a news conference, I tried to make sense of it. Like so much in this divided country, I suspect it is entirely a question of where you stand. His supporters will probably have loved him sticking it to the media the moment he walked into the room. His opponents will have been appalled that he could put the coverage of his own handling of the crisis above the suffering of the American people.

Before I made it into the Briefing Room tonight, I had to have my temperature taken in a tent that's been erected just outside the White House estate on Pennsylvania Avenue. And I had to have it taken again before being allowed to enter the Briefing Room. Good thing they didn't do blood pressure. Am sure a fair few people – participants and observers – would have had very different before and after readings.

14 April

This book was meant to be about the race for the White House, but I fear this pesky global pandemic is hijacking it. So let me get back to the original purpose. Really significant things have been happening in the Democratic Party race, which would have normally had me ringing up programme editors and demanding a prominent slot in their precious running orders.

I realise that in my diary entry for yesterday I made no mention of something hugely significant that happened. The self-styled democratic socialist, Bernie Sanders, has taken part in a joint webcast with Joe Biden – fully endorsing him and urging his supporters to get behind him. Wow.

I had meant to write about it, but in the maelstrom that followed Donald Trump's news conference last night – I didn't give it another thought. And this is me: a Washington based journalist tasked with writing a book about the election. If it is totally passing me by, because our every breathing second is being filled with Covid-19 and the impact it is having on all our lives, how much attention is the November election being given by the average American right now? Not a whole lot would be my guess.

And today the *big* endorsement, if not the most surprising one. Barack Obama weighs in to offer his support to his former VP. The Dems of late have orchestrated things pretty well. Sanders yesterday, Obama today. Elizabeth Warren can only be a matter of time. Certainly, this is far better than four years ago, when the battle between Hillary and Bernie for the nomination was protracted and ugly and ankle deep in bad blood.

As I've said in previous entries, Joe Biden, the presumptive nominee, is almost totally anonymous. So how big a problem is it? In normal circumstances it would be huge. But I've spoken to several Democrats who think that Trump is making such a dog's dinner of his response to coronavirus – the failure to test early, the playing it down, the mixed messages – and it's doing him so much harm that you just let him get on with his daily news conferences. Give him the rope. The more he speaks, the less he is listened to, according to some Democrats. Let him marinade and stew in his own juices.

I had intended that today's entry would be entirely about the Dems – but at his nightly briefing the President has just announced that the US is going to withhold funding for the World Health Organisation. Yep, in the middle of the first global pandemic for over a century, the organisation tasked with fighting it is going to have the financial tap turned off by the WHO's biggest contributor.

But it's a bit more complicated than that. The WHO has not exactly wreathed itself in glory. There's a strong feeling that it has been far too cosy with the Chinese, and has allowed them to get away with – well, murder might be too strong. But certainly their secretiveness over what was happening in Wuhan was not challenged sufficiently. The WHO did not push back. And then the organisation said introducing travel bans – as Trump did on Chinese nationals entering the US – was unjustified. There is also a growing concern in the US State Department at the growing influence that China has in any number of multilateral organisations. This would be a way of making a point.

But it's also impossible to ignore the domestic politics element of this. For the past few days, to Donald Trump's thin-skinned chagrin, he has been getting a mighty kicking over his administration's erratic response to the crisis. The *New York Times* and *Washington Post* have both done lengthy exposés of the fumbles and missteps. What better way to change the subject than put the focus on something else, someone else, somewhere else. Get everyone to look in the other direction. And when it comes to that, nobody does it better, as Carly Simon sang in the theme tune of *The Spy Who Loved Me*.

But like an 'and finally', where the newsreader at the end of the bulletin signs off with a quirky, amusing or heartwarming story, so I am going to go to bed now with a smile on my face – an incredulous one, but a smile nonetheless. The *Washington Post* is reporting that the $1200 cheques going to all low-paid American workers to help them through the pandemonium caused by the pandemic are going to be delayed for a few days. Why? Because Donald Trump wants it to be his name on the cheques, and that is going to hold things up.

Sometimes you really couldn't make this shit up.

17 April

At times I just don't understand. I just can't make any sense of it and want to pull tufts of ever lengthening hair out of my head. Donald Trump last night was backing off, outlining a gradualist, three-stage approach to reopening the US economy and saying it was up to the state governors to decide when to reopen. The news conference had been sane and thoughtful. It didn't answer a lot of questions – particularly around ramping up testing. But it was clearly science led.

Then this morning he puts out a series of tweets which, in effect, called for insurrection against three Democratic-run states: Minnesota, Virginia and Michigan. He sent a tweet to his supporters urging them to 'LIBERATE' those states. Result? Placard carrying, Trump supporting crowds come out onto the streets around their respective statehouses. No social distancing being respected, no one wearing masks or gloves.

All thinking, presumably, that coronavirus (no worse than the flu) is a plot hatched by Democrats, the Chinese, George Soros, the deep state, the liberal elite and the media – name your bogeyman and take your pick – to deprive them of their god-given freedom to be jerks.

I'm guessing the President knows that last night he didn't go far enough to please his base, so today he's chucked them some red meat. Talk about mixed messages. Bloody dangerous and irresponsible ones, one could argue.

19 April

Good news and bad news for Joe Biden in an NBC/*Wall Street Journal* poll. On the upside it shows Biden leading Trump by 7 points among all registered voters (49% to 42%). But remember national polls are largely irrelevant in looking at US politics. Hillary Clinton won three million more votes than Donald Trump in 2016 – but under the electoral college she lost in the states that mattered. Those are the key swing states – the sharp end, if you like. That is where elections are won and lost. And this poll is also good news for Biden. Even when the race is reduced to 11 swing states – Arizona, Colorado, Florida, Maine, Michigan, Minnesota, Nevada, New Hampshire, North Carolina, Pennsylvania and Wisconsin – Biden's combined lead over Trump is 6 points (49% to 43%).

And the demographics are good too. He's winning big among African American voters (85% to 7%), Latinos (60% to 26%), voters aged 18–34 (54% to 31%), women (56% to 35%) and whites with a college degree (55% to 37%). Among white voters he is at 42 per cent – Obama in 2012 was 39 per cent here, and Hillary Clinton in 2016 was at 37 per cent.

But there's bad news too for the former vice-president: while he leads Trump by 20-plus points among voters aged 18–34, they have a net-negative personal opinion of him (25% favourable/44% unfavourable), which is a clear warning sign.

And here's the kicker; the result of having to wear Harry Potter's invisibility cloak. When voters are asked if they trust his statements about the coronavirus, 42 per cent said they weren't aware of his statements. Ouch.

20 April

Let's stay with numbers. And here's a comparative statistic:

Date	Covid deaths in South Korea	Covid deaths in USA
Feb 20	0	0
March 20	150	100
April 20	236	42,300

Anyway, jostling for top story tonight is an announcement from Donald Trump that he is going to ban all immigration while they deal with the coronavirus. Remember the presidential election is only months away. But with 22 million people made unemployed in the last month, who is going to disagree with the President trying to protect American jobs? I see some Democrats accusing him of being a racist and a xenophobe. That strikes me as dumb. While we don't know what the details are of what the President is proposing – and it may be neither does he – I suspect this is a message that will resonate.

Oh, and reports are appearing in the US media that Kim Jong Un is critically ill, maybe brain dead. I ask my lovely former Washington colleague, Laura Bicker, who's now our correspondent in Seoul, what she makes of it – and she says it's all nonsense. Oh well. That's one less thing to worry about.

23 April

I realise as I sit to write this I am in danger of being the boy who cried wolf. It was only a few days ago that I declared the Trump briefing I had been to at the White House the most batshit crazy thing ever. Well, this evening I have been to another one.

This had less of the rolling battles. This didn't go on for the best part of two and a half hours. It had one moment. Just one. But oh my word.

Let me set the scene, the President had brought along an official for whom this was his first outing in the Briefing Room. At the Department of Homeland Security in their research labs they have been conducting a study on the impact of UV light, temperature and humidity on the coronavirus. And the findings were really interesting – and encouraging. The warmer it gets, the brighter it is, the more humid it is, the less long the virus lives on surfaces or in the air. The DHS boffin then took us through the impact that disinfectant had on the virus – how it killed it stone dead within a very short time.

This clearly flicks a switch in the President's head – and very quickly it is open mic night at Trump University medical school, junior common room. He is riffing on what the potential of this might be. If you haven't watched it, this was becoming an improbable episode of *Veep*. The President starts speculating on putting UV lamps inside the human body. My head is spinning. But then he muses on whether you could inject disinfectant into the human body, just like you spray it onto a kitchen surface: 'I see the disinfectant that knocks it out in a minute, one minute. And is there a way we can do something like that by injection inside, or almost a cleaning? Because you see it gets inside the lungs and it does a tremendous number on the lungs, so it would be interesting to check that.'

I honestly think I've misheard. Dr Deborah Birx, the chief medical advisor, doesn't know where to look or what to do. She is studying her shoes so closely and so intently that I think she may be considering a doctoral thesis on them. The Homeland Security guy is looking bewildered. From his quiet laboratory to this. And the outside world is letting rip with a collective WTF! We have had the President advocating the merits of hydroxychloroquine, sure. But that is a recognised anti-malarial drug that may or may not have applications for Covid-19 (actually first proper research says it is potentially dangerous). But injecting bleach into our veins so that we can wash out our lungs? Holy moly.

As the briefing ends I try to get through the blue sliding doors that lead from the Briefing Room into the West Wing to see the press secretary, but the secret service stop me. In lower press – the place where the most junior press officers work – the President has stopped with his advisors. And it looks like a counsel of war is going on. This has gone as badly as any press conference has gone, it seems to me. In the past he has done and said things that have caused people to gasp. He's been insensitive. He's been a bit sexist, or perceived to be a bit racist. But tonight he's said something off the scale dumb.

When I get back to my apartment I scour some fringes of the internet to see if I can find anything that might explain what the President was talking about. My assumption is that although he might have expressed himself clumsily, there must be something sane and credible underpinning the disinfectant idea, or UV inside the body. I can find nothing. And then I go in search of something that – surely – will be much easier to find. The Trump army pitching in to defend their man. But tonight, at least, they seem to have gone AWOL, or have lost their voice.

24 April

I wake around 6am as usual, and with my eyes struggling to focus I check my phone. I want to know first and foremost that all is fine at home in London. And then I quickly scan my emails to see what the news-desk might be planning. This morning I see there's an email from a James Fearnley-Marr. He, I read, is the director of external affairs for the Reckitt Benckiser group, makers of such well-known household brands as Dettol – and in the US, Lysol. The letter contains this state-ment: 'As a global leader in health and hygiene products, we must be clear that under no circumstance should our disinfectant products be administered into the human body (through injection, ingestion or any other route).' The email doesn't mention the President, but clearly the group is terrified that because of what he's said someone, some-where might decide to act on his words.

Un-bloody-believable. Because of what Donald Trump said from the presidential podium last night, a leading manufacturer of bleach is having to issue a statement saying whatever you do, don't try main-lining bleach.

The memes, the jokes are ubiquitous. I have an appointment at 10.30 with Kayleigh McEnany, the President's press secretary. I am expecting the email to tell me that the meeting's been called off, but it doesn't arrive, and so I make my way to the West Wing. It still boggles me that we can walk in, and be so close to the Oval Office. Her door is shut. It opens briefly, but then closes again quickly. After a few moments, the President's chief of staff, Mark Meadows, emerges along with a couple of others. Kayleigh, who looks as though in another life she might have been a Fox News anchor, appears as though she has not had much sleep. She probably hasn't.

With a slightly strained politeness I am told the meeting won't be going ahead, and no, she can't commit to rescheduling later in the day. I never expected it would happen. They are fighting a bush fire that is burning out of control.

A statement is issued by her saying we have taken the President out of context, and trust the media for running with negative headlines.

At midday the President, true to form, gives another version. Yes, he had said it, but it was sarcasm; he was being sarcastic to us reporters in the Briefing Room. Yeah right.

On that night's *Ten O'Clock News* in the 'live' tail to my report I said this:

> Leave to one side whether it is appropriate from the presidential podium to use sarcasm in the midst of a pandemic, but Donald Trump's account is not what happened. I was there. He wasn't speaking to reporters, his comments were aimed directly at his chief medical advisor and the official from the Department of Homeland Security, and he seemed deadly serious. Throughout the day the White House has been scrambling to come up with an explanation that will withstand scrutiny. This isn't it.

I walk from the White House back to Georgetown along an empty Pennsylvania Avenue. I get a notification that that evening's briefing is just getting underway. I will probably miss the first 20 minutes, but will pick it up when I get home. Inside my apartment I turn on the TV, but the briefing is not to be found. Tonight he has come and gone in 20 minutes, and refused to answer any questions.

I wonder whether we are seeing the last of the briefings. The nightly Trump show might well be over, the final curtain. He obviously didn't want to face a barrage of questions on disinfectant. He would have also been subject to further scrutiny over his advocacy of hydroxy-chloroquine. Again and again he touted it as the game-changing drug in the treatment of coronavirus, even though there was no scientific evidence to back it up. Under his orders the US bought millions of doses of the drug – presumably making the manufacturers very rich. But now if you go to the website of the federal agency charged with overseeing the safety of drugs, The Food and Drugs Administration, you will now see this headline: 'FDA cautions against use of hydroxy-chloroquine or chloroquine for COVID-19 outside of the hospital setting or a clinical trial due to risk of heart rhythm problems.' Yes, in some patients, it had changed the game – but in a deadly way.

In truth, well before disinfectantgate some of the President's advisors had become increasingly concerned that his freewheeling, rambling and fact-light performances, far from underlining his stature as some kind of latterday Churchill or Roosevelt, were undermining his position with the electorate. Polls were beginning to suggest that the public was wearying of the nightly displays – too often lacking in any kind of empathy for the thousands dead, too often whining about how meanly the press have been treating him and how hard he's been working.

26 April

This is looking like meltdown Sunday at the White House. Veritable barrage of tweets spitting out from the presidential phone every few moments. A couple of them talk about how journalists haven't deserved the Noble Prizes [sic] they've been awarded. I rather like the idea that we are given awards for our nobility. But it seems that is a misspelling of 'Nobel' prizes – even though of course, journalists don't get Nobel Prizes ... a lucky few in the US pick up Pulitzers. There is another tweet in which the President protests that he has been working *so* hard, and that he hasn't left the White House for months. Well, one, you would expect the leader of the world's pre-eminent superpower to be working hard during a global pandemic (I just can't imagine Roosevelt or Churchill, if they'd had Twitter, complaining about how little sleep they'd had preparing for D-Day). But two, and call me pernickety for facts ... it's just not true. The President was on the terrace of Mar-a-Lago last month with the Brazilian president, he played golf, and a couple of weeks before that he was in India. And one other thing: I know you've been holed up in the White House, but it's not a squalid tenement block in Queens. There are worse places to be hunkered down.

There was another tweet that also caught my eye. In it he said it was a wonderful feeling to know that individual states were loaded up with ventilators. It is indeed a considerable achievement that everyone in the US who has needed a ventilator has had one. But wonderful feeling? What about the feeling that nearly a million Americans have had coronavirus, that over fifty thousand have died and that millions have lost their job? Find me the tweets that empathise with the appalling toll this is taking.

27 April

We need to talk about Joe. Biden, locked away in his basement in Wilmington, Delaware, seems to be a beneficiary of the President's erratic performances. Though he's been mostly invisible to the American public his numbers are steadily rising. He put out a rather good mood-of-America video at the weekend: the Americans could do anything when they came together; their spirit would prevail; and the passage where it talked about the need to end divisiveness was over pictures of Donald Trump. It was slick, if unremarkable.

Today I tuned into Fox News awaiting the start of the Trump briefing (just as an aside – in the morning the press secretary did a quick Q and A with reporters and she announced there would be no press briefing; three hours later she announced there would be one … you get the impression that after disinfectantgate, things have become a little rocky) and the anchor and his panellists are sinking their teeth into Biden and the media. And they have a point.

There is a serious allegation against Joe Biden from when he was in the Senate nearly 30 years ago. Tara Reade, now 56, worked as an assistant to Mr Biden from 1992 to 1993 when he was a senator for Delaware. In recent interviews, she has said that in 1993 her former boss forced her against a wall and put his hands under her shirt and skirt after she delivered him his gym bag. 'There was no exchange, really, he just had me up against the wall,' she told podcast host Katie Halper.

'I remember it happened all at once … his hands were on me and underneath my clothes.' He then penetrated her with his fingers, she said.

Joe Biden is undoubtedly a touchy-feely politician. If you were being positive you would say he is tactile; if you took a different view of him you might use the word 'creepy'. But it is a long journey from creepy to sexual abuse, and in his decades in public life, no one has accused him of the behaviour that Tara Reade is suggesting – or come anywhere close. And remember, Biden would have been thoroughly vetted before Barack Obama made him his pick for vice-president.

Reade filed a complaint against Biden at the time of her departure from his office, and has spoken to reporters in the past – but never levelled this accusation. She had said – instead – the then senator had made her feel uncomfortable. She's chosen pretty explosive timing to go into more detail.

28 April

Today started with my alarm going at 05.45. And for once it had nothing to do with Donald Trump.

When I was a child growing up, there were times when I thought I had two sets of parents. My own, and my mother's best friend Irene

Aitman and her husband Gaby. My mother and Irene had met at the London School of Economics after the war, and both ended up as social workers in the East End. My mother had suffered from polio when she was 11 that had left her disabled. But Irene took her hitchhiking round the South of France at the end of the 1940s. My sister, Rosalind, and I grew up with their kids David, Timothy and Jane spending all our Christmases together, and a good deal of time out at their house in Northwood, Middlesex. When Irene was in her late eighties she would be found birdwatching in Mali, or somewhere equally far-flung and exotic. She painted, she recited poetry, she gardened – and she was an endless source of encouragement and enthusiasm to her own children – and to my sister and me.

Irene died last week at the age of 94. She was an amazing woman, who absolutely squeezed the last drop out of life. She'd never had a day of illness, and up to four weeks before she died she was still going to the supermarket and walking the dog.

Today I am about to get my first experience of a 'zoomeral' – an online funeral, which starts at 11am in London, but 6am here. I can't quite imagine what it will be like, but it is wonderful. Her kids are prodigiously talented – and they do her proud; and the grand-children are magnificent. Despite the fact that none of us is connected in person, our individual computer screens seem able to generate a real warmth and emotion as we celebrate her amazing life. When the service ends I find I am feeling far more emotional than I could have anticipated.

I call Linda in London – who'd also been part of the zoomeral – and have a mighty sob. The sense of mourning I have for someone who was one of the last threads linking me to my parents and my own childhood, is combined with the emotions I think we are all feeling in these slightly dystopian times. What I got from my mother, who was determined that her polio would not define who she was,

was the importance of continuing to look forward, to not be self-pitying. But today I am suddenly acutely aware of the loneliness of not having a hand to hold, not having another person in the flesh to talk to. Washington feels a long way away from my family, and I suddenly feel very isolated from those I love. Emotions that I have been able to keep a lid on for these past few weeks – by keeping busy with Trump and all his doings, by trying to enjoy the adventure of cooking and cleaning and ironing (things that I haven't done much of in the last few decades), by trying to stay well – come pouring out.

But Linda turns the tears of anguish into laughter. She tells me I have lived out a classic anxiety dream as reality. I ask what she means. I'd had my computer propped up in bed so that I could watch the events unfold, but I hadn't considered that I could – would – be seen too. So I hadn't got dressed. At the end of the service the rabbi asks those who have been part of the online congregation to pass their good wishes on to the family mourners, which I do with a good deal of emotion, and far too little self-awareness.

I have gone to a funeral dressed in my pyjamas. And have spoken to the mourners in my pyjamas. That is *exactly* the sort of thing I have anxiety dreams about: arriving at school to sit my exams with no clothes on, going to do an important interview, but realising I am only wearing a pair of underpants, going into a studio to read the news, but I have forgotten all my scripts so I am trying to remember what each story says, and it is all coming out as a terrible, incoherent jumble – and I bet everyone reading this has their own version, tailored to their own lives. But now I have lived the dream (or nightmare), so to speak.

I think Irene would have laughed. For someone who works in television, failure to consider the visuals was a pretty rudimentary error.

Back to the 'real world' – America passed a million cases of coronavirus today. What a terrible milestone.

1 May

It was trailed last night, but I wake up to the MSNBC breakfast show *Morning Joe* and their exclusive with Joe Biden from his basement in Wilmington. He is going to break his silence on Tara Reade. This is not the usual web-cam stuff that we've seen for the past few weeks, as he tries to get a foothold in the national debate. Now at the precise moment when he probably wants least publicity, pre-coronavirus levels of production have gone into this. There is a proper link, and Joe Biden is on camera facing Mika Brzezinski, who is in the studio (actually she is in the garage of the house where she and her husband and co-host Joe Scarborough live in Florida – instead of old tennis rackets, bikes and tool boxes they have lighting gels, risers and backdrops). Mika is prosecutorial. She has a series of forensic questions that she puts to Biden. And he has one emphatic statement: 'No, it is not true. I'm saying unequivocally it did not happen.'

He absolutely denies the charge, leaving no wiggle room. He is careful not to get into a slanging match with his accuser. He doesn't question her motives or her integrity. He says he wants any Senate records opened up that will reveal her complaint – if there is one – from nearly 30 years ago. In fact, he is happy for any Senate records about him to be shared publicly. But one area where he pulls back is on opening up the papers – the Biden archive, if you like – he has handed over to the University of Delaware.

This feels risky. Hard to gain traction when you protest that you want total transparency ... except for the bits where you would prefer things remain opaque. Biden's position is made more complicated because of his stance over Christine Blasey Ford, the college professor from California who came forward to accuse Donald Trump's choice for a vacant Supreme Court seat, Brett Kavanaugh, of sexual abuse. Over that Biden had said at the time: 'For a woman to come forward in the glaring lights of focus, nationally, you've got to start off with the presumption that at least the essence of what she's talking about is real, whether or not she forgets facts, whether or not it's been made worse or better over time.'

To which the only sensible question is: what's the difference? What's the difference between the believability of Christine Blasey Ford and Tara Reade? Surely, following the logic of that statement through, she has to be believed – that what she is saying is 'real', just like Professor Blasey Ford.

This is where the subject of sexual abuse seems more uncomfortable for Biden than it ever was for Donald Trump. Why? Well yes, Donald Trump has been accused of worse, by far more women – and is captured on tape in the infamous *Access Hollywood* tape boasting about sexual assault, sexual conquests and what he can do to women. But Trump had never been a champion of women's rights beforehand. There aren't the #MeToo sympathising quotes that you can play back to him. Unfortunately for Biden, in his case there are.

And sure enough, Trump campaign Twitter supporters are on it. I then see this exchange between two women, which just makes me almost wish the coronavirus doesn't go away, so we are not subjected to another six months of this. The first tweet is from Mercedes Schlapp – she used to be at the White House as Donald Trump's director of strategic communications, and now has a senior position on the Trump re-election campaign. She is feisty and smart. Although I do remember sitting in her West Wing office when she was still in the administration, while she challenged me over Brexit, and – how can I put this politely – her vehemence on the subject and the strength of her views on Britain leaving the EU seemed to be in inverse proportion to her knowledge about it. The reply is from Neera Tanden. She is Democratic Party establishment through and through. She is president of the liberal thinktank, Center For American Progress, has worked closely with the Clintons, served in the Obama administration, and appears regularly on cable TV advancing Democratic Party causes.

> Schlapp: 'Will the Democratic women Senators ask for the release of @joebiden documents from the University of Delaware? They are turning a blind eye to Tara Reade's story and the #MeToo movement. #DoubleStandard.'

> Tanden: 'Hey @mercedesschlapp, they don't contain personnel records. But now that you mention it, will Trump allow all the backstage video of The Apprentice to go public? Because there are serious allegations of rape, assault and racism he faces and victims have said there's taped evidence.'

In the midst of the pandemic, this somehow seems so ghastly, irrelevant and pathetic. Let's just hurl great clods of mud at each other – but from a socially distanced six feet apart. As if choosing the next president to guide America – and possibly the world – through the aftermath of a global pandemic is a question of who has the least-worst sexual assault allegations levelled at them.

You might think that the last thing the Trump campaign would be doing would be applying a poker to the embers of this particular fire. The appalling *Access Hollywood* tape nearly cost Trump the presidency – he was hours away from withdrawing from the race. But though some of the attacks in US politics may be crude, the thinking behind them is sophisticated, if unattractive. Obviously, you can't have Trump out there in the vanguard leading the attacks on Biden over Tara Reade's allegations. That might be too much for people to stomach. But there is nothing to stop the campaign team, the willing surrogates, and the ever loyal – and utterly shameless – Don junior from wading in. As they are.

Let's move swiftly from sexual assault allegations to polling demography. Where is Donald Trump at his weakest? What is his exposed flank? We saw it in the midterm elections in November 2018, we've seen it in a lot of polling data since then – Trump is doing really badly among white, college educated women, who live in the suburbs. A majority – 53 per cent – embraced (maybe not the right word) him in 2016 – but they have been alienated by his language, by his antics, by his boorish behaviour since then. A *USA Today* poll I saw a couple of days ago had those who thought Trump was honest and trustworthy at 31 per cent– but Biden was at 47 per cent. So, if by going hard on the Tara Reade allegations you can chip away at that number by getting these voters to think ill of Biden too, then that is a result. Even if you simply have the effect of disillusioning them, so that this key demographic turns out to vote in lower numbers, then that would be a positive outcome too, if you are part of the Trump campaign. Remember, something that Trump did very effectively in 2016 is work on the insight that to do well you don't need to transform in a positive direction the way people think about you, so long as you can alter in a negative direction the way people see your opponent. As with Hillary Clinton, so now with Joe Biden. And where is Biden's weakness? It's among the mostly young, super-liberal voters who backed Bernie Sanders or Elizabeth Warren. If these people become even more dubious about Biden, how are they going to be persuaded to vote for him?

You go into elections to win. Remember Bismarck's dictum about laws and sausages …? It is even more so if you substitute the word 'laws' for 'election campaigns'. And the Trump campaign are not going to miss a beat, or blush an embarrassed blush, in going after Biden – with Tara Reade the tip of their arrow.

3 May. Six months until polling day

Mike Pompeo, America's Secretary of State, has been on the TV this morning. And it seems he has taken into the studio with him a prop – a stick that he has sharpened to poke China in the eye with. We all know that unlike Las Vegas, what happened in Wuhan didn't stay in Wuhan. A coronavirus which has affected billions, infected millions and killed hundreds of thousands, is claiming a new casualty: US/China relations. On the American side there is growing fury about China's secretiveness, and – for the moment at least – an unsubstantiated charge: that this didn't originate in a wet market in the city, but in a government laboratory. He was asked whether he was convinced it had come from the lab. This is his answer:

> There is enormous evidence that that's where this began. We've said from the beginning that this was a virus that originated in Wuhan, China. We took a lot of grief for that from the outside, but I think the whole world can see now. Remember, China has a history of infecting the world and they have a history of running substandard laboratories. These are not the first times that we've had a world exposed to viruses as a result of failures in a Chinese lab. And so while the intelligence community continues to do its work, they should continue to do that and verify so that we are certain, I can tell you that there is a significant amount of evidence that this came from that laboratory in Wuhan.

Now maybe that would have been a bit more offensive to the Chinese if he'd called them a bunch of dirty dogs, but not much. These words from America's top diplomat seem calculated to wound a proud nation.

Against the backdrop of the Lincoln Memorial, Donald Trump this evening has again raised the potential death-toll in the US to perhaps as many as a hundred thousand. But each time he does that, there is more scrutiny of his own erratic handling of the crisis. With an election six months away, having someone else to blame – the Chinese, the World Health Organisation – has become politically essential.

But it's not just about electoral politics. There's a deep unease in the White House that the Chinese are exerting way too much influence on multilateral bodies – such as the World Health Organisation and the World Bank – and a sense that America needs to re-assert itself. The coronavirus pandemic is becoming a defining and unsettling moment in the relationship between the world's two economic superpowers. Last week stock markets fell sharply on the threat by Donald Trump to take unspecified retaliatory action against the Chinese. Further tariffs? We don't know.

But China is giving as good as it gets. A cartoon lampooning the Americans has been posted by the Xinhua news agency in English. It ridicules how appallingly (in Chinese eyes) the Americans have dealt with the outbreak. The deterioration in relations has been rapid – in the early stages of the outbreak, Donald Trump spent his time lauding President Xi, for the steadfast way he had dealt with the crisis, for his transparency. And through January and February he saluted the great friendship between the US and China.

We're not hearing much about that now.

4 May

I am flying back to London tomorrow, which has filled me with so many emotions. Excitement overwhelmingly to see the family – and the dog! Anxiety too, though – I feel that over these past couple of months I have got myself into a rhythm. I only go to the supermarket once a week; maybe the office a couple of times. The few people I see are maintaining social distancing as fastidiously as I am. And no one has been into my apartment since I got back from Hawaii. So I feel kind of safe. When we've gone out to film we wear masks and carry hand sanitiser with us at all times. And maybe some sadness – everything feels so epochal at the moment that I have no idea when I will be back in DC, and I will miss being here and reporting this extraordinary story.

One of the things that has changed most for me these past few weeks is how routinised life in lockdown has become. I eat at the same times. One of the nightly news shows at 6.30, gin and tonic at 7, dinner at 8 (always with music and not with TV); a box set for a couple of hours (I have got through *Narco*, *Unorthodox*, *Ozark* and, a little belatedly, *Broadchurch* – I felt I needed something English in the mix). My son Max and his wife Kate will call from Sydney around 10pm, when they're having their lunch. And I will go to bed at around 11.30.

And then I will do it all again the next day, to the point where I have no idea what day of the week it is, as one seems so much like another.

The morning ritual is a long walk along the canal towpath, and then returning on the cycle path than runs alongside the river. When I first got back from Hawaii, Washington was still wearing its dark, winter clothes. The trees were only just coming into bud, it was cold. But each day a little bit more of spring has sprung. And now the trees are in full leaf the banks are bursting with colour – buttercups, daisies, thistles. And with every day that passes something else has changed – fewer and fewer planes overhead – so the incessant sound of jet engines has been replaced by birdsong.

It has given me such delight to see the birds, busy gathering twigs, digging around in the mud on the edge of the canal – all totally oblivious to what the human beings who walk alongside their habitat are going through. This morning I saw a beautiful pair of American goldfinches hunting out thistle seed. The other day there was a really striking red-winged blackbird flying fast and low over the canal. There are the wonderful dusty red cardinals, darting in and out of the hedges, and my favourite sighting was a pair of blue jays digging in the mud, who seemed utterly unbothered by my approaching. So beautiful, and yet so nasty in the way they treat other birds and their nests.

After about a mile and a half there are some wooden steps that go down from the canal to the paved cycle path running alongside the Potomac which takes you back into the city. Here this morning there is a duck supervising her ducklings in the grass. In a tree that has been stripped bare of all foliage, cormorants seem to spend the whole day just sitting on the branches, watching the world go by, like the old Cuban men you see playing dominoes in the parks in Miami. The other day I saw a snake – but I am unable to tell you the make and model. And two deer stepped out in front of me early one morning – which seemed to startle them as much as it did me.

This daily walk has helped keep me sane. It really has. A delicious hour without news, without emails, without texts and without the incessant Covid chat. The passing of the weeks, though, cannot only be measured by buds coming into bloom. It can be measured too by the way we humans are behaving and interacting (or not).

When I first start walking here in mid-March no one was wearing a mask – now the majority of us are. We now walk as far apart from each other as possible. I find myself wanting to shout if someone comes too close. Like governments which spark conflict by unilaterally declaring that the waters for 25 miles around their coast are off limits to foreign fishermen, I want to declare a two-metre exclusion zone around myself. Neurotic? Moi?

5 May

Am sitting writing this aboard a British Airways Boeing 787 about to take off and fly to London from Washington.

I was worried that the flight might be crowded and my two-metre exclusion zone would be not just compromised but smashed to pieces. I needn't have worried. I have just asked the lovely cabin services director, Susie, how many passengers there are on the flight. There are 14 – just 14 of us aboard a Boeing 787. It's ridiculous. There is one other person in my cabin, as far away from me as would be possible. This is like having your own private jet.

I am told that there will be no meal or drinks service on the flight, so that human contact is kept to a minimum. I hadn't realised this would be the case, and I didn't eat before I left home. I am about to feel disgruntled, but Susie tells me that if I like, I can nip off the plane – just take my boarding pass – and go back into the terminal to get myself something from a fast food outlet that's open. What? Are you being serious? She is. That has never happened to me before.

But before I can get my wallet out of my rucksack in the overhead bin, one of the BA staff has volunteered to go for me – and within five minutes I have a double cheeseburger and fries delivered to my seat. What phenomenal service from a whole bunch of people who are living with all the anxieties of coronavirus that everyone else is having to cope with, but also the high possibility that their livelihoods are about to come to a crashing and unexpected end.

In the US last Sunday 135,000 people got on planes. It sounds a lot, but on the same day a year earlier, that figure was 2.5 million. So down roughly 95 per cent. The airline industry is cratering, and it's hard to see it coming back any time soon. The Treasury Secretary Steve Mnuchin gave an interview on Fox yesterday, which won't have done anything to lift the spirits of airline executives. He just couldn't foresee when the travel ban would be lifted.

I guess before all this kicked off I would go to Dulles Airport, just outside Washington, about every six to eight weeks – either to fly back to the UK, or to some other destination around the world (don't tell Greta). I think if you blindfolded me and dropped me on the kerbside at departures I could find my way to the BA check-in desk, through to TSA pre-check security, onto the train that takes you out to the B gates, and up the escalators to the shopping concourse, where I would then go up one level to the British Airways lounge until the flight was called. And with blindfold still in place I would have found my way – with ease – to gates 42 or 44 where all the BA flights go from.

It is so familiar to me as a place. But today it just felt eerie, alien even. The whole place was a ghost town. Like a neutron bomb had gone off and killed all the people but left all the buildings intact. I was the only person on the train. The corridors of glass, marble and chrome that stretch as far as the eye can see were empty, the rows and rows of seats by departure gates devoid of any humanity. All the shops were shut, aside from a newsagent/confectioner and the Wendy's burger bar where dinner came from.

I always love looking at departure boards when I am in an airport. They always speak to me of the infinite possibilities of the world. I've travelled widely over the course of my career, but there are so many places I haven't been, that I still thirst to go to. I have always had the fantasy that one day you could go to an airport and instead of having a booking to somewhere, your boarding pass would allow you to go *anywhere*. You simply decide when you get to the terminal. Should it be Lima? Or maybe Laos? No, I think it's going to be gorillas in Rwanda. I'll take the flight to Kigali, please.

Tonight, my BA flight is the only one to any destination in Europe. No Paris. No Frankfurt. No Geneva. No Rome. No Amsterdam. There is an Ethiopian Airlines flight to Addis Ababa, and Qatar Airways is flying three times a week to Doha. And that's it.

In the space of two months the wiring that had us all so interconnected has been ripped out of the wall, leaving loose, frayed cables all over the floor. The US has shut itself off from the world, and appears in no hurry to change that. I've got four hours left till we arrive into London.

Right. Lights out. Eye shades on. Good night

When I come out of the double doors that transition the space between airside and landside, there is no one there. None of the usual hubbub. Costa coffee is closed. No Uber drivers, no nameboards, no Addison Lee chauffeurs. No people holding welcome home banners or standing around with bouquets to greet loved ones. There is just one person and one dog. Linda and Alfie. God it is good to see them.

6 May, London

I am still in a bit of a jetlagged fog. Still disorientated. I drive our little Fiat 500, and London feels empty and lifeless, like Washington. But a lot feels so different. I can't believe how few people are wearing face masks. It's unbelievable. In the US you would not be allowed to go into a supermarket without some form of covering over your mouth and nose, no matter how improvised. Ditto riding on public transport. But here in Britain the advice from the government is they're not necessary. There is this – to my mind – lackadaisical argument that if people start wearing masks then they will start to feel invincible and disregard social distancing guidelines. Or worse, they will take away vital PPE equipment from doctors and nurses. Well, if we were all going out to buy the latest, state-of-the-art N95 mask with go faster stripes down the side, then maybe. Would that we could, but rightly we can't. But in DC your mask is a statement that you are taking coronavirus seriously. You still give other people wearing a face covering a wide berth. It is not about no one being able to infect you; it is about *us* saying we are conscious of the danger of infecting each other.

Honestly, I'm dumbfounded. In the US I have been tuning in from home to the Downing Street briefings, which are so different from the contentious and occasionally bizarre press conferences we've been getting at the White House. The British ones are sober, and slightly dull. Very British, I guess. They are held in the grand, wood-panelled dining-room of Number 10, and each day a politician introduces the briefing, invariably flanked by the chief scientific officer and chief medical officer – all appropriately socially distanced. Reporters' questions come in via video screen, ensuring there are none of the pyrotechnics and verbal brawling we've had at the White House. All of that is to the good. I don't believe the British government is playing politics with the pandemic – a charge that can easily be levelled at politicians of all stripes in the US. The UK government is not trying to second-guess the scientists, in the way that Donald Trump has done with, to take one example, his insistence on promoting hydroxychloroquine. There is an earnestness about the way they seem to want to go about things.

All of which makes the decisions the Boris Johnson government (ministers and advisors alike) has made all the more surprising. I guarantee that within a couple of weeks they will be telling people travelling on the tube or going into supermarkets that they *should* be covering their faces. Is Britain going to carry on *ad nauseam* with zero checks at the border? Almost certainly not. Are they going to carry on limiting testing only to essential health workers? No. Because that way they will never get things under control. Even the definition of the symptoms of coronavirus – a cough and a fever – seem hopelessly limited when so many people are talking about a loss of taste and smell as one of the tell-tale signs of Covid-19, and those are considered as indicators in other parts of the world. It seems that everything – I mean everything – that this government has decided to do has been two weeks too late. It's as though they can't see a curve without deciding to tuck in behind it. I couldn't believe that when I got back to the US from Australia everything was shut. But not in the UK. Lockdown came ten days after the US – even further behind Europe.

For all the chaos and noise getting there, in the US they really have ramped up testing, sourcing PPE, made sure there are enough ventilators to go around. In the UK (and I know this will sound terribly unfair to all the civil servants and ministers and special advisors who are probably working their butts off) it feels that we go from long and languid periods of complacency to panic in the blink of an eye. Shutdown, testing, school closures, masks, quarantine, you name it. The much-vaunted Rolls-Royce that is meant to be the British civil service is not purring away in perfect harmony. The engine is spluttering, the gearbox is grinding, and the exhaust pipe is belching out thick black smoke.

Who would have thought the elite super-league of pandemic players would be Taiwan, South Korea, Singapore, Germany, Finland, Australia, New Zealand and Greece? Who'd have chosen them for their fantasy football team?

This is not being anti-government. Not in any way. I am desperate for the BoJo administration to succeed in its battle against the virus. Just as when I fasten my seat belt on a plane and it moves out onto the runway, I invariably give up a little prayer that there is no drama and that the captain delivers us to our destination safely. There are still parts of the world where there will be a spontaneous eruption of applause from passengers, as the wheels screech onto the tarmac at the end of a flight. An expression of pure existential relief and release. So, I want those in charge to get us to the other side of this with as few deaths as possible and as little long-term damage to our economy and society as can be reasonably expected. Captain Johnson and your team in the cockpit, and in engineering maintenance and air traffic control, I am rooting for you, but feeling exasperated.

10 May

It is Mothers' (I am never sure where the apostrophe goes for this particular day – is it for all mothers or just yours?) Day in the US – and Donald Trump appears to be in the mother of all moods as he is firing off a fusillade of tweets on a range of issues – but he is unleashing something else: OBAMAGATE – his capitals not mine. 'The biggest political crime in American history, by far!' he declares. What this crime is is not immediately apparent. But it is all wrapped up with the FBI investigation into his former National Security Advisor, Michael Flynn – even though that happened *after* Donald Trump had taken office, so quite what role Barack Obama played is also unclear. But it loosely revolves around the conspiracy theory that the outgoing president used his last weeks in office to target incoming officials and sabotage the new administration.

It is worth just adding, insofar as Michael Flynn is concerned, that he pleaded guilty to lying to the FBI, although a new defence team have moved to have the sentence quashed on the grounds that the FBI sought to entrap him. Trump and his acolytes have played up recently disclosed FBI documents from interviews with Flynn, claiming they show he was the victim of 'dirty cops'. One handwritten note from the FBI's then director of counterintelligence said: 'What's our goal?

Truth/Admission or to get him to lie, so we can prosecute him or get him fired?'

But quite how you get that to lead to Barack Obama's door is not yet clear. I suspect that part of this is tactics – one of Joe Biden's strongest suits is the eight years he spent as loyal wingman to Barack Obama. Undermine Obama, and you undermine Biden. But there is also an aspect of it is that is visceral. Trump loathes and detests Barack Obama – and it probably all stems from the White House Correspondents dinner in 2011, when Obama mercilessly mocked Donald Trump's fixation with the utterly discredited 'birther' conspiracy – the allegation that Obama had been born in Kenya, and therefore America's first African American president was not legitimate. Donald Trump was in the audience that night, and clearly was not enjoying the opprobrium that was being heaped in his direction.

It would merit proper psychological investigation, because at times it does seem that the Trump presidency is driven by a single desire to undo anything that is considered to be part of the Obama legacy. It is as though Donald Trump carries a screwdriver in his pocket and wherever he sees a plaque with Barack Obama's name on it, he unscrews it and throws it in the bin.

But Trump taking on his predecessor so directly is not without risk. Barack Obama still commands a lot of public support. Can't help feeling that while the attacks on America's first black president might get the juices flowing for some of his more atavistic base, Republican strategists will be a good deal more wary.

Nevertheless, this is what Donald Trump does so effectively: hurl an insult and see if it sticks, see what traction it gets. 'Obamagate' is now a thing. Not a thing with definition, and it's still not clear what the greatest crime in American political history is – but maybe it will all become obvious and apparent.

Happy Mothers' Day.

11 May

The White House is probably one of the most closely guarded buildings in the world. Snipers are on duty on the roof and adjacent buildings. Heavily guarded fences with a mass of electronics keep out intruders, secret service officers swarm around the perimeter. There are no-fly zones over the building, there are secret tunnels and bunkers. The US Marine Corps guard the entry to the West Wing, and yet undetected the coronavirus has snuck in.

At the weekend it was announced that a senior aide had tested positive for coronavirus. Any mystery about who it might be was quickly dispelled by the President. 'She's a wonderful young woman,' Trump said. 'Katie tested very good for a long period of time and then – all of a sudden – today she tested positive. She hasn't come into contact with me but spent some time with the Vice-President.'

The Katie in question is Katie Miller, the Vice-President's communications director, and a spokesperson for the coronavirus task force. And without going into an organogram of the executive branch, Katie Miller is married to Stephen Miller, who is probably the most influential, controversial – and the longest serving – policy advisor to Donald Trump. The upshot is that the VP, Mike Pence, is now in a version of quarantine – and so too are the three key figures on the coronavirus task force, including Dr Fauci.

News of this came one day after one of the US Navy valets to the President had tested positive. These are the people who serve Donald Trump in his private quarters in the residence. No wonder White House staff are uneasy. Kevin Hassett, the President's top economic advisor, was blunt: 'It is scary to go to work. I think I'd be a lot safer if I was sitting at home than I would be going to the West Wing. But, you know, it's the time when people have to step up and serve their country.'

Am I surprised? Not really. When the President at his briefing a few weeks ago said that his coronavirus task force had just announced that all Americans should wear face masks where social distancing was a problem, he made plain he wasn't going to be wearing one. Meetings went ahead in the Cabinet Room and Oval Office. Crews and photographers would be there along with reporters asking questions. And though the President is a famed germophobe, he kept shaking hands for long after it was deemed safe.

One of the things that's amazed me since I've been reporting from Washington is the unbelievable access we have to the White House, if you have one of the hard passes, which are like gold dust. With it I can enter the grounds – once I've been through security and, as of four weeks ago, had my temperature taken. I went to see the President's press secretary at the beginning of this month. She meets with the President daily. Her office is probably 12 paces away from his. I and any other journalist with a hard pass can go there, without an invitation or an appointment. My colleagues at Westminster have no such access to Downing Street. When I went in no one was wearing a mask. It is a rabbit warren of offices where social distancing is impossible. Yet despite not having been tested for coronavirus I am able to walk within about five metres of the Oval Office. It's astonishing.

As a result of these latest cases, White House staff are being told that from today they have to wear a face mask … and some should consider working from home. From now on coronavirus testing is being introduced for senior staff on a *daily* basis, where you get the results back in 15 minutes. There will be temperature checks for everyone else too.

This all at a time when the President is pushing to open the US economy. But if this is the benchmark of what it takes to keep your office/factory/depot functioning safely and Covid free, is there a company – large or small – anywhere in the US that could offer this to its staff?

The news conference takes place in the Rose Garden – only this time everyone is wearing a mask. Well, one person isn't ... do you really need me to tell you who that is?

15 May

The Tara Reade allegations haven't gone away, but you feel they are going away. The PBS programme *Newshour* spoke to 74 former Biden staffers – 62 of whom were women – who'd worked for him over the course of his career, to see whether the allegations fitted a broader pattern of behaviour, and whether his behaviour towards the opposite sex was viewed as problematic. None said they had ever been subjected to any form of sexual assault or approach from Joe Biden. And perhaps equally significant, given how gossipy the environment is when you are working in a Senate office, none said they had heard any rumour or whisper of such behaviour from him.

Also, this research threw up a very different narrative as to why Reade had been fired. It wasn't because she'd made allegations of sexual assault. It was because she wasn't very good at her job. Another former Biden staffer has come forward to say she had told him that her departure was because of the way a medical issue had been handled.

Other journalists digging into her past have found evidence of her giving conflicting accounts of various incidents in her life where things she has claimed have not withstood scrutiny. For his part Joe Biden has given another interview today in which he said that this November people should vote with their heart. 'If they believe Tara Reade, they probably shouldn't vote for me. I wouldn't vote for me if I believed Tara Reade.'

18 May

Oh wowzers. Donald Trump has put his money where his mouth is. Well, not literally – but he has put hydroxychloroquine where his mouth is. He's just told journalists he is taking the anti-malarial drug that he has been touting for so long as a treatment for coronavirus. But he is taking it as a prophylactic to prevent the disease. This despite the fact that the federal government's own Food and Drug Administration has warned of the adverse effects of doing so. That it should not be used outside of a clinical setting and that it can cause deadly heart arrhythmia. A study by the Veterans Affairs department – which is the nearest thing the US has to an NHS with its network of hospitals dedicated to treating current and former servicemen and women – found that 'an increased overall mortality was identified in patients treated with hydroxychloroquine alone'.

The President blasts the VA study, insisting that anecdotally he's heard good things about it. And he again repeats his view that what do you have to lose from trying it. Well, your life, perhaps?

But as if the President's announcement wasn't enough of a jaw dropper, what happened next was even more so. As the US cable channels pick up from the announcement, the anchor on Fox News – a station that can so often seem less devoted to journalism than cheerleading for Donald Trump – is uncharacteristically blunt. 'If you are in a risky population here, and you are taking this as a preventative treatment … it will kill you,' says the presenter Neil Cavuto. 'I cannot stress enough. This will kill you.' I suspect the President had to up his dose on blood pressure tablets having heard the Fox guy say that.

There is now a feeding frenzy for more information from the White House about when he started, what dose, for how long. There is a lot of doubt from Trump watchers that he is telling the truth. That his medical team wouldn't have allowed it. That he has made a public show of saying this to show – once again – his independence from the scientists and the experts. Eventually, late in the evening some sort of clarification is forthcoming from the physician treating the President. Commander Sean Conley writes in a memo to the President's press secretary: 'After numerous discussions he and I had regarding the evidence for and against the use of hydroxychloroquine, we concluded the potential benefit from treatment outweighed the relative risks.'

Call me cynical, sceptical, a doubting Tom – whatever you like. But does this statement confirm the President *is* actually taking hydroxy-chloroquine? It just says they discussed it. Maybe I have become too jaundiced – actually, maybe it would help treat that too ...

22 May

Joe Biden has given an interview to a radio breakfast show, contain-ing this exchange, with Charlamagne tha God, a black co-host of the syndicated radio show *The Breakfast Club*. The former Vice-President tries to cut short the interview, because, he says, his wife, Jill needs to use their basement studio:

Charlamagne says: 'Listen, you've got to come see us when you come to New York, VP Biden. It's a long way until November. We've got more questions.'

'You've got more questions?' Biden replies. 'Well I tell you what, if you have a problem figuring out whether you're for me or Trump, then you ain't black.'

Whoosh! The firestorm that erupts is fast and predictable. How dare Biden say that you aren't properly black if you vote for Donald Trump? South Carolina's senator Tim Scott – the only black Republican in the upper chamber – tweets: '1.3 million black Americans already voted for Trump in 2016. This morning, Joe Biden told every single one of us we "ain't black".' Trump says the comments are arrogant and condescending.

It is dumb, arrogant and out of touch for Biden to have said this. In fairness to him, the campaign is quick to realise this is a major boo-boo. He is quickly out with a shovel to clear up the mess of his own making. 'I shouldn't have been such a wise guy,' Biden tells the US Black Chambers, an African American business group, a last-minute addition to his schedule for the day. 'I shouldn't have been so cavalier.'

Biden also said he would never 'take the African American community for granted'. Perhaps that is the more revealing part. Democrats have long been accused of taking the African American community for granted, and not doing anything like enough to help.

26 May

Here we go again. In Minneapolis a video has emerged of a white police officer casually placing his knee on the neck of an unarmed black man, George Floyd, as he lies on the ground gasping, 'I can't breathe.' The police officer keeps his knee lodged against the 48-year-old man's neck for a long time after he's become unresponsive. And he dies. This just doesn't get any less shocking.

I would like to think that the victim's race wasn't a factor, and that justice would be colour blind (as if) in deciding what sanction to take against a law officer who had overstepped the mark. But that would be to fly in the face of reality and the evidence. This video *is* truly shocking, and *is* immediately causing ripples.

I started my posting to the US as North America Editor in August 2014, and one of my first deployments was to Ferguson, Missouri, after the killing by a white police officer of an unarmed black man,

Michael Brown. And after that there was the killing of 11-year-old Tamir Rice in Cleveland as he stood in a children's playground with a toy gun. There was the death of Eric Garner, selling counterfeit cigarettes in New York, who was wrestled to the ground and put in a chokehold by the cops. And on and on the weary list goes: Freddie Gray in Baltimore, Philando Castíle in Minnesota, Walter Scott in Charleston, South Carolina – each a stain on the way law is enforced, each a cause for further African American resentment. The victims black, the policemen white. And though investigations are held, the one common thread is that invariably there is no action taken against the officers in question.

27 May

The US passes 100,000 Covid-19 deaths. It's an uncanny and almost tragically perfect piece of symmetry: the number of US servicemen and women killed in Korea, Vietnam, Iraq and Afghanistan – over an aggregate 44 years of fighting – is exactly the same as the number of Americans who've now lost their lives to coronavirus in just three months of America's war against the hidden enemy, as Donald Trump likes to refer to Covid-19.

In New York, the richest city of the wealthiest country on the planet, we've seen nurses heading into intensive care units to treat Covid patients wearing bin liners as PPE, because that is all they had. We saw the ER consultant putting on his ski goggles to examine a patient, because the hospital didn't have the right face masks. We saw mass graves being dug on a small island in the Bronx to accommodate all those who'd died with no next of kin, or with no money for a funeral. It reminds me of the inscription on the tomb of the unknown soldiers in the Commonwealth war graves: 'Known unto God'.

America, this almighty superpower, with enough weaponry to blow the planet to smithereens many times over, was looking ragged and not in control of events in its own backyard. It's hard to see this chapter of America's story being regarded as another moment of this nation's greatness.

Now that America has reached this grim milestone of 100,000 dead, what of the future? In public opinion there does seem to be a head versus heart battle going on. Science pitted against gut instinct. The role of the state against the rights of the individual. It seems a phone app that can track and trace your movements is the vital tool to prevent a second wave of the virus, but it relies on a sizeable majority of the population handing over their personal data for it to be effective. Will that happen? In a country whose founding fathers in drawing up the Constitution fretted about the dangers of the state becoming too mighty, I just cannot see it (and this goes far wider than pro and anti Trump divisions). And what if, please God, an effective vaccine is found? You can be sure that the anti-vaxx brigade (and remember Donald Trump was once one of its advocates) will be out in force, stirring up doubts about the science, the medicine, the state, big brother – you name it.

Donald Trump has boasted repeatedly in the past couple of months that no country has done more coronavirus testing than the USA – 'It's not even close,' he says. No country has built more ventilators or supplied so much PPE to its front-line workers. The President has claimed that other world leaders are jealous of what the US has managed to achieve. Really? Germany, South Korea, Taiwan, Australia, New Zealand, Greece envious? Hard to believe somehow. No country has had more deaths, more infections. And that too, so far, is not even close.

May 29

Predictable that America has woken up to news of rioting overnight in Minneapolis and other cities after the death of George Floyd. Two days ago America passed 100,000 deaths in the novel coronavirus. Now America's oldest disease – racial division – is spreading wildly again.

Of course, we've been here before: go back to the 1950s and the unrest caused when paratroopers – the famed 101st Airborne after their heroics on D-Day – had to escort nine black children to their classrooms at what had been a white school in Little Rock, Arkansas. That came after the Supreme Court ruling upheld the decision in the case of Brown versus Board of Education that segregation was inherently unequal. There were the Watts riots in Los Angeles in 1965 that resulted in 34 deaths.

After the murder of Martin Luther King in Memphis, Tennessee, unrest spread to 125 cities across America. The country had not seen anything like it. And again the army was mobilised to help bring peace to the nation.

Spool forward to Miami 1980, when there was violence after four white police officers were acquitted of beating a black motorcyclist to death. 1992 saw the rioting sparked by the film emerging of four white police officers beating up a black motorist, Rodney King. All sparked by predictably similar ingredients.

In all these cases the president of the day, Republican or Democrat, has sought to find the words that would reassure and defuse the tensions on the streets; that would act as balm. Not Donald Trump.

Twitter for the second time in a week has taken on the President. The President's overnight tweet that 'when the looting starts the shooting starts' was deemed to be an incitement to violence – so if you went to the President's timeline, you would have seen this from the Twitter organisation: 'This Tweet violated Twitter Rules about glorifying violence. However, Twitter has determined that it may be in the public's interest for the Tweet to remain accessible.' Just think about it: a president of the United States cautioned for inciting violence.

The phrase the President used is freighted with history, although it is arguable whether Donald Trump was aware of its provenance. It was spoken first by a Miami police chief in 1967 during the civil rights struggle at a period when unrest had come to the streets. Walter E. Headley said, 'There is only one way to handle looters and arsonists during a riot and that is to shoot them on sight. I've let the word filter down: when the looting starts, the shooting starts.' It was seen as inflammatory and confrontational. Now Donald Trump had borrowed that language.

Meanwhile in Minneapolis itself, in an act of what can only be described as knuckle-headed idiocy, the Minnesota State Patrol arrested a CNN film crew, broadcasting live from the scene of the violence. The reporter, who was the very model of politeness and respectfulness, who said he would move to any position that the police asked him to go – but was black – was handcuffed and taken away, along with his crew. America is wearing an ugly face today.

Donald Trump has now tweeted again, trying to reframe his 'when the looting starts the shooting starts'. What he intended was that it should be read not as a threat, but as a cautionary tale: 'Looting leads to shooting, and that's why a man was shot and killed in Minneapolis on Wednesday night – or look at what just happened in Louisville with 7 people shot. I don't want this to happen, and that's what the expression put out last night means …'

That is as near to an admission of regret as you are going to get from Donald Trump. Clearly there are advisors in the White House who are cautioning the President over his use of language.

He's also just given a news conference on severing all relations with the World Health Organisation, and new measures against China –

but, at this time of national peril, he chooses not to answer a question on the situation in Minneapolis. It is the dog that doesn't bark. And all the more striking for that.

30 May

Overnight in the US there have been more eruptions of anger. An outpouring of fury at what has happened in Minneapolis. There are protests. There is violence, more fires, more tear gas, more burning – some of it coming close to the White House as protestors gathered in Lafayette Park, just across the street from 1600 Pennsylvania Avenue. There were clashes with the police and secret service, as the President watched from inside his heavily fortified lair. If on Friday night his tweets were designed to mollify, today they are more like Molotov cocktails. He talks about the lines of defence and how the baying mob was kept back. And then he tweets about what would have awaited them if they had got over the White House fence: they would have been greeted, he says, 'with the most vicious dogs, and most ominous weapons, I have ever seen. That's when people would have been really badly hurt, at least. Many Secret Service agents just waiting for action.'

It was hard to see this as anything other than the President almost salivating at the prospect of a fight. A Clint Eastwood in Dirty Harry mode standing over someone and taunting them to 'make my day'. But there is some calculation too.

I was on Radio 4's *PM* programme, and there was a member of Black Lives Matter, the civil rights organisation, being interviewed before me. She wouldn't condemn the burning and the looting; she said property mattered a lot less than justice. Fine, but can you justify the torching of people's businesses when they haven't been part of the problem?

This sort of response is perfect for the Trump campaign. If what happened in Minneapolis is all about racism, white supremacy, institutional indifference, the injustice suffered by black people, then it's an argument that Trump loses, and loses badly.

But if it becomes about the mob, the radical left and anarchists hijacking the protests, lawlessness, people frightened to go out – then Donald Trump will reheat the message from 2016, when he pitched himself as the law and order president to the American people. I have just reread the speech he made at the Republican Convention in Cleveland. This is what he said:

> Americans watching this address tonight have seen the recent images of violence in our streets and the chaos in our communities. Many have witnessed this violence personally, some have even been its victims. I have a message for all of you: the crime and violence that today afflicts our nation will soon – and I mean very soon – come to an end. Beginning on January 20th of 2017, safety will be restored.

It was a dystopian picture that he painted, but his central message resonated. And if this goes on, he hopes it will work this November too – though it's more problematic when the violence has happened on his watch.

31 May

The violence is spreading. This is reaching 1968 levels. And unpleasant groupings are hitching their wagons to the outrage felt by African Americans over the death of George Floyd: right-wing agitators, left-wing agitators, and a lawless element who want to go shopping without the inconvenience of paying.

This is now a full-blown crisis. But not just one. This is three crises rolled into one. It is as though the 1918 Spanish Flu pandemic has morphed into the economic collapse of 1929, which in turn has enveloped the nationwide riots of 1968 which followed the assassination of Martin Luther King. Each magnifying the effects of the other. So, it is not surprising, when there are thirty million Americans unemployed and there are record long lines at food banks, that people are coming out onto the streets. The burned-out buildings and the looting will just exacerbate the economic crisis that the country already faces. And the problem with rioters and looters is that they tend not to take much notice of social distancing guidelines. The looters piling into smashed-up shops are not saying to each other, 'We need to keep two metres apart.' And that in turn is leading public health professionals to worry that the wave of protests is going to lead to a second wave of coronavirus outbreaks.

And for African Americans everyone of these crises is hitting them harder: they are more likely to die from coronavirus, more likely to suffer injustice at the hands of the legal system, more likely to be the worst hit by the economic downturn.

A new factoid has emerged which is getting a lot of traction. On the first night that the riots hit Washington, President Trump moved to the secure underground bunker in the White House. His critics are seeking to depict him as a tin-pot dictator cowering from his people; a man, who, for all the tough talk, has not only got a mop of yellow on top of his head, he has a streak of yellow running through his body. He will be hating this publicity. The coward in chief.

The President is seeking to blame weak Democratic Party mayors and governors, the lawlessness of the left-wing mob – the anarchists. And of course us, the media. But surely the time is going to come when he has to address the legitimate concerns of a section of the population who feel that on every level, at every turn, the chips are stacked against them.

In January 2017, in that dark inaugural address, Donald Trump made a promise: 'This American carnage stops right here and right now.' Cast your eyes over American cities this evening and you can see the smoke rising into the sky while the broken glass crunches under your feet, and the residual, bitter taste of tear gas lingers uncomfortably on your tongue.

DC has taken on the appearance of a war zone. After last night's looting every shop in Georgetown is boarded up. Police cars are everywhere, Black Hawk helicopters are hovering low over the city. And as you move closer to the White House it becomes more militarised. Trucks carrying troops seem to be everywhere. Humvees are on street corners. Washington's demeanour is new and deeply concerning. And perhaps the most arresting image of all: the lines of National Guard officers lined up on the steps of the Lincoln Memorial, fanned out across the spot where Martin Luther King delivered his 'I Have a Dream' speech, and in the shadow of Abe – America's unifier.

1 June

What a day. But let's not talk about the day. Let's just stick to one hour, because although it means omitting a round-up of the overnight violence and mayhem, this one hour in the early evening of Washington is worth the price of admittance alone.

The President is going to make remarks in the Rose Garden. At around 6.35 he emerges to address the nation. A debate has been raging among his advisors on the tone to take – father of the nation, consoler in chief, the man to bind the nation's wounds? Or toughtalking, no nonsense, law-and-order hard man? The President went with his gut. It was the latter. There was a secondary debate over whether he should make an address at all. Some were thinking that it would change nothing and end up making the President look weak, as his appeals for a halt to the protests fell on deaf ears. The argument runs that you don't make a set-piece address to the nation until you have something to announce that will address the racial tensions that have convulsed the country. Others, though, were sensing a backlash from his conservative base, who felt that he had disappeared and wasn't taking a grip of the crisis.

'I am your president of law and order,' he declared. 'Where there is no justice there is no liberty.' He warned that the army would be deployed on the streets if the local mayors and governors didn't get tough with the rioters and the looters. Earlier in the day he'd read the Riot Act to the governors on a call where he said they would end up looking like 'jerks' for the way they had acted. The President told them, 'You have to dominate ... you have to do retribution.' One called it an 'unhinged tirade'.

In the Rose Garden the sentiments were the same, but spruced up and put on autocue. He said he would mobilise every available federal force, both 'civilian and military', to put an end to the violent protests sweeping the nation. Then came the order to governors and mayors to establish 'an overwhelming law enforcement presence' until the protests have been extinguished – and he threatened to send in the US military to 'quickly solve the problem for them' if they fell short – an extraordinary exertion and extension of federal powers. This is a promise to use the powers of the 1807 Insurrection Act, to deploy the might of the US armed forces to suppress American citizens. He ended his remarks by saying he would be going to pay homage at a very special place. That's all he said.

All the time this address was going on you could hear muffled thuds and bangs being picked up on his microphone. And that was because federal law enforcement officers from a variety of different agencies – not the local Washington police – had moved in against a crowd of peaceful protestors across from the White House with stun grenades, rubber bullets and tear gas. The daytime protestors are very different from those who come out at night. The crowd this evening were sitting, kneeling and chatting. They were not goading, nor spoiling for a fight. This was the Whole Foods crowd out protesting – the US equivalent of Waitrose or M&S. An Australian reporter was live on air when the police moved in. Her cameraman gets whacked in the face by one of the law enforcement officers. There was no discussion, no negotiation – no appeals to clear the area. They just went straight in, batons flailing, rubber bullets firing, stun grenades erupting, tear-gas spreading to clear the area: Lafayette Park, H Street, that runs parallel with Pennsylvania Avenue, and 16th Street. It soon became apparent why.

Out of the White House strode Donald Trump, to leave his fortress and walk across the park and H Street to visit St John's Episcopal Church, which stands on the corner of 16th and H. It is the so-called Church of Presidents (every president has worshipped there since James Madison) and had been vandalised the night before. Huge numbers of plain clothes, secret service officers accompanied him. Riot police had created a cordon-not-that-sanitaire, and up he strode to this famous place of worship. As they got there, daughter Ivanka opened her white leather, designer handbag and produced from it a bible, which he then proceeded to hold up awkwardly. Was it his bible, a reporter asked. 'It's just a bible,' the President replied.

There was no prayer, no reading from the bible. This was a photo op pure and simple. A bible. A graffitied church. A steely-jawed president posing for the cameras. It was all about the visuals to make Donald Trump look tough, no matter how many unarmed and peaceful protestors had to be forcibly swept out of the way like street litter to make this happen. But if it was all about the visuals, then there were profound conceptual flaws in the thinking, the design and the execution.

The innocent protestors exercising their First Amendment rights being tear-gassed and rubber-bulleted out of the way, for a start. Then the use of a bible and a church as props. And lastly, lined up outside the church were the President, his daughter and a handful of other senior administration officials. Not one even off-white face among them. What a photo-call of white power this was at a time when the African American community is hurting.

I'm racking my brain to think of another single act of this presidency that comes close to this for its sheer brazenness, for its shock value. The memes on social media are sharp. A photo of him alongside Adolf Hitler, with the Nazi leader also brandishing a book; another of him alongside a photo of Mussolini in a strikingly similar pose. Maybe the depiction of Donald Trump cowering in the panic room in the White House basement while America burned was too much for him to bear. It will become the searing image of this period of time. Look strong at all costs. Use a bible, use a church. Do whatever it takes.

The church authorities had been given no warning that he was turning up, and the episcopal bishop of Washington was seething. The Right Rev. Mariann Budde said, 'I am outraged ... and was not even given a courtesy call, that they would be clearing the area with tear gas so they could use one of our churches as a prop.' And warming to her theme in a radio interview she went on, 'Everything he has said and done is to inflame violence. We need moral leadership, and he's done everything to divide us.'

Support is decidedly thin on the ground – though two predictable voices came out to say how brave and fearless he was – sons Don junior and Eric.

2 June

It's not quite like a prisoner exiting solitary confinement, blinking at the searing brightness of sunlight – but it's not far off. After months in the basement of his home in Wilmington, Delaware, Joe Biden has surfaced – and not only are his eyes adjusting to the daylight, the mask that has been serving almost as a muzzle is allowing him to be heard.

And what a contrast he paints of what a Biden presidency would look like compared to the incumbent. His speech in Philadelphia is excoriating of Trump. 'Is this who we are? Is this who we want to be? Is this what we want to pass on to our children and our grandchildren? Fear, anger, finger pointing, rather than the pursuit of happiness? Incompetence and anxiety, self-absorption, selfishness?' And after the events of the night before at Donald Trump's photo-shoot, the presumptive Democratic nominee warmed to his theme: 'The President held up the Bible at St John's Church yesterday,' Mr Biden, a practising Catholic, said. 'I just wish he opened it once in awhile instead of brandishing it. If he opened it, he could have learned something. That we're all called to love one another as we love ourselves.' And he accused the President of putting power above principle; the demands of his base above the needs of the American people.

It was a big return to the national stage, and one that Democrats had been waiting for.

Let no one say there isn't a clear choice facing America in November. Mr Joe 'Empathy' Biden, against Mr Donald 'Tough Guy' Trump. I do a report on the radio. The only thing I can think to say that these two have in common is that they are both in their seventies.

3 June

Mark Esper is Donald Trump's defence secretary, and was the man put in charge of militarising the nation's capital, with the deployment of thousands of National Guard troops – and all sorts of other branches of federal law enforcement – many of them wearing no insignia or identification tags as they lined up with their riot shields and batons. But he has just gone and done something that few members of the Trump cabinet have dared, and even fewer have survived. He's disagreed openly with the President. On Monday evening, after the worst rioting in the US in decades, the President said he was prepared to use the 1807 Insurrection Act that would allow him to deploy the might of the armed forces within the US to restore order. At a Pentagon news conference the defence secretary made clear that he opposed what the Commander in Chief, Donald Trump, was proposing, telling reporters: 'The option to use active duty forces in the law enforcement is a matter of last resort and only in the most urgent and dire of situations. We are not in one of those situations now. I do not support invoking the Insurrection Act.'

If history is anything to go by, Mark Esper will now be a marked man. But the President may feel he can't sack him just yet. Trump has won few friends for his handling of the crisis. Republican senators have chosen a sullen silence. There is a very funny but excruciating sequence of clips of an MSNBC star reporter, Kasie Hunt, door-stepping Republican senators as they go into a caucus meeting. She seeks their opinions of what happened outside St John's Church. One of the most senior and loyal to the President, Senator Ron Johnson from Wisconsin, claims he can't comment because he hadn't been following it, and didn't see what had happened. I guess if you were living in a cave and been blindfolded and wearing the best noise cancelling headphones that money can buy, then maybe you could have a feeble stab at the 'I saw nothing' defence. But a serving US senator?

And if the intervention of Mark Esper wasn't enough, his most distinguished predecessor at the Pentagon has spoken out too. James Mattis, the four-star marine general who was the 'big catch' appointment in Trump's first cabinet, but who parted company with the President over his decision to withdraw troops from Syria, has piled on the pressure. All the more remarkable because since leaving office, Mattis has remained silent. Not any more. He says he's 'angered and appalled' by the President's handling of George Floyd's death. Of the military tactics, he says that troops are being ordered to violate the constitutional rights of citizens to protest. General Mattis said he could never have dreamed of that happening. But his attack goes wider than that. 'Donald Trump is the first president in my lifetime,' he writes, 'who does not try to unite the American people – does not even pretend to try. Instead he tries to divide us.' And to twist the knife he adds, 'We are witnessing the consequences of three years without mature leadership.'

More worrying for Mr Trump is a Reuters/IpsosMori poll suggesting that only 33 per cent of Americans approve of his handling of this crisis. For all the controversies of the Trump presidency, for all the turmoil, noise and brou-ha-ha, for all that the President's fortunes seem to fluctuate wildly with dizzying highs and harum-scarum lows, his approval ratings stay on a remarkable flat line: they scarcely ever drop below 40 per cent. They rarely rise above 45 per cent. But if this poll is accurate – and yes, I grant you all the caveats that should be given to one piece of opinion research – then this is profound. And dangerous for him. An erosion of support from his base like this is the last thing he can afford. There are some state polls too that make equally grim reading: he is underwater in Wisconsin, a must win state, and neck and neck in Ohio and Texas – both places he won easily in 2016.

Maybe the remarkable Teflon coating on the Trump presidency is starting to scratch and chip.

5 June

Epic piece of trolling of the President by the Democratic mayor of
Washington, Muriel Bowser. Overnight she's had painted on the
street outside St John's Church in giant yellow letters 'BLACK LIVES
MATTER'. And has renamed that section of 16th Street, with the
church on one side and the famous Hay Adams hotel on the other,
'Black Lives Matter Plaza'.

6 June

There are huge protests in Washington in support of George Floyd; in
support of reform. There are demonstrations around the world. But it
is clear how the Trump campaign is positioning itself on this. A 'ques-
tionnaire' has been sent out to his supporters to find out what they
think. But the questions are leading, to say the least:

1. Do you agree with President Trump deploying the National Guard
    to communities where Democrat leaders have proven ineffective?
2. Do you support President Trump's fearless resolve when he walked
    to St John's Church – a historical church that was set on fire by
    rioters the night before?
3. Did you know that Joe Biden's campaign staff is financially
    supporting rioters?
4. Do you believe that the Fake News is biased against President
    Trump's efforts to restore law and order in our communities?

Not exactly subtle, is it? The President is doubling down on his tough
'I am your president of law and order' approach. And there has been
a blizzard of tweets over the past few days – but two stand out. Both

are short, and both have the cap lock on. One says 'LAW AND ORDER' – that's pretty straightforward. The other one is even briefer. It says 'SILENT MAJORITY'.

This is clearly what Donald Trump's gut is telling him. I cannot tell you how many rallies I went to in 2016 where his supporters would come up to me and whisper, 'He says what I'm thinking but I'm not allowed to say.' In other words, these Trump supporters shared his sentiments, but dared not express them as raucously as he did for fear of being un-PC and falling foul of the 'thought police'. Ignore the number of demonstrators on the streets, would be Donald Trump's instinct. Count those who are staying inside their homes. And even there, the President's obsession with the size of crowds comes to the fore after these huge – and peaceful – demonstrations in Washington. 'Much smaller crowd in DC than anticipated,' he tweets, as if to suggest that the high-water mark of this has now passed. He also says the forces of law and order have dealt with it easily – in other words, these protestors aren't up to much. Am not sure that is the best way to defuse tension – but there again, maybe it's not meant to.

But his pollsters are telling him it is all far more serious than that. His numbers don't look good.

11 June

There is growing outrage about Donald Trump's plan to go to Tulsa next Friday to hold a rally. The reasons are almost too numerous to list, but let's have a go. Next Friday in the US is known as 'Juneteenth'. It is a public holiday known as Freedom Day, and takes place on June the 19th. It commemorates the events in June 1865, when Union general Gordon Granger read federal orders in Galveston, Texas, that all previously enslaved people in Texas were now free.

Holding a rally for a predominantly white audience – and in Tulsa, Oklahoma, it is going to be a more overwhelmingly white crowd than normal – when tensions are still so high over the Black Lives Matter protests, when the President still hasn't had anything meaningful to say on the issues driving BLM, might just seem a touch on the insensitive side.

Not only that, but Tulsa has just marked the 99th anniversary on 1 June of what has been deemed the 'single worst incidence of racial violence in American history'. It was a massacre that left an estimated 300 black people dead and thousands injured, as a white mob rampaged through an affluent and thriving predominantly black area of the city called Greenwood. So the optics of coming to Tulsa look less and less propitious.

The California Democratic senator, Kamala Harris, has just tweeted, 'This isn't just a wink to white supremacists – he's throwing them a welcome home party.'

And then there is the not inconsequential issue of coronavirus. This will be an event for 15–20,000 people packed tight in an enclosed arena. It just flies in the face of *all* the public health advice set out by the experts who've been advising the President about the spread of the disease. The head of public health in Tulsa has urged him to postpone. And perhaps most bizarre of all is this – the disclaimer being sent by the Trump organisation to all those who go online to try to get tickets:

Disclaimer: By clicking register below you are acknowledging that an inherent risk of exposure to COVID-19 exists in any public space where people are present. By attending the rally, you and any guests voluntarily assume all risks related to exposure to COVID-19 and agree not to hold Donald J. Trump for President, Inc, BOK Center; ASM Global; or any of their

affiliates, directors, officers, employees, agents contractors, or
volunteers liable for any illness or injury.

In other words, this might give you coronavirus, but don't blame us.
Isn't this the height of irresponsibility?

15 June

Hurrah. I have finally heard that I have been granted a travel waiver.
After a good deal of stress and impatience and frustration, it seems I
can return to the United States.

I really hadn't fully appreciated just how complicated, tricky and
bureaucratic it would be when I left Washington in May. As it turns
out, when an American president makes a proclamation it really is a
very big deal. There's no nod-and-wink 'Don't worry, Jon, we'll sort
you out.' This is the President declaring that borders are closed and no
one without a US passport or a Green Card gets in. This is new territory for me, and – I suspect – untrodden ground for the staff at the
embassy in London – who I have to say I can't praise highly enough.
They made it their mission to assist. Yes, Carson Wu, Matt Goshko
and J.P. Evans, I am talking about you. And while I am handing out
herograms, I ought also to mention Britain's new ambassador to the
US, Karen Pierce, and one of the diplomats there, Emily Slifer. They
also helped nudge the process along.

After making some tentative inquiries it becomes clear that this
is going to be quite a faff. It turns out the consular staff and press
people have to make a formal declaration to the State Department
and Department of Homeland Security in Washington explaining
why it is in America's national interest that Jon Sopel be allowed to
return. Now let me say, there is no person alive who thinks I am more

important than I do – but even I would struggle to write a declaration about why America's national interests would be seriously compromised by my not being there.

How I would love to get hold of what was written. That would definitely be framed and hung in the toilet. I've booked myself a flight for Thursday.

18 June. Departure day

This is a day of very mixed emotions. Totally relieved – finally – to have permission to go back to Washington. But actually lockdown life in London has been strangely enjoyable, if that doesn't sound a paradoxical thing to say. Nice food. Good wine. Company. Walks on Hampstead Heath, which is one of London's gems. Lots of reading. Box sets. And two 1,000-piece jigsaws: one of Europe and one of the US. Fitting really.

And obviously really sad to be saying goodbye to Linda, Anna and the dog. And just like three months earlier in Australia, who knows when or where or how we will next be able to get together. That uncertainty is the worst bit of all this. And the total loss of the control that for years we have taken for granted: if I want to go somewhere I book a flight and fly there – bish, bash, bosh. I realise I am feeling anxious. On shpilkes, to use the wonderfully descriptive Yiddish word.

When I thought that the waiver might not be forthcoming from the Americans, I studied other options for getting back into the US via a third country. According to the rules, so long as you have been out of the UK for two weeks, you should be able to get in via a country where there are no restrictions imposed by America. I looked at all the places where Covid-19 has been managed most effectively: South

Korea, Vietnam, Singapore, New Zealand, Australia, Thailand. But I couldn't get into any of those countries. Everywhere I looked I drew a blank. The world may be your oyster, but coronavirus has clamped the shells firmly shut.

I think this inability to be master of our own destiny weighs heavily on all of us – well, maybe not the dog. He's more concerned about retrieving his ball, which is stuck under the sofa. News then comes through that Vera Lynn has died at the age of 103. On a day where it is pouring with rain outside (I think the first day of continuous rain since I have been back), and where the air is heavy inside, on radio and TV all you can hear on any channel is the forces sweetheart singing 'We'll Meet Again'. Oi Vey (to use a second Yiddish phrase). In a movie this bit would be edited out as being too cliched.

Linda takes me to the airport where we try to talk about anything other than any of this. Boris, Trump, football season resuming etc.

Heathrow is a ghost town. Only four check-in desks in the whole of Terminal 5 are open. As you walk into the terminal, staff are there handing out masks and dispensing hand sanitiser. As expected the friendly BA counter staff tell me I cannot fly with the visa I have, but they ring the US Department of Homeland Security people who work at the airport, and they confirm I am good to go. Only a handful of flights are leaving Terminal 5 today. One flight each to Milan and Madrid, one to Hong Kong and a couple to the US. Only a W.H. Smith's and a Boots are open (although that does at least allow me to stock up on Cadbury's chocolate to take back to Washington).

There are only around 40 passengers on the flight over. Nearly all Americans repatriating. It is eerily quiet everywhere. The plane moves off the stand and straight onto the runway, and up into an empty sky. All the BA cabin crew are wearing masks, and no drinks are being poured, no food dished out. Drinks come in sealed bottles, and food comes in wrappers.

At Dulles Airport there is now a health station before you get to Passport Control. I have my temperature taken, and the guy at the desk tells me to 'try and quarantine if you can'. That seems a long way short of a command. I am told to take my temperature twice a day and to contact my physician if I fall ill. But it seems quarantine is not being strenuously enforced.

Anyway – enough about me. You haven't bought this book to have me rambling on about my worries and woes. All is good in my apartment, and a colleague has kindly done some shopping for me. A cup of tea and shower and bed.

19 June, Washington. Juneteenth

While I have been packing up from London and flying back to the US, Donald Trump has been having quite a week. And not in a good way.

I remember a conversation I had with Tony Blair (I hate name-droppers, as I once said to the Queen over tea) and we were discussing the difference between politics as it is depicted on television – in particular we were discussing the brilliant Aaron Sorkin drama *The West Wing* – and the reality. Blair was making the point that in TV drama politics is episodic: a problem arrives on the desk of Jed Bartlet, his officials struggle and fight over the best way to deal with it, and by the end of the episode the problem is resolved or it has all gone pear-shaped. And then the next week a new storm hoves into view and we see Josh, Toby and CJ reaching for their sou'westers and battening down the hatches. But the former British PM says it just isn't like that. Multiple problems are being dealt with at any one time. There are no neat beginnings and even fewer neat endings.

Donald Trump is having one of those weeks. For a start, although he was due to be holding his first rally in Tulsa today, he caved on that and has moved it to tomorrow – a rare example of the President bowing to public opinion. Twice this week already the Supreme Court has ruled against him. First it agreed to extend equal rights in employment to people who are LGBTQ. Then it threw out the President's tough immigration plans to overturn Obama-era legislation and kick out the so-called 'dreamers' – the children of illegal immigrants who came into the country without papers, but are now working and paying taxes. On both Trump had expected his conservative majority Supreme Court to back him. But they went their own way.

Meanwhile the first excerpts have appeared from John Bolton's memoir, *The Room Where It Happened*, his account of the 18 or so torrid months he spent as Donald Trump's National Security Advisor. It is unsparing of the President. There has been no shortage of books about the 45th occupant of the White House – I might have contributed a couple myself to this oeuvre – but this is the first written by someone who has had such up-close access. And it confirms the picture painted by so many other books – but this is written in vivid technicolour. He says the President is not fit to hold the office, that he doesn't read his briefs, that he can't distinguish between his interests and the national interest. And on and on it goes: how he tried to persuade President Xi to buy lots of US soybeans, as that would help his re-election efforts. Seeking help from a foreign leader to help him win a second term was exactly the 'misuse of office' charge laid against him in the impeachment proceedings. And Bolton details bits of stunning ignorance from the Commander in Chief. He apparently didn't know that Britain was a nuclear power, and he thought that Finland was part of Russia.

For Trump the problem with Bolton is that he can't be dismissed as a former Wall Street quasi-Democrat, as some early departees were branded. He is the conservatives' conservative. Hawkish, bright and, yes, difficult. He is the sort of man who can start a fight in an empty room. As bristly and prickly as his famous moustache. But what marked Bolton out compared to many other Trump appointees was that he had long experience of government; this was a man who could find his way round some of Washington's Byzantine corridors, and knew how to get things done. That said, with this book Bolton has done that rarest and most difficult of things. He has united the Trump White House and Congressional Democrats in fury and outrage – when was the last time that happened?

Bolton kept his powder dry during the impeachment hearings and refused to testify – even though he corroborates the Democrats' central charge about the President's behaviour in respect to Ukraine. And he details how the President was a repeat offender with other countries. To pose what I think can now be called the Mrs Merton question: what was it about a $2 million book advance that led you to keep this information from Congress, and instead save it for publication/serialisation? Am not sure that passes the smell test.

Trump has tweeted furiously about Bolton with his usual range of vim, vigour and venom: the familiar hallmark of the Trump riposte to anyone who dares criticise him.

The latest polls also make grim reading too for the President. I am going to gloss over the headline numbers, but they are bad. What really interests me is 'negative partisanship'. The figures suggest that the main reason roughly two-thirds of those who will vote for Donald Trump will do so is because they like him; a third will vote for him principally because of their fear of Joe Biden. But among those who say they will back the veteran Democrat, those numbers are reversed. Two-thirds are motivated to vote for Biden because they loathe/fear Trump. And talk to political scientists and they will tell you the negative emotion is the most powerful. In 2016, there was not widespread love of Trump; there was a powerful antipathy towards Hillary Clinton. Or look at the UK general election in 2019. How many voted for Boris Johnson because they were terrified/horrified by the prospects of a Corbyn administration?

And this underlines another problem the Trump campaign is having. The attacks on 'crooked' Hillary in 2016 – whether fairly or unfairly – resonated. Wherever I travelled I found this really strong, almost visceral, dislike of the former secretary of state. But Biden? The attacks so far on him for being 'sleepy' don't seem to be finding the target. The other thing that has happened is that Biden is almost invisible. I described this phenomenon earlier as having been made necessary because of the 77-year-old needing to shelter in place during the height of the Covid outbreak. Now it is my firm belief that keeping him hidden from view is deliberate strategy. He does seem sleepy and low energy. He does mangle his words and is guilty of crimes against the English language (though Donald Trump has form here too); he is gaff-prone and liable to slips and fumbles. So keeping him somewhat sheltered is working wonders. The hidin' Biden strategy.

Biden doesn't seem to stir up many emotions at all. He doesn't make people get hot under the collar or go red in the face. He seems to stir up a whole lot of apathy. That would be a major problem if Donald Trump was doing well and winning approval for his handling of the coronavirus outbreak, and the issues around George Floyd. But he's not. The more Donald Trump becomes an out of control fireball, likely to burn up on re-entering the earth's atmosphere, the more it makes sense just to stand well back – and let all the world's camera lenses focus on the light show. Or, as one forlorn and despondent Republican said to me about the easy position Biden now finds himself in, there is no need to murder someone who is committing suicide.

Indifference to Biden may be his biggest advantage.

20 June, Tulsa rally, Oklahoma

This has been the most remarkable, bizarre and occasionally surreal day. And if you want to follow the arc of it, I commend you to look at two photos. The first is a picture of the President arriving on Air Force One into bright sunshine in Tulsa. Look at Donald Trump's face as the door opens. He is cheerful, skittish, fooling around at the top of the steps. He is making faces to the cameras. He's almost dancing, now that he's out of Washington and doing his favourite thing in the whole world – soaking up applause. Is he happy to be on the road again, and attending his first rally? He's delighted. Throughout the week the build-up has been unbelievable. The campaign message is that around a million people have registered to attend at an arena that seats only 19,000. So the campaign built another giant stage outdoors and it is announced that the President and VP will give two rally speeches – one inside the BOK arena, and another to the thousands outside. It is, to borrow a very Trumpian phrase, going to be HUGE.

Except it's not. It's just a little bit tiny.

I did point out, when the claims were made that a million would be attending, that that is roughly two and a half times the *total* population of Tulsa, but never mind. The campaign got well and truly punked by the TikTok generation. Thousands of young people registered to attend, with absolutely no intention of ever turning up. It turns out my cameraman's daughter and all her friends signed up; my producer's sister and her mates registered. But the Trump campaign were oblivious. It led to braggadocious over-hyping pre-rally; and po-faced pique post-rally.

My initial thought about it was that this is funny but not that worthy of comment. But it is. It is more than a prank. It is a sign of young people – in very large numbers – getting involved. It is a form of political action that left the highly sophisticated, and supposedly social media savvy, Trump campaign team with egg all over their face. Involvement of young people in the election could be a crucial determinant. If, as I suspect, for many this is their first taste of engagement like this, they will have come away with a bit of a taste for it.

The reason I thought at first this wasn't that important was that the bigger story was how few people had turned up for the rally. Donald Trump and his campaign team were guilty of that most elementary of political mistakes – they had over-promised and under-delivered. Not the other way around. The arena is nowhere near full. Only around six thousand people have shown up. The outdoor rally space is an empty car park with a stage. The campaign is left to put out appeals on social media for supporters to turn up, while staff quickly start dismantling the outdoor space.

First things first. Some are seeking to suggest the reason for the low turnout is the mass TikTok sign-up. But that has nothing to do with it. If a million are able to sign up, then clearly *anyone* can sign up without restriction. The fact is that the Trump supporters have chosen to stay away, and this prompts two uncomfortable thoughts – each with quite profound implications for the campaign. The first is that the Trump rally – such a sure-fire sell-out in its 2016 iteration – has lost some of its lustre, some of its appeal in 2020. Remember this is meant to be the all-singing, all-dancing relaunch of the Trump campaign. But the engine has spluttered and misfired, the ignition sequence has been halted – and the spaceship is sitting on the launch pad, lift-off aborted. With Commander Trump ready to give a rocket to his staff.

That is, those staff who are still there. Six campaign staff and a number of secret service agents have contracted coronavirus while setting up this rally – which all public health officials have advised against. In Oklahoma the number of cases is rising sharply. And this is the second uncomfortable thought: Donald Trump may have decided that coronavirus is now a thing of the past – but clearly the thought of spending the evening in an indoor arena for hours on end, with no social distancing, where hardly anyone will be wearing a mask, is sufficient deterrent for thousands. It suggests that there is a distinct wariness and caution among an awful lot of people. It's not just the snowflakes of liberal America who are worried, but everyone. And that brings a renewed focus on Donald Trump's handling of the pandemic.

To the rally itself. On coronavirus he makes jokes about it, and calls the disease 'Kung Flu'. It is jarring. A description that many Asian Americans find deeply offensive and racist. And with the numbers who have the disease ticking upwards, the President claims that is because there is too much testing going on in the US; that he has told his officials to slow down the testing operation.

Despite speaking for nearly two hours, not once did he mention George Floyd or the police brutality that led to his death. Instead he focused on the protestors – the mob, as he calls them – and how his 2020 rival Joe Biden would be in their pocket. This was stirring the culture wars pot, not an attempt to unify. At no point does he address the grievances of so many African Americans about injustice and discrimination.

Though the speech goes on and on, there is next to nothing about what the President plans to do if he wins the election in November. No roll-out of policies, no ambitions set for the next four years. No road-map or anything approaching one. As John Bolton charges in his book – the President is fixated on winning, not governing.

And then it was over. You can't fault the 74-year-old president on his prodigious energy levels. I can't imagine what it would be like to go on stage and keep talking for that long. Backstage reports are emerging that Trump is incandescent; seething that so few have turned up. Numbers are everything to him. Small numbers are unconscionable. On social media his surrogates are spinning what seems like the most lamentable line: the fact that Trump's opponents are laughing so much and ridiculing the rally to such an extent is proof of just how successful it was. Er, no.

And that brings us to the second photograph. It is a long, weary flight back from Tulsa to Washington. Marine One touches down on the South Lawn of the White House at a shade before 01.00. As the President walks down the steps he is not walking so much as trudging. He is dishevelled and disconsolate. His tie is undone, and it hangs limply round his neck. Everything hangs heavily. He is unsmiling and looks spent. I have never seen Trump look like this. I have seen him crowing and overbearing. I have seen him frustrated. We've all seen him angry. But never broken. And tonight he looks broken. The contrast with his arrival in Tulsa is stark. He looks like a man who has spent a long night at the casino and put all his chips on red. But it's come up black.

24 June, Washington

Easy to become obsessed with polls and there are going to be dozens of them between now and November, but this one, in the *New York Times*, seems significant. First, because of its scope – it's not just a nationwide poll; it is a series of state polls too, focusing on the six key swing states where the election will be decided. And second, because of what it suggests. But before I go any further, let me add all the health warnings and provisos. Think of this as like the Ts and Cs on radio commercials that go with financial advice, where the voice-over artist speaks extremely fast while talking about how shares can go up as well as down. *This is a snapshot in time over four months out from the election. This is not a guide to what will happen.* Right. Health warning over.

The poll is dire for Donald. Or, to be more precise, the series of polls is dire for Donald. According to the nationwide poll Biden is at 50 per cent, Trump at 36 per cent – that is dismal. But nationwide polls, I would argue, are pretty meaningless. Remember that four years ago Hillary Clinton won the popular vote by three million, but she lost the electoral college. The polls that matter most are those in the key swing states: Florida, Arizona, North Carolina – and the three decisive states from four years ago, Pennsylvania, Wisconsin and Michigan. Here the story is not much different – Biden is at least 6 points ahead in each of these states. And if you dig into the data a little deeper, there are a series of indictors, which for the Trump campaign not to take extremely seriously would be an act of foolish complacency. His support among the over 65s has fallen sharply. And women are decisively moving towards Biden. Yes, Trump retains strong support among non-college-educated white men. And on the issue of management of the economy, he retains a lead over Biden. But as the *New York Times* puts it: 'Among a striking cross-section of voters, the distaste for Mr Trump has deepened as his administration failed to stop a deadly disease that crippled the economy and then as he responded to a wave of racial-justice protests with angry bluster and militaristic threats.'

25 June

Tonight I've had my first dinner out since I was together with Max and Kate in Australia, back in the middle of March. We sit outside at Café Milano in Washington, one of the 'to be seen' venues in Georgetown. Cutlery comes in sealed polythene bags. Bread is served individually in paper bags. The menu and wine list you scan onto your smart phone. All the waiting staff wear masks, and Perspex dividers are erected around our outdoor table so that the serving staff don't come too close. It feels odd, sure, but wonderful to be out in the world again.

Would love to tell you who I was with, but that would be breaking the confidence of the evening. And, obviously, I would have to kill you. Suffice to say they are extremely well connected. One had been for dinner the night before at the home of Treasury Secretary Steve Mnuchin. Another had been meeting during the day with the people running the Biden team. Two have worked inside the White House at senior levels.

Overriding view is that Trump is in serious trouble and that Biden seems on course for victory. But a lot of unease about what a Biden presidency would mean, and whether he would be a lame duck the moment he's elected. There's lively debate over who he'll choose as VP – consensus is on Kamala Harris. Other names in the frame don't have sufficient seniority. There's debate whether markets would crash once he's elected. One says it's inevitable – investors would take fright at the regulations that would be re-imposed by Biden if he won; another says markets wouldn't move – the markets will love that big government would be back with lots of spending. But all express concern that he will be weak, and will be pulled to the left.

Then one of the people at the table who has served at a senior level in a Republican administration, and is still well-connected, offers this thought: he says if Trump is well behind come Labor Day (the bank holiday at the beginning of September that marks the transition from summer into fall) then Trump might pull out, rather than face defeat in November. He says he's heard a few people saying Trump's psychological make-up is such that he wouldn't be able to accept the moniker 'loser'. This would plunge the Republican Party into chaos so close to an election – but the general view is that would not bother him one little bit.

One of the people at the table gives very positive reviews to Treasury Secretary Steve Mnuchin. Says he is masterful at playing Trump, is straight dealing with business leaders, and also won the confidence of leading Democratic politicians. Am told Mnuchin won't promise what he can't deliver.

Also heard a fabulous vignette of the negotiations that went on to secure the massive economic rescue package for the US economy at the height of the pandemic. It required Congressional approval, and that meant Mnuchin had to spend hours in the office of the Senate minority leader, the New York Democrat, Chuck Schumer. Mnuchin has a line open to the Oval Office, as the President needs to approve line by line what is discussed. Whenever there is a new demand from Schumer, Mnuchin relays it to Trump. And each time, the President asks the same question: will it make the stock market go up? If Mnuchin says it will, it gets approved; if he says it won't, it doesn't.

There is also discussion over how hopeless and stupid some on the left of the Democratic party are when it comes to branding. In the wake of George Floyd's death, why would you name your policy 'defunding the police' – if you want to lose the white, suburban, college-educated women who abandoned Trump in the midterms, if you want to wave goodbye to independents and moderate Republicans, this seems a sure-fire way to do it.

One of those around the table had earlier in the day hosted a Zoom call for clients with George W. Bush and Bill Clinton. Bush was pressed on whether he would vote for Trump in 2020. He swerves. But then he is pushed to say what he thinks about the current president. A twinkle comes to Bush's eye: 'People say I hate Donald Trump. That's not true. I love him.' And then with a perfectly timed pause to allow that to sink in, the former president goes on: 'Yeah, I love him … because Trump makes me look like Thomas Jefferson!'

26 June

Another day, another unwelcome record, with more cases of coronavirus recorded in a single 24-hour period than ever before. Thirty of
America's fifty states are heading in the wrong direction with numbers
surging. And some of the most populous are really badly affected. In
Florida yesterday they recorded nearly 9,000 new cases – an increase
of over 60 per cent on the previous day. It all makes grim reading –
across the United states 125,000 people have now died, with a total
of 2.4 million cases. And the Centers for Disease Control, the federal
government agency, says the real figure for those who've contracted
Covid-19 may be ten times higher than that. Today for the first time in
weeks the coronavirus task force held a news conference – it was led
by the Vice-President, Mike Pence, who couldn't bring himself to use
the words 'face mask'. He talked about facial coverings as a last resort.
Dr Anthony Fauci, the senior infectious disease advisor to the administration, was much more forthright. You really don't get the impression
that the scientists have the ear of the administration any more.

The President keeps insisting that the reason the numbers are
surging is because of how much testing the United States is doing.
But few public health experts share that analysis – they say there is
community transmission – and several states are urgently considering
what additional measures might be needed to halt this. A number are
looking to apply the brakes on opening up their economies. Far from
flattening the curve, America seems to be fattening it.

28 June

There is a retirement community in Florida called The Villages – and
it seems that among the old people driving around there in their golf

carts there is disharmony. A protest takes place in support of Black Lives Matter. So pro-Trump retirees don their MAGA hats, unfurl their flags, and form a convoy of buggies to be the counter-protest. It is laced with profanity – on both sides. Donald Trump, on his way out of Washington that morning to play golf, where he will forego his armoured Cadillac in favour of his own golf cart, retweets approvingly.

The trouble is, the first thing you hear with absolute crystal clarity on the video he's retweeted to his 80 million followers is one of the Trump supporters shouting 'White power!' It's unbelievable at any time that a President would want to give succour to such an overt display of racism – but now? In the wake of George Floyd? In the wake of so many protests?

The tweet stays up for three hours before it is taken down. As soon as I see the Trump retweet I ask on Twitter whether this is deliberate, accidental, or careless. Remember, at no point has the President expressed a word of support for Black Lives Matter protestors. He was sympathetic to the Floyd family in the immediate aftermath of his death, and said those responsible must be brought to justice. But about the protests that followed, and the concerns about racial injustice and the scourge of racism, nothing. So all that we have is the President retweeting approvingly someone shouting 'white power'.

And though repeated requests are made for information from the White House, all we get is a mealy-mouthed statement saying the President hadn't heard the man shouting 'white power'. Hmm. But for three hours it is the most extraordinary gift to that part of his racist base. It is one of the longest dog whistles ever. At no point do the White House or the President choose to disavow, even less condemn, the sentiments expressed. Point blank refusal. So, I go back to my tweet from early on this morning – was this deliberate, accidental, or careless?

30 June

Anthony Fauci is up before a Senate Committee testifying on the outbreak. The session has been going on for quite some time, but it's comparatively late on when he starts answering questions from Senator Elizabeth Warren, and it is then that he chooses to unload and unleash. He says that America is going in the wrong direction, that the situation is not under control, and warns that unless things turn around, America will soon be experiencing 100,000 new cases per day. Per day. About a month ago if you looked at the graph for the US, it was much the same as Canada, the UK and Europe. There was that very steep rise in cases in March and April, and then the much more gradual descent down the mountain on the other side through May. But too many states in the US took that as their cue to move their foot from the brake to the accelerator. Beaches opened, bars opened, restaurants opened – and whoosh, the fire has rekindled. And in each of the last few days we have seen record after record smashed for the number of new cases recorded, eclipsing everything at the worst of the outbreak.

What I find unbelievable is that Donald Trump seems to have nothing to say about it. If you think how he was front and centre of every announcement during the early phases of this in March and April, he is at the moment totally schtoom. Mum. Silent. Not a word. He joked about the names for coronavirus in Tulsa, but has said next to nothing since.

And it's being noticed around the world. The world's pre-eminent superpower may still be the United States, but what a stinging rebuff to the country's reputation that Americans will be banned from travelling to Europe, because of the administration's handling of the coronavirus outbreak. The US joins Russia and Brazil on the banned list, on the naughty step – while citizens from countries such as Morocco, Rwanda, Algeria and Uruguay, where levels of Covid-19 are much lower, will be allowed to travel to the EU.

What will infuriate the White House even more is that China passes the admission test as well – although the EU is demanding reciprocity. European Union diplomats will be anxious to convey to Washington that this is a decision taken purely on epidemiological grounds. Whether Donald Trump sees it the same way is another matter. He is no fan of the European Union over its trade practices, and has been making threatening noises before this decision.

1 July

Received a lovely invitation from the Irish ambassador to go to his residence this weekend for a barbecue. Dan Mulhall and his wife Greta have been over to our house, and he is excellent company, a good tennis player – and a great lover and connoisseur of Irish poetry. I think it is only going to be me and the Mulhalls for dinner. But what times we are living in. This is the text of the email I get from his PA.

Dear Jon,

As part of the new reality we're living in, we have had to change the way gatherings are hosted at the residence. This includes a safe food handling and distancing protocol. In this regard, may we ask you to let us know your choices for food and drink per the below menus. If you have a dietary restriction, please let us know.

1. Steak and chicken wings
2. Salmon and chicken wings
3. Plus sausage to the above?

Drink on arrival?
Gin and tonic, beer, wine (what colour) or other

Dinner drink ... wine what colour?

Water – natural or sparkling

Only in-house staff will assist during this gathering. They are
required to wear a mask and gloves.

Last week I got an email from a spa in Dupont Circle where I had
once gone for a massage. The letter is a notification to announce their
re-opening. It is then a list of the health and safety measures they are
– prudently – taking to prevent either their masseurs or you catching
coronavirus. The stipulation of things that clients of the spa need to
do before you arrive and how you prepare for your massage makes me
think that multi-organ transplant might be more straightforward. I
feel stressed just reading the instructions. Can't believe that having a
massage there will be that relaxing, which sort of defeats the purpose.

2 July

Governor Abbott of Texas imposes masks as mandatory. There is an
irony here. Abbott made Obama's life hell when he was president by
repeatedly taking the federal government to court for its overreach. He
did it dozens of times. He was quoted as describing his job thus: 'Get
up, go to work, sue the federal government. Go home.' He relished
being the libertarian thorn in the side of the big government ambitions of Barack Obama. And the lone star state loved their governor
for taking on the man in Washington.

Under Abbott's leadership, Texas was one of the first states to open its doors in the country. He's a Trump loyalist through and through. But coronavirus is now ripping through the state, to such an extent that the governor has felt it necessary to make it mandatory for anyone in public to wear a mask. Abbott is now being eviscerated on social media for being a weakling who's given in to the liberal mob.

3 July

It is a steamy hot evening when I go to Ambassador Mulhall's for dinner. I have packed a pair of shorts in the car in the forlorn hope that the ambassador might have foregone the long trousers. If prizes were given for social distancing engineering, this garden in Kalorama would win. Three tables are set up in an equilateral triangle in the garden. I will be sitting by myself at a small round table; the ambassador and his wife, Greta, are sitting next to each other at a small square table. There is a third table (round) where another couple will sit. We are all more than two metres apart. There is a fourth table quite a way away where the meals we have ordered (I went for the steak and chicken wings, seeing as you ask) will be served. And we take it in turns to go up. On our tables are the drinks that we ordered. We are close enough together for conversation not to be strained, and no one is having to shout. And this being an Irish gathering, there is no shortage of chat.

Most conversation focuses on November and what is likely to unfold. Like all conversations I have had in recent days there is a general feeling that Trump – at the moment – is in serious trouble. And again there is the suggestion that if Trump is convinced come Labor Day that he is going to lose, he will walk, rather than go down in flames. I get a more detailed elaboration of that story – the theory, according to someone who has worked closely with Donald Trump until very recently, is that he will come out and say the polls are rigged against him; that postal votes will lead to widespread electoral fraud. But when he quits the race he will say he can't get a fair hearing because of the way the media is stacked against him, with even Fox News an unreliable ally. And according to this theory, he will go off, set up Trump TV and run again in 2024. And if he wins he will have done a Grover Cleveland, the only president to serve two non-consecutive terms. You've got to admit it's a helluva theory.

The other consensus (I want to say around the table, but around our three tables) is that the greatest challenge the Biden campaign faces is keeping their man free of Covid-19. There is a lot of discussion about who his pick will be for VP. She (Biden has confirmed it will be a woman) has, more than ever, to be someone who's ready to step up to the presidency immediately. And let's face it, American voters would be mad not to have in their mind Biden's age. If he wins the election, on his first day in the White House he will be older than Ronald Reagan was when he left at the end of two terms – and I remember thinking Reagan was a fossil when he first came to power. Biden is an old man.

Washington dinners tend to be early. Arrive around 6, leave at 9. In the ambassador's garden everyone is still going strong at 11.15. I get home just as Donald Trump is finishing his speech at Mount Rushmore. It is an unforgettable address. I ought to say at this point that speeches delivered by presidents over Independence Day weekend are all about how the differences that separate Americans are much more inconsequential than all that unites them. It is about American exceptionalism and the 'city upon a hill', the phrase from Jesus's Sermon on the Mount that has been used by US politicians to signify the idealised dream of America as that beacon of hope.

This speech was not that. It was a throwback to Trump's 'American carnage' inaugural. In the wake of the Black Lives Matter protests, the backdrop was the move to ban Confederate flags, the attempts to topple statues – the so-called 'cancel culture'. This was a speech not of one United States, but Us and Them.

> We will expose this dangerous movement, protect our nation's children, end this radical assault and preserve our beloved American way of life. In our schools, our newsrooms, even our corporate boardrooms, there is a new far left fascism that demands absolute allegiance. If you do not speak its language, performance rituals, recite its mantras and follow its commandments, then you will be censored, banished, blacklist persecuted and punished … Make no mistake, this left-wing cultural revolution is designed to overthrow the American Revolution. In so doing, they would destroy the very civilisation that rescued billions from poverty, disease, violence and hunger, and that lifted humanity to new heights of achievement, discovery and progress. To make this possible, they are determined to tear down every statue, symbol and memory of our national heritage.

That is a small flavour of it. It is a call to arms to wage cultural wars. The issue of why so many Americans took to the streets in every city across every state in the USA is not addressed.

It is the playbook of Richard Nixon from 1968. The so-called Southern Strategy that propelled 'Tricky Dicky' to power, when America last underwent such a period of searing social unrest over racial injustice. What is implicit in all of this is the scarring subject of race. Black and white. It is a call to the white working-class. It is a call to what Donald Trump calls the silent majority

The Trump campaign mark 1.0 was to fight the election on the economy, but with 11 per cent unemployed now that's going to be a hard sell. Mark 2.0 was to cast Donald Trump as the Churchillian war leader who steered America to safe waters during the coronavirus outbreak – but America is distinctly storm-ravaged right now, and sailing ever closer to the rocks. So mark 3.0 looks like it is going to be an old-fashioned us and them, culture wars confrontation.

4 July

Happy fourth. I spend a wonderful day out on the Chesapeake Bay with friends, and unplugged from politics.

6 July

If there was any doubt that Donald Trump wanted to fight this election on culture wars issues, it has been dispelled today. At the centre of it Bubba Wallace, NASCAR's only top tier black driver. A noose was found in his garage at a race track a few weeks back. Wallace didn't report it. NASCAR did, and called in the FBI. They found that this wasn't a hate crime as the rope door pull, while most definitely in the shape of a noose, had been there for months, and long before that garage had been allocated to Wallace. End of matter? Well, no.

This morning the President tweeted this: 'Has @BubbaWallace apologised to all those great NASCAR drivers and officials who came to his aid and were willing to sacrifice everything for him, only to find out that the whole thing was just another HOAX. That and flag decision has caused lowest ratings EVER!'

There is a lot to unpack here. First of all, it wasn't Wallace who made the complaint about the noose found in his garage. NASCAR decided to investigate after it was reported to them – so quite what

Wallace needs to apologise for is not exactly clear. Secondly, the implication is that even if he *had* found a noose and decided to take action, he didn't really have the right to protest. I mean, you don't want a black driver getting uppity, do you? And the final line about flags suggests that Donald Trump thinks that the decision to ban Confederate flags from NASCAR – a sport that is overwhelmingly white and some might say 'redneck' – shouldn't have been made. The Confederate flag is a symbol of the era of slavery, the banner that the Southern states held aloft in their fight against the North in the Civil War over the move to end slavery.

Donald Trump followed this up by attacking moves by two of the most famous teams in American sport to change their names, under pressure from advertisers and sponsors – the Washington Redskins football team and the Cleveland Indians baseball team. Donald Trump is declaring it is weak of the two fabled franchises to surrender to political correctness.

As for Bubba Wallace, the driver hit back saying that hate should be met with love … even when the hate is coming from the president of the United States. The Lincoln Project, a highly effective grouping of anti-Trump Republicans, was even more pointed, saying that the President won't wear a mask, but has no problem with putting on a white hood.

7 July

Tulsa Trump rally postscript: the head of public health for the city in Oklahoma, Dr Bruce Dart, reports a big spike in coronavirus cases, which he says are most likely caused by the rally two weeks ago. One of Trump's most prominent black supporters, the millionaire businessman Herman Cain, has been admitted to hospital with the disease. He posted photos at the time of the rally saying what a great time he was having. Not so much now. We've all become familiar with the idea of the 'super-spreader' – who knew you didn't even need to have Covid-19 to fit that category? Eye roll emoji.

9 July, Supreme Court

Are we about to see Donald Trump's tax returns?

This is not the outcome the President wanted. Far from it. Despite a conservative majority on the Supreme Court, it's voted 7–2 to reject Donald Trump's assertion that he enjoys absolute immunity while he remains in office. That will allow a New York prosecutor to pursue the President's private and business financial records. 'In our judicial system, the public has a right to every man's evidence,' said John Roberts, the chief justice, who wrote today's judgement. On the question of whether Congress should be able to access the President's tax returns, the Supreme Court fudged that. But Donald Trump is furious. Rat-a-tat-tat came the tweets from an angry Gatling gun.

However, if you look at this through a political lens I'd say it hasn't been such a bad day for the President. Unlike all his predecessors in the past 50 years, Donald Trump has refused to let the American public see his tax returns – and has done everything he can to keep them secret. This has given rise to a whole cottage industry of theories about the reason for his reluctance: they show he's nothing like as rich as he has claimed; they show he's in hock to the Russians ... It has become an arm wrestle – and because the media demand to see them, he is determined to defy his tormentors. Who knows?

But if the President's ultimate objective in this Supreme Court case is to keep his finances under wraps and away from prying eyes until after the November election, he's probably succeeded – the Supreme

Court has kicked this back to lower courts to sort out. And in Chief Justice Roberts's written opinion, he enumerates the various legal paths open to Trump. And there are a lot of legal blocking manoeuvres open to the President's lawyers that could stretch this way, way into the future.

He might have lost the legal battle, but he seems to have won the political one

Today we've also seen Joe Biden unveil his economic proposals under the slogan 'Build Back Better'. He wants to use the power of government spending to spur manufacturing in the US – something not seen, he claims, since the great Depression and World War 2. 'Throughout this crisis, Donald Trump has been almost singularly focused on the stock market – the Dow and the Nasdaq. Not you and not your families,' Biden said. 'If I am fortunate enough to be your president, I'll be laser-focused on working families, middle-class families like I came from here in Scranton, not the wealthy investor class. They don't need me; working families do.'

Biden is promising a 'buy American' approach, including $400 billion in new spending over four years. He would tighten the rules on those products that can bear the stamp 'made in America'. Companies that receive federal research grants won't then be able to manufacture whatever the product is overseas, and pass it off as American.

The proposal to use the power of federal government procurement to kickstart the economy looks a lot like a plan envisaged by the Massachusetts senator, Elizabeth Warren – even if her plan was more narrowly focused on clean energy.

The proposals get a mauling from the Trump campaign. This is socialism, they say, and will lead to a massive increase in taxes. But they should be flattered. The focus on 'building back better', boosting US manufacturing, moves to stifle off-shoring – yes, they are more Keynesian than anything Donald Trump would propose, but they are nonetheless a variation of his America First, protectionist policies from 2016. The Biden proposals show just how much Donald Trump has reshaped the political debate on globalism and free trade. We seem to have travelled a long way from the Trans-Pacific Partnership and all those other proposed deals of the Obama years.

10 July

It's been a blissfully quiet day. No calls from work. A minor flurry that Donald Trump has cancelled a rally he was due to be holding in New Hampshire, citing a tropical storm that was due to hit.

But all hell breaks loose this evening. The White House has announced that the President is commuting the sentence of Roger Stone. I feel that, like so much I report on, it is simultaneously startling and not in the least bit surprising. The White House puts out a long statement raking over the 'fake' Mueller investigation witchhunt; how Stone had been so cruelly and unfairly treated.

Reading this stuff you would think Roger Stone had spent his early life in a Jesuit seminary before becoming Mother Theresa's assistant. But anyone less hair-shirt it is hard to imagine. By his own description and admission he is a dirty trickster, a provocateur; he is a practitioner of the dark arts in politics. On his back he has a tattoo of his great hero: Richard Nixon. And his philosophy seems to be why hit above the belt when you can strike more effectively below it. And he's a dandy. Always extravagantly dressed, with homburg hats and foppish suits. In a previous life he was probably a peacock. When I interviewed him at the Republican Convention in Cleveland four years ago it was clear that he was loving every minute of the limelight and attention that came with being a Trump *consigliere*. And he had for years and years been a close confidant of the President.

It was his role during the 2016 Trump campaign that brought him to the attention of the Mueller inquiry. He would be found guilty of a long list of charges. And his trial started off as flamboyantly as you would expect. He emerged from court, arms outstretched, giving a victory sign with both hands – an homage to Nixon. He posted on Instagram the picture of the judge, while next to her head was what appeared to be the crosshairs of a gun sight. Funnily enough the judge, Amy Berman Jackson, didn't think it was that funny.

Stone was found guilty of witness tampering, obstruction and a number of counts of lying under oath. He had worked with Julian Assange to bring the stolen treasure trove of Clinton campaign emails into the public domain – the emails had come from Russian intelligence. This will give you a flavour of Stone. When rumours started circulating that he had been the point person with the Russians to get these damaging emails into the open, he wrote to a magazine saying this: 'I myself had no contacts or communications with the Russian State, Russian Intelligence or anyone fronting for them or acting as intermediaries for them. None. Nada. Zilch. I am not in touch with any Russians, don't have a Russian girlfriend, don't like Russian dressing and have stopped drinking Russian Vodka.'

Do you see what I mean? Not exactly a shrinking violet. I could fill pages and pages with Stone stories, but it would be a distraction. Suffice it to say when he was found to have lied on oath to Congress – who was he lying to protect? The beneficiary of Stone's stonewalling (or deception) was the President – who on this Friday night has decided to commute his sentence.

Given all the President's other problems – with polling, with coronavirus, with Black Lives Matter concerns – this was a remarkable decision: to invest so much capital in someone who is hardly the most *sympathique* character in the political jungle, and who most people, Republicans and Democrats, thought had it coming.

Mitt Romney, the only Republican senator to vote for Donald Trump's conviction at his impeachment trial, tweets: 'Unprecedented, historic corruption: an American president commutes the sentence of a person convicted by a jury of lying to shield that very president.'

11 July

Forgive me a moment of self-indulgence. Today is the first anniversary of Max and Kate. We should have been in Europe together. Instead they are in Sydney, I am in DC, and Linda and Anna in London. And there is nothing that any of us can do about it. Talk about scattered …

I am going out to Middleburg in Virginia for lunch with Tom and Katty. Katty Kay is the incredibly impressive presenter of *Beyond 100 Days*, and one of the regular voices on the MSNBC breakfast show, *Morning Joe*. She is that rare British beast – someone much more famous here in the US than I suspect she is in the UK. Tom Carver, her husband, I have known for over 30 years. We started our careers together at Radio Solent. They have a lovely, slightly tumbledown old cottage in the countryside. To reach it you drive a mile and a half along an unmade road, then follow a dirt track for a couple of hundred metres, and it is there on the right. Suffice it to say, slightly in the middle of nowhere. On my way up the gravel track I see a coyote – my first ever sighting of one. It stares at me in my car and then in no particular hurry skulks off.

We sit out on the porch. There are butterflies fluttering all over the garden. And a bluebird is commuting between trees making a lot of noise. It is only 50 miles from Washington, but feels a lot further. And as we sit there, with Tom and me about to go and play tennis, the most incongruous of sights. A number of young, white men with big, bushy beards pass on horseback, dressed as Confederate soldiers, presumably as part of some Civil War re-enactment. When they see Katty they all doff their hats. We are back in 1863, and the Battle of Middleburg. Bizarre. In the age of George Floyd and Black Lives Matter, with the heightened attention to statues and flags, you don't really expect to come across the Confederacy on a Saturday lunchtime in July.

I drive back to Washington late afternoon. And the big breaking news is that – finally – Donald Trump has put a mask on, and has allowed himself to be seen and filmed wearing it. He has gone to the Walter Reed military hospital in Bethesda. After ripping into Biden for his insistence on wearing one, and slamming a reporter for being 'politically correct' for keeping a mask on while asking the President a question at a White House briefing, Trump has succumbed – three months after the White House Coronavirus task force told Americans to put on a face covering to reduce the risk of transmission.

It comes as a poll is put out which finds that 67 per cent of Americans say they think he has mishandled the health crisis. So, the issue which has sparked a new frontier in the culture war is resolved (sort of). It's OK to wear a mask. But at what price? Can you imagine what a difference it would have made if that sort of lead had been given early on? Dare one say, how many lives would have been saved? The virus is still ripping through the sunshine states in the South and west, and only now is the President saying to people it's OK to wear a mask. It's not a liberal plot. However, it's hard to avoid the conclusion that given these poll numbers the President's conversion to the efficacy of a face covering may have more to do with political necessity than public health considerations.

12 July

And what is absolutely 100 per cent, Waterford crystal clear is that the sight of the Don donning a mask has nothing to do with a new-found admiration for, or acquiescence to the ministrations of, Dr Anthony Fauci. The strained relationship between the scientist and the populist is at breaking point. Just to spool back, Fauci, more than any other medics who are part of the coronavirus task force, speaks his mind. He doesn't go out of his way to jab the President in the ribs – but nor does he acquiesce. He's no nodding dog on the back shelf of a car. In recent days he has said that the US is not doing as well as many other countries – remember the White House line is that no one is doing better than America (even though the most cursory glance at the figures will tell you that is not true). He has said the worst is far from over, when Trump wants to insist it's just a small brush fire that will be quickly extinguished. He has predicted the US could reach 100,000 new cases per day – something that seems likely to be borne out. And Trump has let it be known that Fauci hasn't briefed him for two months. In other words he's been marginalised.

But here's the problem for the White House. Who is the most trusted person in the administration when it comes to how to deal with the coronavirus outbreak? Take a bow Dr Anthony Fauci. According to a *New York Times*/Siena College poll, 67 per cent have faith in him. And how many trust Donald Trump? Well, according to the poll a meagre 26 per cent. That you can be sure is a situation the President will not find to his liking. If one were being logical, one might argue that it's fantastic to have someone on the team who commands such trust and support from the American public – and that therefore we ought to do all we can to burnish his reputation.

But this is the capricious Trump White House. Donald Trump had said the other evening that Fauci didn't get everything right. So, the

Washington Post asked, what is it that he has got wrong? To which the press office would on any other day of the year be expected to say, 'I don't know, I haven't asked the President.' Or, 'the President and Dr Fauci work very well together.' Or, 'any disagreements they have are extremely minor.' Or, 'we have no comment.' Or, 'piss off you fake news scumbag, go to hell and stop screwing up my Sunday.'

Instead, perhaps motivated by a genuine and compassionate desire to help the *Washington Post* – or a determined effort to undermine Fauci (it's one of the two – I'll leave it to you to decide) – the White House comms shop answers the question. Not only do they answer the question, they send over a lengthy document detailing all the areas where the considered view of the scientific super-brains in the White House is that Fauci has screwed up. It looks exactly like the sort of dirty-ops research you do on an opponent in an election. A dossier of shame. Not something you produce on your chief infectious diseases specialist, who is spearheading the efforts to find a vaccine.

This is the 79-year-old who has served as the director of the National Institute of Allergy and Infectious Diseases since 1984. The man who has served six presidents; has spent half a century trying to keep the country safe. Regardless, the *Washington Post* was given an on-the-record (although delivered anonymously) quote that 'Several White House officials are concerned about the number of times Dr Fauci has been wrong on things.'

This needs deconstructing. Several? This is a classic smear tactic. You don't say who the people are. You just make sure that it comes across as a wide swathe of opinion in the administration, and not just one disgruntled person. There is something else – because the official has given this quote 'on the record', this is a sanctioned hit, and not a rogue freelance operation.

The *Post* was then given a lengthy list of the scientist's comments from early in the outbreak. Those included his early doubt that people with no symptoms could play a significant role in spreading the virus – a notion based on earlier outbreaks that the novel coronavirus would turn on its head. They also point to public reassurances Fauci made in late February, around the time of the first US case of community transmission, that 'at this moment, there is no need to change anything that you're doing on a day-by-day basis'. And on and on the dossier went. He'd been against the travel ban from China, but the President went ahead with it anyway. He'd been against masks, but had changed his mind.

And if you are thinking this might be special treatment being given to the *Washington Post*, let me disabuse you of that. When other news organisations contacted the White House, they were given the same on-the-record quote – and the same list of Fauci shortcomings. This is a concerted effort to take him down. And disingenuous too. If the evidence of his failure is the advice he gave at the early stages of the outbreak, then that is pretty harsh. The opinions that Fauci was giving were based on the science at the time; when people knew little about the idiosyncrasies of this particular coronavirus. And let's face it, he never recommended that people inject themselves with disinfectant.

I suspect Fauci, having worked for six administrations, has seen pretty much all there is to see when it comes to dealing with politicians – but maybe nothing quite like this. If he goes to bed tonight feeling that he's been hung out to dry, he's right. He has.

13 July

The Washington Redskins are one of the biggest names in American team sport. But the club has also aroused the greatest controversy – going back decades. In 2001 its owner, Dan Snyder, vowed that he was never going to change the name of the football team. He is still the owner of the franchise today, but now in the wake of the death of George Floyd, and the growth of the Black Lives Matter protests, the climate has changed. And where that change is most notable is among corporate backers. American boardrooms want to be seen to be taking a lead, and their threat to withdraw multi-million-dollar sponsorship deals is an effective lever. It is hard to argue – to call a Native American 'a redskin' would be considered a racial slur. But in America's toxic culture wars debate this has strong political overtones. Last week Donald Trump accused the club of being weak and giving in to political correctness. Nevertheless they made the announcement of the change this morning, via a tweeted press release – from their account, with the handle @redskins.

14 July

The tormenting of Fauci goes on. And it's even more unbelievable. Today in the newspaper *USA Today*, there's an op-ed from senior White House trade advisor Peter Navarro, laying into Fauci – along similar lines to what we saw at the weekend – but the difference this time is that there is a name attached. But here's the thing: according to the White House, Navarro had not sought authorisation for this hit. It was a freelance operation.

In any normal political operation this should result in one of two things. Either the views expressed by Navarro are shared by the President and had been quietly authorised by him – in which case you fire Fauci, on the basis that he has lost the confidence of the President. Or you fire Navarro for such a gross act of insubordination. Instead the communications director says that Navarro owes Fauci an apology. And that is it.

Makes me think that Navarro, far from freelancing, is – on this occasion – His Master's Voice. In the midst of this pandemic, where the number of states with a surge of coronavirus cases is growing terrifyingly, what a decidedly odd strategy to undermine the credibility of your chief infectious disease specialist.

17 July

Madness (part 278). In Georgia the Democratic mayor of the biggest city, Atlanta, has made it mandatory to wear masks. Georgia is one of those Southern states where numbers have been climbing alarmingly. And the mayor, Keisha Lance Bottoms, who has gone down with coronavirus herself, is one of those under consideration to be Joe Biden's running mate. Her decision to make face coverings compulsory follows what a number of other cities and towns in the state have done – and what has been adopted by other states as a whole – including ones with Republican governors. But now the uber-Trumpian state governor, Brian Kemp, has decided to sue Lance Bottoms over making masks mandatory. This as the head of the Centers for Disease Control has said that America's coronavirus nightmare could be dealt with if for the next four to six weeks all Americans wore a mask all the time.

The politicisation of wearing a mask is one of those things I am still struggling to get my head around.

This evening I go out for dinner with my BBC colleague Tom Geoghegan and his old university mate, Geraint Vincent, who is now a reporter for ITV. It is a steamy hot evening as we sit on the balcony of a restaurant on the Georgetown waterfront. We drink quite a bit, and eat a bit less. I go home quite merry, and think it will be a good idea to have a wee dram of whisky before bed.

Well, it seemed like a good idea until I see the flash that John Lewis, the legendary congressman, has died of pancreatic cancer. He was one of the towering figures of the civil rights movement in the 1960s. He had a booming voice and an integrity that few in Washington can match.

He was one of the original 'Freedom Riders' who challenged segregation on public transport across the South. The riders were attacked and beaten for their trouble – but the rides changed the way people travelled and paved the way for the Civil Rights Act of 1964 and the Voting Rights Act of 1965. He also shared the platform with Martin Luther King Jr at the 1963 March on Washington, when MLK delivered his 'I Have a Dream' speech. In 1965 he had his skull fractured by white policemen in Selma, Alabama, as civil rights protestors tried to cross the Edmund Pettus Bridge. He was last seen in public with Washington's mayor a few weeks ago as they inspected the Black Lives Matter Plaza, the area opened across from Lafayette Park, where police had forcibly ejected protestors in support of George Floyd.

I remember, a couple of years back, giving a talk to a group of sixth-form politics students, over from the UK. I ask them what they have planned for the week. The teacher tells me that they will be going to Congress and will have a sit-down meeting with John Lewis. *The* John Lewis, I reply, somewhat startled. Yes, the teacher tells me. He meets our students every year.

After the whisky I now drink quite a lot of coffee to straighten myself up ahead of a late night/early morning chat with Martha Kearney for the *Today* programme.

18 July

There is an outpouring of grief over Lewis's death. Heartfelt tributes from across the aisle. And they are led by all the former presidents. The

White House orders the flag to fly at half mast. The communications director issues a message of condolence. But from President Trump nothing. He has gone off to play golf. As condolences turn to consternation over the presidential silence, he does eventually tweet a desultory message: 'Saddened to hear the news of civil rights hero John Lewis passing. Melania and I send our prayers to he and his family.'

This is possibly a harsh observation to make. But the last time he went to play golf, Donald Trump retweeted a man shouting 'white power' and left that post up for several hours, before removing it – and then without apology. This time over the death of a hero to much of the black community he chooses to say nothing for several hours, and when he does say something it is the bare minimum. If you are a believer in 'white power', how much are you going to love the optics of that?

19 July

Trump has done a sit-down with Chris Wallace from Fox News. If you see the words 'presidential interview' and 'Fox News' and automatically think 'easy ride', allow me to disabuse you. Chris Wallace is consistently the best interviewer (to my mind) in America today. He manages to remain scrupulously polite, with an apparently deferential manner – while being absolutely deadly. There is so much about this interview that is fascinating – both in what the President actually says, and what it reveals about his mindset.

Perhaps the most bizarre section is when the President says he doesn't want to say that he thinks Biden is senile – but does his best to say exactly that. Then he brags about how well he did on his cognitive test, and how he is much sharper than Biden. Here's the exchange with Wallace:

TRUMP: Well, I'll tell you what, let's take a test. Let's take a test right now. Let's go down, Joe and I will take a test. Let him take the same test that I took.

WALLACE: Incidentally, I took the test too when I heard that you passed it.

TRUMP: Yeah, how did you do?

WALLACE: It's not – well, it's not the hardest test. They have a picture and it says 'what's that?' and it's an elephant.

TRUMP: No no no … You see, that's all misrepresentation.

WALLACE: Well, that's what it was on the web.

TRUMP: It's all misrepresentation. Because, yes, the first few questions are easy, but I'll bet you couldn't even answer the last five questions. I'll bet you couldn't, they get very hard, the last five questions.

WALLACE: Well, one of them was count back from 100 by seven.

TRUMP: Let me tell you …

WALLACE: Ninety-three.

TRUMP: … you couldn't answer – you couldn't answer many of the questions.

WALLACE: OK, what's the question?

TRUMP: I'll get you the test, I'd like to give it. I'll guarantee you that Joe Biden could not answer those questions.

WALLACE: OK.

If that was the most bizarre section of this compelling interview, the most tendentious was what he said on the coronavirus outbreak, where he again insisted that America's testing regime was the envy of the world. He also claimed that America had the lowest mortality rate for the disease (not borne out by the facts); that the US only had more cases than Europe because Europe had stopped testing. Wallace was doing his best (and for the most part did it brilliantly) to fact-check the President as one false claim was made after another. But Trump went back to a refrain that we've heard again and again – the disease will one day just disappear.

TRUMP: I'll be right eventually. I will be right eventually. You know I said, 'It's going to disappear.' I'll say it again.

WALLACE: But does that – does that discredit you?

TRUMP: It's going to disappear and I'll be right. I don't think so.

WALLACE: Right.

TRUMP: I don't think so. I don't think so. You know why? Because I've been right probably more than anybody else.

One other thing from the interview that stands out is when Trump is asked whether he will accept the result of the election. His answer is unequivocally equivocal: 'I have to see. Look, you – I have to see. No, I'm not going to just say yes. I'm not going to say no, and I didn't last time either.'

I think for a lot of Democrats and some Republicans, comments like that send a shiver down the spine.

20 July

Portland, Oregon. We need to talk about what is happening here. Protests have been going on for weeks. But unfortunately the death of George Floyd and the Black Lives Matter issues have been overtaken by those who just like to protest – often violently. In a familiar pattern anarchists and hangers-on have hitched their wagon to the endless protests. Pretty it is not.

But this has become a testing ground for Donald Trump's get tough, law and order policies. And forget the rights of states and cities to determine their own policies – the President has sent in federal agents to deal with the situation. Their mission is to protect federal buildings and property. Fair enough. But who are these people dressed in full camouflage uniforms, like active duty troops – but with zero insignia, no names? Federal agents, but from which agency? They look like the snatch squads or secret police you might see in an oppressive, authoritarian regime. They are driving unmarked vehicles, under whose aegis are they operating? What are their rules of engagement? What are their powers of arrest? What training do they have to deal with protestors? Far from seeking de-escalation, to use the jargon, they seem to be spoiling for a fight.

A navy veteran who has the temerity to ask some of these federal officers just those questions – and tries to do so politely – is given a mighty beating, first with batons and then pepper spray. He suffers a broken arm. There is growing unease within the Pentagon that people dressed as active duty soldiers are deploying overwhelming power against the civilian population, even though the right to peaceful protest is enshrined in the Constitution.

You just have the nagging feeling that this is exactly the made-for-television confrontation that Donald Trump has wanted to engineer to highlight his wider political narrative – there is the path to lawlessness and anarchy if you vote for Biden; and there is a tough guy in the White House right now who will push back against the unwashed, lawless mob. What is playing out on the streets of Portland, Oregon, is the President's Mount Rushmore speech made flesh.

21 July

The coronavirus briefings are back. But not as we knew them. This time Donald Trump is flying solo, with no phalanx of health experts around him. And it is data driven with lots of charts. He is sticking to the script. And in questions he's keeping it brief – both in the answers he gives and the number of questions he takes. The headline is that it's going to get worse before it gets better; and strong support for face masks – although he's not wearing one. This couldn't be more different from what went before.

23 July

Woke up this morning
Got out of bed
Got me a bad case of the Covid blues

I unloaded to Max last night. Am fed up with being alone in this apartment. Am fed up that I don't know when we can all get together again. Am fed up that Linda can't get here. Am fed up that we can't get to see Max and Kate in Australia. I have no idea how coverage of this bloody election is going to pan out – I have visions of never being able to leave DC. Arrgghh.

But have just been immensely cheered by another Donald Trump clip from another interview that he's done with Fox. For two minutes and four seconds in the interview he is reprising the cognitive test he's just done. He takes the bewildered but straight-faced (hope he gets a bonus for pulling that off) interviewer through his answers, telling him how one in particular got him mega points And he keeps saying Person. Woman. Man. Camera. TV. And apparently you get asked that again – and again he recites the incantation: Person. Woman. Man. Camera. TV. He claims that the testers are amazed and ask him how he does it. 'It's because I'm cognitively there,' he tells the interviewer, who is still strictly observing the White House No Smirking policy.

The latest polling data from Florida is catastrophic for the President. The Quinnipiac University poll has him down 13 points. This is a state he was hoping wouldn't even be in contention in November. No wonder we're seeing such a change in tone on the need to tackle coronavirus.

Nothing to do with the election, but there is the most stunning take-down by Alexandria Ocasio-Cortez of a Republican congressman who'd called her 'a fucking bitch' on the steps of the Capitol. The congressman, Ted Yoho, had given a non-apology apology about it the previous day. AOC's response is devastating. She calmly and articulately eviscerates him. It is a speech for our age.

It is early evening now. It's breakfast time in Australia. Bedtime in the UK, and I have just received an email from the US embassy informing me that Linda has been granted a waiver to come into the US. Fantastic news. Max comes on the group What'sApp and says we should have a family Zoom. Seems he has something he wants to say. We agree – and before we get on the call, a video clip lands in our inboxes of a little thing wriggling around inside Kate's tummy. So, the big news we had about Linda getting a waiver to come to the US is well and truly outshone by the down-unders and a future baby Sopel – and impending grandparenthood. Yikes.

I hope I can be a fit and proper grandparent. Just keep reciting it: Person. Woman. Man. Camera. TV.

24 July

What a week. It's as though, in January 2017, Donald Trump was given a shiny, new car. The best, most beautiful car the world has ever seen. And in this week in July he made an important discovery about it. It has a reverse gear. It was an extra on the car he never thought he'd need and certainly never intended to use. But on Monday he put the car into reverse, and wrestle as he might with the gearstick and the clutch, he can't stop the blasted thing from going backwards.

Or to change the metaphor, and borrow the language used this week by Boris Johnson to describe his Labour opponent – the President has had more flip-flops than Bournemouth beach.

A quick recap. Masks – which the President used to deride as politically correct – are now an act of patriotism and should always be worn when social distancing is impossible. Coronavirus, which only a few days ago was being described in most instances as a bad case of the sniffles, is now something altogether more serious – and it is going to get worse before it gets better. Two weeks ago the President was insisting that all schools had to reopen, and threatening to take away their funding if they didn't. He's now saying in some of the worst hit cities that wouldn't be appropriate – and sounding much more empathetic towards parents wrestling with the decision about whether to allow their children to resume in-school education.

And the really big U-turn came last night on the Republican Convention in Jacksonville, Florida. The President loves a crowd. A raucous, adoring crowd. The original plan had been to hold the event in Charlotte, North Carolina. But when the governor of that state said there would have to be social distancing the President went ballistic, went after the governor, and announced huffily the Republicans would go somewhere else. Jacksonville would be the venue for the tickertape and hoopla, and thousands of cheering and whooping Republicans. Except now it won't be.

It was a stunning and painful reverse, and one the President made with the heaviest of hearts. The announcements have come on three consecutive nights of revitalised White House coronavirus briefings – now with Donald Trump flying solo, and not flanked by his medical advisors. But they have also been much more disciplined than when the President would spend a couple of hours at the lectern, musing on anything and everything – most memorably on whether disinfectant and sunlight should be injected into the body to treat coronavirus.

I was at that memorable briefing with the President, and I was back again this week for his briefing on Wednesday night. This time around he was in and out in less than half an hour, stuck to the messages he wanted to deliver (OK, no one had anticipated the bizarre foray into the legal difficulties facing Ghislaine Maxwell), and answered a handful of questions. He didn't get riled. He didn't get into fights. He did what he came to do. And then was off.

All I would say is that Season 2 is nothing like as much fun as Season 1 – though the episodes are much shorter.

I sat discussing this one evening this week in the garden of someone closely involved in the doings of the administration. It was an insufferably humid evening and the thunder rolled around the city. We spent a time discussing the psychology of the President (yes, a common topic). And this person was making the point that he has an old-fashioned macho need never to appear weak. Even though he knows at times it would be smart to give ground and concede, that is unconscionable.

But if we are still playing pop psychology with the President's brain – whose cognitive strengths we now all know: person, man, woman, camera, TV – there is one thing worse than being weak. And that is being a loser.

And though in public – for fear of looking weak – the President insists his campaign is winning, and the American people love him, and polls that show him sinking underwater are fake news, the reality is altogether more uncomfortable.

Let's just take Florida, where Donald Trump was to have made his Convention acceptance speech. It is the epicentre at the moment of the appalling surge in coronavirus cases. With its population of 21 million, last week it was diagnosing more new cases per day than the whole of the European Union (population 460 million). That merits a Twitter friendly 'wow'. But Florida is also ground zero for US presidential elections. Just think Bush versus Gore in 2000. It was a state Trump won comfortably in 2016. It was a state he thought he would breeze in November. But the latest Quinnipiac University poll has Joe Biden 13 points ahead. Thirteen. That is massive. And there is a whole pile of other key swing states which show Donald Trump lagging behind.

What hasn't changed in the past week is the science. You can be sure that his long-suffering public health advisors have been banging on about the same things like a broken gramophone. Masks, distancing, avoiding crowds. It may be that the President has had a

Damascene conversion to listening to his doctors. Possible, but I have to say unlikely.

If we're looking for a significant 'thing' it is this: last week Donald Trump fired his 2020 campaign manager, Brad Parscale, and installed a new one. And it appears Bill Stepien has sat the President down and given him the ice cold bucket of water. That the polls are awful, and going in the wrong direction; that all is not lost but quickly could spin out of control. That a change of direction and tone is urgently needed, particularly when it comes to anything and everything to do with Covid-19.

It is worth inserting one proviso here. I don't know Bill Stepien – who gets very good reviews. But brilliant though he may be, there is a bit of a pattern when the President makes a new appointment: for the next two or three weeks he does what he is told – but then reverts to going with his gut; going with his instinct. The things that he will tell you have served him best throughout his long and colourful career. But we are in new territory.

For three and a half years the President has been able to define his own reality; to bend and fashion facts to suit his own narrative. The coronavirus has been unimpressed by his efforts. This has been a foe like none that Donald Trump has faced. And he has had to bend to its will. Not the other way round.

What has happened this week is that what the polls are showing and what his scientists have been repeatedly calling for are totally aligned. And he really doesn't want to be a loser in November.

The spectre of these 180-degree turns has brought much guffawing from liberal commentators. The man who only knows how to double down, now doubled up in the pain of these very public reverses.

But they should be more cautious. The conversion may be insincere; may well be born of polling necessity – but what a lot of Americans will see is their president behaving rationally and normally; making decisions consistent with the scale of the threat the American people are facing – and Americans are fearing. But, I hear you say, surely they won't forget about all those things the President said in March and April when he played the pandemic down and urged the reopening of the US economy prematurely?

Well, all I would say is that the circus moves on quickly; everyone seems to have incredibly short memories. Who talks any more about Mueller? Or Russia? Or impeachment? The beam of the lighthouse doesn't stay long in any one place. With our impatience for new developments, for new storylines and plot twists, we seem to suffer collectively from attention deficit disorder. And this president understands that better than anyone.

Some will no doubt write that this has been the President's worst week ever. If he wins in November it will come to be seen as his best.

27 July

A fascinating little get-together at a foreign embassy. It is the nearest thing I have seen to a party in the last five months. There must have been – ooh – 20 or 25 people there. OK, there is as much hand sanitiser as there is champagne, but frankly any champagne is welcome. And the invitation stresses that the evening will be conducted according to Centers for Disease Control guidelines.

Nevertheless, the ambassador has also managed to pull in some pretty A-list Trump team members. I'll come to them in a minute. My evening started off with what I thought was a fairly depressing conversation with a senior American diplomat who had served his country under successive administrations – both Republican and Democratic. He has served as an ambassador in some of the world's most dangerous places, before coming back to the State Department.

But he has now resigned over his concerns that the engine-room of American diplomacy was being hollowed out, and was being overly politicised.

I ask whether he would do an on-the-record interview for the BBC. He declines. He says he will talk to me off the record, but is too fearful that if he appears on camera, his life will be upended. 'This is a highly vindictive administration,' he tells me. So you serve your country fearlessly in places where you put your life on the line, but you return to Washington, and though the First Amendment guarantees your right to speak your mind, you are too fearful to do so.

I have a long and hugely enjoyable conversation with the President's senior advisor, Kellyanne Conway – one of the handful of people who have been with him since the beginning. She tells me that she believes the polls showing the President to be behind Biden – that is something that Donald Trump won't acknowledge – are correct. But she makes the analogy that America is on a blind date when it comes to Biden. They've heard he's good-looking and charming but haven't yet met him. And, she argues, the race becomes a different thing when he emerges from his basement. I push back, saying that is an analogy that only takes you so far. He was Veep four years ago; he's been in American public life for more than four decades. He may be bland, he may be vanilla, he may be old – but it's hard to argue that the American people don't really know who he is. Though where she does have a point is that voters are going to look at him with much greater scrutiny when they are contemplating him as their next president.

Another interesting conversation is with Trump's former chief of staff, Mick Mulvaney. He's still involved in the campaign, and is due to take up the position as the President's envoy for Ireland. He puts it succinctly. He says if November's election is about Trump versus Trump (in other words a referendum on him), then he loses; but if it's about Trump versus Biden, then he has a chance – but he says the sand is passing through the hour-glass quickly.

I get home slightly giddy from having been out in the world again (and maybe the Bellini at the end wasn't strictly necessary), and Twitter is lighting up. It seems that the fact-driven discipline shown by Donald Trump last week is gone. The President is retweeting approvingly a doctor from Texas who is arguing that hydroxychloroquine is a cure for coronavirus, even though there have been no randomised tests which prove it is of any use at all. And the advice of the federal Food and Drug Administration is that it should not be used outside of a medical setting because it might lead to heart arrhythmia.

I feel I have watched this movie so many times.

Over these three and a half years I have given probably an unhealthy amount of mental space to Donald Trump – his motivations, the rationale for his policy decisions – and normally I can find an explanation for what he does. But the one thing I have never been able to figure out is his unfailing admiration for Vladimir Putin, where the President is endlessly forgiving, and always giving him benefit of the doubt. Add to that his unswerving – and some would say absurd – advocacy for hydroxychloroquine, on the basis of zero science.

28 July

Stella Immanuel, today is your day. You are up in lights. You are an overnight internet sensation. She is the doctor who was retweeted by the President last night advocating hydroxychloroquine as a cure for coronavirus. In a video posted online the Cameroon-born doctor from Texas is seen in her white coat, flanked by a number of other doctors. It is exactly what the President wants to hear. She also says face masks are unnecessary. Donald Trump Jr retweets her comments approvingly, as does the President. Less impressed are Facebook and Twitter, who remove the video, as it transgresses their misinformation policies. Twitter also slap a temporary ban on Trump junior.

A little investigation into the background of Doctor Immanuel might have given the Trumps cause to pause. You see her views are somewhat outside the medical mainstream. Five years ago, she alleged that alien DNA was being used in medical treatments, and that scientists were creating a vaccine to prevent people from being religious. Other claims include blaming medical conditions on witches and demons, who she says have sex with people in a dream world. 'They turn into a woman and then they sleep with the man and collect his sperm … then they turn into the man and they sleep with a man and deposit the sperm and reproduce more of themselves,' she said during a sermon in 2013. Ah yes, the demon semen …

Now some might ask how is it the President retweets someone with views that are as nutty as a fruitcake? But when challenged, the President doubles down (as an aside, I wonder how many times I have written this sentence), saying, 'She said that she had tremendous success with hundreds of different patients, I thought her voice was an important voice but I know nothing about her.'

In the new fact-based, data-driven, keep-it-real White House, the President has allied himself with Dr Immanuel.

FOOTNOTE: After Facebook took down her video she posted again, this time saying that unless the video was restored, Jesus Christ would destroy the media giant's servers. At time of writing, they still seem to be up and running.

30 July

It is another split-screen moment in a split-screen country. On one side of the screen a solemn but still uplifting scene is playing out at the Ebenezer Baptist Church in Atlanta, Georgia, where three former presidents have gathered to bid farewell to congressman John Lewis. This hero of the civil rights movement, and the man who came to be known as the conscience of Congress over his fight for voting rights, is being given what is, in effect, a state funeral. Powerful orations are delivered by presidents Clinton, Bush and especially Obama, as he reflects on how the blood of Lewis was spilled on the bridge to Selma so that every black man and woman should have the right to vote.

The current occupant of the White House chose not to pay his respects. He didn't go to the lying in state in the Capitol rotunda; he didn't make the journey to Atlanta. Instead, in perhaps the most unprecedented and incendiary tweet of his presidency – and, yes, I appreciate that's a high bar – he suggests November's election should be postponed. His concern is that postal votes, which will be used much more widely because of coronavirus, will be a source of massive fraud – even though that is how Donald Trump himself votes.

Now it is just worth recalling that in 1864, at the height of the American Civil War when Confederate forces were closing in on the capital, Abraham Lincoln insisted that the election go ahead. Ditto Franklin Delano Roosevelt during the Second World War. So what is going on here? I offer you two theories:

1. Trump is lagging badly in the polls. He is underwater, and seemingly sinking. Of all the scenarios I can see playing out late on election night on 3 November, one I find particularly hard to imagine. If Trump loses, I just cannot foresee him getting on the phone to Joe Biden and saying congratulations, well done Mr

President-elect, you won fair and square. How can I help with the transition? Just as he did in the Fox News interview he gave a week or so ago to Chris Wallace when he said he might not accept the result of the election, he is sowing doubt; alerting his supporters to the possibility of defeat, but saying to them if he loses it will be because of theft, not a fair fight. This is dangerous stuff. The peaceful transfer of power is what marks out liberal democracies from autocratic regimes. But Donald Trump by these comments seems to want to cast doubt on the potential results before a ballot is cast.

2. This is classic distraction. This morning has seen the publication of the worst GDP figures for a single quarter in American history. The economy is cratering. The growth of five years has been swept away in the second quarter of 2020. Donald Trump's plan was to go to the country on his towering economic achievements, but coronavirus has put a stop to that. America last night also passed the grim milestone of 150,000 Covid deaths – a country with 4 per cent of the world's population has racked up 24 per cent of the world's deaths. It would be entirely understandable if he wanted to set a diversionary fire so we all look the other way. And quite possibly he wanted to draw attention away from John Lewis's funeral, aware that many of the eulogists there would have had the absentee president in their cross hairs.

The ridiculous thing is that delaying the election is not something the President has any control over. It is for Congress to decide. And there is not a cat's chance in hell that lawmakers there will vote for a delay. And just imagining for a nanosecond that they did, it would not make that much difference to the President, as the Constitution lays down that after four years his term expires. In other words, at the end of 20 January 2021, he's out. He's an ex-president.

But it is another occasion where the President is tearing at the fabric of the Constitution, which three and a half years ago, during his inauguration, he promised to uphold. We have been here before – and these moments tend to be met with an embarrassed silence by the Republican leadership, who fear the consequences of getting into a fistfight with Trump, and so will cross the street to avoid having to speak to a television camera. But not today. From the leader of the Senate, Mitch McConnell, downwards, Republicans of all shades are coming out to affirm that the election will be held on 3 November. No ifs or buts.

31 July

Sometimes I feel that Aaron Sorkin, the creator of *The West Wing*, has taken over the script-writing of this presidency. With perfect synchronicity the Chinese-backed governor of Hong Kong has just announced that she is delaying the territory's legislative council elections because of coronavirus. Look at the symmetry – just as the President is calling for delay in the US elections, so the authorities in Hong Kong do the same.

There is a press briefing at the White House with the President's spokeswoman, Kayleigh McEnany, and I am one of the pool reporters down to cover. It seems the obvious question. 'Does the President support what the Chinese-backed administration in Hong Kong are doing in postponing the elections?' I ask her. Ms McEnany shuffles through her notes and reads a stinging condemnation of the anti-democratic sentiments of the Chinese. How dare they try to postpone an election!

It is brazen. There is not a flicker on her face that shows recognition there might be any irony in what she is saying, having spent the earlier part of the briefing defending the President's call to postpone this November's election.

It is worth digging out the recording to see what happens next. Without pausing for breath, as if there is no comma or full stop she stares at me and starts talking about the bravery of American first responders in dealing with the coronavirus outbreak. Doctors this, nurses that. It was a two-minute monologue that had absolutely nothing to do with what I asked her. Talk about non sequitur.

This is clearly the rehearsed emergency ripcord you pull when things are looking shaky. Go to your back-up notes. Go to back-up. Now. Quick. Quick. Quick. Change subject. Change subject!

And then, having delivered her homily on the front-line first responders, she turned on her heels and left the Briefing Room, without giving me – or anyone else – the chance to ask the obvious follow-up: so what's the difference between what the President is proposing and what they're doing in Hong Kong? She did it seamlessly. Or shamelessly. One of the two.

3 August

Another Trump interview, and another massively uncomfortable encounter. The days of the free ride seem to be over. It has set the heather alight. What is remarkable about this interview on the *Axios* news website is how much it has been remarked upon, given that – on the face of it – it is so unremarkable: interviewer sits down with politician and asks questions. Politician is evasive and makes baseless assertions, so the quizmaster says things like 'What do you mean?', 'What's your basis for saying that?' or 'Why?' I mean, isn't that what we do in interviews?

But it *was* exceptional because that is not how Donald Trump is normally interviewed; it is not what normally happens; it is not how people behave before him. But there was something else too. Trump is highly selective about who he allows himself to be interviewed by (declaration of interest: despite repeated efforts, and coming very close once, he has not done an interview with me – although he has answered a lot of my questions at news conferences). If I were to put a number on it, I would say that he gives 90 to 95 per cent of his interviews to the Murdoch-owned Fox News network – and he always knows well who is interviewing him.

With the *Axios* interview, he knows Jonathan Swan too. The charming Australian (at one point in the interview, Trump looks at him during an answer he is giving and says 'Look at that smile') has been a force of nature in Washington. He is fabulously well connected and, though an outsider, has cultivated the key players in the White House like an insider. In other words, Trump thought he knew what he was getting when the two men sat down together in the White House.

But Swan will have watched closely a couple of weeks earlier the presidential interview in the sweltering heat of the Rose Garden with Fox's Chris Wallace. Wallace, like Swan, was not there to give the President a free ride. Wallace is old-school courteous – but as sharp as a Gurkha's kukri knife. What was new about these two interrogations was that for the first time that I can recall the President is fact-checked in real time. And each interview has its jaw-dropping moment.

In the Wallace interview, the President asserted that Joe Biden would cut funding to the police. Wallace said that wasn't true. So the President stops the interview to allow White House officials to go off and find the killer quote: but they can't. A delicious moment for Wallace. In the *Axios* interview, the President produces a sheaf of papers with graphs and tables to prove how well the US (and he) was dealing with the coronavirus outbreak. But it is clear that Trump has little idea what the tables show, and isn't across the detail, as he declares that America is 'lower than the world'. Swan shows his incredulity with a range of facial expressions that a Kabuki actor would have been proud of.

What these two white men doing the interviews have in common is that they are … two white men. If you have sat in as many White House briefings as I have you know the President does not react favourably to being challenged like this by women. He very quickly gets hot under the collar. He was so 'triggered' by a brilliant 20-something female CNN reporter, Kaitlan Collins, that just before one press conference, White House staff tried to move a male reporter into her allocated front row seat so she would be pushed to the back of the room, and not in Donald Trump's eye-line. There are endless more examples.

I did wonder whether anyone from the White House would say to the President after the Wallace and Swan interviews, 'That was awful, and you need to prep better for these sort of encounters' … but I feel confident I know the answer to that.

I recently had drinks with a senior advisor who told me that he had told the President to do fewer interviews and briefings. Only speak out when you have something specific to say, he counselled. There was a period when the advice was taken – in late April Donald Trump stopped his coronavirus briefings after he had mused in one of them about injecting disinfectant into the human body to cure Covid-19. But the more significant faction in the White House is the one that believes there is no such thing as too much Donald Trump – and that grouping is led by Donald Trump.

After these two difficult interviews it was no surprise to see the President turn up the next day on *Fox & Friends*, the popular and everso Trump-friendly breakfast show. There, for the best part of an hour, the President sounded off without interruption. Answers could be four or five minutes long, and there would be zero interruption. It was a lovely warm bubble bath for Donald Trump, after the cold, needle spray shower that he'd been given by Wallace and Swan.

In the 2016 election, Donald Trump would just ring up programmes and be put directly on air, where he would be given the easiest of free rides, as he bullied and bulldozed his way through interviews. But the Swan/Wallace exchanges have shown America's rather deferential and, dare I say, obsequious interviewers that there is a more rigorous way of doing things.

But at least he's coming out and continuing to face the questions. That's more than can be said of the reclusive Joe Biden – hidin' Biden – who rarely ventures out of his Wilmington basement cocoon.

2020 may be the election fought by one candidate who can't stop talking, and another who never wants to start.

5 August

How exciting, I have an email from Marjorie. Marjorie is our travel agent who does all the BBC's flight bookings within the US, and it is literally months – months – since I have heard from her, because since the coronavirus lockdown I have not flown anywhere internally. But here is my ticket to go to Milwaukee, Wisconsin, where the Democratic Convention will begin in just under two weeks' time.

We are going to go a couple of days early, and film in one of the parts of this key swing state that backed Trump in 2016, but voted Democrat in the midterm elections in 2018. And then we will cover the main speeches of the convention – the Obamas will speak on different nights; Biden's pick for VP will be on the penultimate night; and Biden on the last night.

This morning Donald Trump has announced that he would like to make his acceptance speech from the White House, a massively controversial suggestion. The White House is government property, paid for by the taxpayer. It is not a setting for a party convention speech; just as it would be unthinkable for Boris Johnson to make his Tory party conference speech from inside Downing Street.

The President also keeps up his barrage about postal voting and how it will lead to fraud, chaos – and make America a laughing stock around the world. Except, what is this? He has just tweeted that mail-in ballots will be fine, just fine in Florida. No other state is mentioned, just Florida. I wonder what it is about the sunshine state with its tens of thousands of Republican voting, old, white people who prefer to vote by post that marks it out? It is so transparent – the Republican leadership in Florida has been growing increasingly restive about the President's assault on postal voting, because they fear that without mail-in votes, the Republican candidates don't stand a chance. Forget American exceptionalism. We now have Floridian exceptionalism.

Wouldn't you know it? Into my inbox drops the email from the Democratic Party announcing that for reasons of public safety at a time of pandemic none of the keynote speakers will now actually travel to Wisconsin to deliver their speeches; they will give them remotely – including Joe Biden. So what is the point of us going, if public safety is the issue? There isn't any. We ring Marjorie and cancel our flights.

If this is what campaigning is going to be like during coronavirus, how do you run an election? November is going to be a daunting challenge.

9 August, Bethlehem, Pennsylvania

A road trip. Yesterday, I and John Landy, my brilliant Australian cameraman and friend, and Morgan Gisholt Minard, a prodigiously talented, young producer and lovely human being who grew up near Boston, actually got in the crew car and headed north on a three-hour drive to rural Pennsylvania. It is one of the states that Hillary Clinton lost in 2016, but which is now trending decisively in Biden's direction.

The wealth of this Pennsylvania town was tied inextricably to the Bethlehem Steel Company. As it prospered, so did the town, and during the twentieth century it grew and grew to become one of the nation's foremost shipbuilding and steel producing companies. Its steel is to be found on the Golden Gate Bridge, the Empire State Building, the Hoover Dam, Alcatraz prison, the Verrazano bridge, Madison Square Garden – and on and on the list goes. It's almost easier to list the famous landmarks in the US that *weren't* built with Bethlehem steel.

But with the rise of foreign competition, and globalisation, and cheaper imports, the company went into steep decline. This was the story of industrial decay that Donald Trump railed about in 2016; the story of decline that he promised to reverse. On the edge of the town is the former steelworks, dominating the skyline, but now shuttered and decaying, a rusting monstrosity that looks like a stage set from a *Mad Max* movie – all pipes and chimneys and furnaces, slowly disintegrating. A vivid, soaring graveyard of America's industrial past. But the steel jobs have not returned.

We are gathering material for a piece we want to do on disaffected Trump voters switching back to the Democrats. The polls have Biden up 9 points in Pennsylvania. A massive turnaround from four years ago. But my instant take-out: those that adored Donald Trump in 2016 still love him. It is hard to find defectors. But in 2016 there were large numbers of Trump voters who either lied to the polling companies about their voting intention or weren't contacted by them, so maybe in 2020 something similar is happening. The polls might have Biden out in front – but show me the switchers. Interesting: we speak to Democratic Party organisers in different Pennsylvania counties, and ask them if they've identified people who've moved from Trump to Biden who we might be able to interview. They're unable to point us to anyone.

11 August

There's growing speculation that today will be the day that Joe Biden announces his running mate. Emily Maitlis reckons we should do a special *Americast* ahead of the announcement where she, Anthony Zurcher and I stick our necks out and make our predictions. It looks set to be an exercise in humiliation.

As the tension builds, a variety of so-called frontrunners confirm that it is not going to be them. They have been contacted by the Biden team with a 'thanks you so much for your application to be running mate. But after a highly competitive process where the quality of the applicants was incredibly high we have decided on this occasion blah blah blah etc ...'

It looks like we are playing skittles, where the last one standing will be declared the winner. But soon the name emerges. A tweet from Joe Biden confirms it: 'I have the great honor to announce that I've picked @KamalaHarris – a fearless fighter for the little guy, and one of the country's finest public servants – as my running mate'.

Kamala Harris, the California senator who had an Indian mother and Jamaican father, would be the first woman of colour to run for one of the highest offices in the land. It's a moment of history, and feels momentous in its own way. The other women under considera-tion are quick to offer their congratulations and support. For a party that at times finds it easier to form a circular firing squad than unity, this afternoon they keep their guns firmly trained on Donald Trump and the need to beat him in November.

And what is my first reaction? I give myself a high five. In our *Americast* recording earlier that day, that is what I predicted. Yes, she had given Biden a hard time during the debates; yes, she will harbour her own ambitions to succeed him in 2024 – but remember that the job of the pick for vice-president is to be the tip of the spear in the election battle. And Joe Biden, still bearing the scars where she lacerated him in the early Democratic Party debates, has decided to go for someone who is smart and is tough.

Her time on the Judiciary Committee earned her rave reviews from Democrats. She was tough with Brett Kavanaugh during his controversial confirmation hearings. And even the Attorney General was given a pummelling as she very quietly and elegantly wielded her prosecutorial scalpel against the chubby and increasing ruddy Bill Barr.

The Trump campaign is quick off the mark with a video branding her as 'phony Kamala'. I can't help thinking that is a bit tame and lame. After the 'crooked Hillary' moniker, and his trashing of his Republican opponents in 2016 – who can forget Little Marco, Lyin' Ted and Low Energy Jeb? – this seems a touch on the mundane side.

12 August, Wilmington, Delaware

The first event of the Biden/Harris ticket will be in his home town of Wilmington, Delaware. It has been Joe Biden's home since he entered public life, and it is where he launched his first Senate bid nearly half a century ago. It is a two-hour drive (on a good day) from Washington up the I-95. But when he was elected senator for the state Biden would return each night by train, rather than stay in DC – earning himself the nickname Amtrak Joe. So much so that Wilmington station is now officially named the Joseph R. Biden, Jr., Railroad Station.

His house is in a leafy suburb, set back from the road on a winding lane of large, expensive properties, with a guard-house at the end of the short drive. The head of the secret service detail comes out to speak to us, and ask what we are doing. He is courteous and helpful. But let's hope the presidential candidate doesn't believe in portents. A terrible storm has cut a swathe through the area, with trees down all over the place, and some have even fallen onto these well-appointed homes. The first house on the road has the trunk of an enormous tree protruding through the lounge.

Kamala posts on Twitter a very cute video of Biden asking her to be his running mate. 'Are you ready to go to work?' he asks. 'Oh my god,' she replies, 'I am so ready to go to work.' The release of this is quickly being lapped up by all the cable news channels – including Fox. The Dems are playing this roll-out pretty impressively.

Biden and Harris are to hold their first event at the Alexis I. Du Pont High School in the city. But the event which is due to kick off at 3.50 is delayed. And delayed. Then a thunder storm comes through, temporarily shutting off the power inside. The few reporters in the gymnasium quickly start filing that the power cut means the air conditioning is off, and the place is becoming very clammy. This wasn't part of the script.

Nevertheless, when they do get on stage it all goes smoothly – if oddly. The speechwriters have created a text for both Biden and Harris where you sense written into the text in italics are lines like 'pause for applause'. But of course there is no applause; there is only a handful of journalists in the room to witness the event, plus a few key advisors. There is the sound of silence. Outside the gymnasium – where I am – quite a crowd has gathered, but the speech isn't being relayed out, and as the rain comes down, so the mix of curious onlookers and committed supporters start to disperse.

Introducing Senator Harris, Biden says, 'This morning, all across the nation, little girls woke up, especially little black and brown girls who so often feel overlooked and undervalued in our communities, but today, today just maybe they're seeing themselves, for the first time, in a new way – as the stuff of presidents and vice-presidents.'

There is one message though above all others they want to ring out – that they are ready to go from day one. Ready to serve.

Let's fit in a quick 'and finally' to finish today's bulletin. (Presenter arranges face into bewildered grin.)

And finally, the US administration is changing the rules on water pressure that comes out of showers after the President complained that bathroom fittings were not working to his liking. The Department of Energy is issuing new guidelines on the volume of water that can come out of taps. It follows this presidential complaint: 'So what do you do? You just stand there longer or you take a shower longer? Because my hair – I don't know about you, but it has to be perfect. Perfect.'

Good night and thanks for watching.

13 August

Today has all the maddening complexity, inconsistency and bizarreness of covering this president. I give you three bits of evidence.

First an interview he has done with Fox Business Network – where, in terms, the President makes clear that he is going to starve the United States Postal Service of additional cash, so as to make mail in ballots impossible. 'If we don't make a deal, that means they don't get the money,' Trump tells the anchor. 'That means they can't have universal mail-in voting; they just can't have it.' Just think about that. The reason that millions want to vote by post is that in a time of coronavirus it is far safer than queuing up at a polling station for hours. But the President wants to scupper that.

Except – and here is the breaking news … it's just been confirmed that Donald Trump and Melania Trump have registered for absentee ballots – a postal vote, by any other name – so they can vote in Florida. Timing. You just can't beat the timing of this.

And, separately, the President also gives air to a preposterous and arcane theory that Kamala Harris might not be eligible to be vice-president because of the immigrant status of her parents when she was born. Never mind that the accepted meaning of the 14th Amendment is that anyone born in the US has the right to US citizenship. A conservative constitutional lawyer has raised the question in the *Newsweek* magazine [a comment piece that the *Newsweek* editorial board would later apologise for publishing], and Donald Trump gives the theory a push. He is smart enough not to endorse it overtly – that might bring charges of naked racism – but he gives it a mighty push by raising it and not dismissing the notion. Nevertheless, a lot of media outlets accuse the President of being racist for this stance.

He has after all got form. Donald Trump for years perpetuated the pernicious myth that America's first African American president was illegitimately in the White House because he was really born in Kenya. He wasn't. He was born in Hawaii. His birth certificate would be produced to prove it. But still Donald Trump pushed this particular falsehood relentlessly, until suddenly at the outset of the 2016 campaign he dropped it. Without apology.

He also talks about Harris as 'mean' and 'nasty', 'a mad woman' and 'condescending'. He is on a roll this morning. He also calls a female news anchor 'a ditzy airhead'. And a Democratic congresswoman 'not even a smart person'. It is all pretty misogynistic.

And then I see a tweet from the President with a declaration attached that the White House has brokered a peace deal between Israel and the United Arab Emirates. It is breathtaking. It comes out of the blue. A president who seems pathologically incapable of keeping a secret, has kept all of this under wraps until now, when it is ready to be unveiled. This is a huge deal. The only two other Arab countries to recognise Israel were Egypt in 1979 and Jordan in 1994. And both of those deals were with neighbouring countries, and had been achieved as a means of avoiding further war. But here was a Gulf nation, an economic powerhouse in the region, agreeing to normalise relations with Israel out of political choice. What a stunning achievement by Trump's White House, and by his son-in-law Jared Kushner. And the intriguing thing is that I get the impression that the WH is confident there might be other countries who will sign similar deals with Israel. This would be a game-changer in the Middle East.

Who would have thought it? When Jared Kushner was put in charge of bringing peace to the Middle East, the idea that this pampered property kid from New York would be able to move the dial a millimetre was greeted with incredulous, side-splitting mirth. But here was a big win. A significant win.

And to put this in the context of 2020, Israel enjoys much greater support in the US than it does in Europe. A deal that makes Israel safer and more secure is going to play well with Jewish voters – and, dare I say, more particularly with evangelical voters, the most pro-Israel of all.

So, in one day, a racist conspiracy laced with sexist overtones, an overt attempt to drive down turnout in an election, and a significant step towards peace in the Middle East. Go figure!

17 August. Day 1 of the Democratic Convention

How do you start a party in an empty room? That is not to be flippant, but it is in a nutshell the conundrum the Democrats face this week as they *don't* gather in Milwaukee for their convention. Campaigning in a time of Covid is challenging. Every four years the balloons are inflated, the confetti is sliced and diced into a million different pieces, all ready to rain down on tens of thousands of delegates dressed in red, white and blue, packed tight into an arena. Not this time. There is no coming together.

But for two hours this evening, the Democrats have put on a show, a TV spectacular. It is a bit glitchy, but I thought – given the challenge – it was pretty impressive. And a lot of thought has gone into the boxes the party wants to tick. It is the Democratic Convention as you've never seen it. The national anthem is sung by someone in every state, on what looks like an ever-expanding Zoom call; the Pledge of Allegiance is given by Joe Biden's grandchildren. There were the prominent Republicans switching sides – most notable among them John Kasich, the former Republican governor of Ohio. Four years ago he had fought Donald Trump for the Republican nomination for president. Today he is endorsing Joe Biden.

But equally the Biden campaign has to look over its left shoulder too. There are the progressives, the 'green new deal' supporters, the young people not ashamed to call themselves socialists, and for them Senator Bernie Sanders came on and gave a full-throated endorsement of Biden. This feels very different from four years ago, when the discord between Sanders and Hillary Clinton supporters was absolutely evident as Dems gathered at the convention in Philadelphia.

There was a moment's silence led by the brothers of George Floyd, whose death brought protests across America and the world. There was strong focus on coronavirus – and a lacerating address from a young woman in Arizona, who spoke of the death of her father from the virus. Kristin Urquiza said that he had been a fit 65-year-old, and 'his only pre-existing condition was trusting Donald Trump'. And for that, she said, he had paid with his life. If the aim of the Democrat schedulers is to create viral moments, that line was an absolute zinger. It hit the target.

But no doubt who the star of the show was: the former First Lady Michelle Obama unloading on the sitting president. 'Donald Trump is the wrong president for our country,' she said. 'He has had more than enough time to prove that he can do the job, but he is clearly in over his head. He cannot meet this moment. He simply cannot be who we need him to be for us.'

And then she trolled him with the dismissive words he had used when describing the death toll from coronavirus in that *Axios* interview: 'It is what it is.'

I was in the House of Commons press gallery when Margaret Thatcher's long-suffering deputy, Sir Geoffrey Howe, finally turned on his bullying mistress and delivered a resignation speech of such understated venom that it would set in motion the events that eventually brought about her demise. It was that speech, with the elaborate and very funny cricket metaphor, which brought the wry observation that it was a speech that had taken 15 minutes to write – and ten years to deliver. I had the same feeling listening to Michelle Obama. This was clearly something she had been wanting to get off her chest for some time.

19 August

At the Democratic Convention, tonight belongs to Barack Obama. The former president is speaking, symbolically, at the Museum of the American Revolution in Philadelphia. It is a powerful speech, searing in its content – and the unwritten convention that a former president doesn't attack the incumbent goes out of the window and down the street:

I have sat in the Oval Office with both of the men who are running for president. I never expected that my successor would embrace my vision or continue my policies. I did hope, for the sake of our country, that Donald Trump might show some interest in taking the job seriously, that he might come to feel the weight of the office and discover some reverence for the democracy that had been placed in his care.

But he never did. For close to four years now, he's shown no interest in putting in the work; no interest in finding common ground; no interest in using the awesome power of his office to help anyone but himself and his friends; no interest in treating the presidency as anything but one more reality show that he can use to get the attention he craves.

Donald Trump hasn't grown into the job because he can't. And the consequences of that failure are severe: 170,000 Americans dead, millions of jobs gone while those at the top take in more than ever. Our worst impulses unleashed, our proud reputation around the world badly diminished and our democratic institutions threatened like never before.

The speech goes wider, talking about the threat that, in his eyes, American democracy is now facing. But it is his attack on the President that will garner the headlines. And as Obama is saying this, slowly and deliberatively, this pops up on my Twitter feed: 'WHY DID HE REFUSE TO ENDORSE SLOW JOE UNTIL IT WAS ALL OVER, AND EVEN THEN VERY LATE? WHY DID HE TRY TO GET HIM NOT TO RUN?'

In full caps lock mode, late on Wednesday evening, this is the President's considered response.

20 August

Today is Joe Biden's big day. A career that has spanned nearly half a century, and this will be the most important speech that he's delivered. But the news gods have another delicacy to serve up before this evening's main course in Wilmington, Delaware.

And I have resolved to bid for the film rights. Steve Bannon – this time four years ago Donald Trump's campaign director, and after the election his White House chief of strategy – has been arrested and taken into custody. It's nearly a ten on the Washington jaw-dropper index.

The *faux* shabby, endlessly cynical, right-wing nationalist and fighter for the downtrodden white working class is arrested on a 152-foot yacht (so half a football pitch) of a Chinese billionaire off the east coast of the US. When I had gone to interview him a year ago at the border wall that he had managed to fund through private donations, he was keen to show off what could be done. How the determination of ordinary Trump supporters could be used to get things done, where government fell short.

Through their Go Fund Me page, 'We Build the Wall' Bannon and his partners had managed to raise $25 million. They pledged that every cent raised would be spent on the wall. Well, it seems that wasn't quite true. According to the indictment, rather large sums of money found their way into the pockets of Bannon and his cohorts, allegedly defrauding a mass of gullible Trump supporters. Bannon was taken into custody.

One of the others arrested, Brian Kolfage, is accused in the indictment of syphoning off enough money to pay for 'home renovations, payments towards a boat, a luxury SUV, a golf cart, jewelry, cosmetic surgery, personal tax payments and credit card debt'. The boat called *Warfighter* was used to sail in one of the President's beloved boat parades – where pleasure craft owners sail in convoy, their Trump 2020 flags fluttering in the breeze. Some of this stuff you couldn't make up.

Bannon joins an impressive roster of key Trump people to find themselves on the wrong side of the law (Paul Manafort, his predecessor as campaign manager, Rick Gates, Manafort's deputy, Michael Cohen, Trump's personal lawyer, Michael Flynn, the first national security advisor … and on it goes). But from the President – this time – there is little sympathy. Trump says he never approved of the privately funded section of the border wall, and calls it 'showboating' – which, given where the money came from for *Warfighter* and what it was used for, seems an uncannily apt description.

Meanwhile, in Wilmington, Delaware, they're getting ready for the final night. In the Chase Center where Biden is to speak, only a couple of dozen journalists and his key staff will witness it. Outside they have built a pop up drive-in cinema. I have visions of *Grease* or *American Graffiti* but can't quite envisage young couples making out, popcorn getting spilt over the back seat of the Chevy convertible, as they listen to Biden.

The impressive thing is that the Democrats seem to have managed to make a Covid convention work. Arguably it is a vast improvement on the normal way of doing things. No doubt it's been helped by a roster of big names – tonight the Chicks (formerly the Dixie Chicks, but who changed their name because of the Confederate association) are on hand to sing a most stunning a cappella version of the national anthem. Julia Louis-Dreyfus, the brilliant comic actress from *Veep*, is the moderator of the evening – with I think a whole pile of misfiring jokes about Donald Trump.

But what has made the week a success – and made it stand out – are the hitherto anonymous Americans with stories to tell. This evening it is Brayden Harrington, a 13-year-old kid with a stutter. It's a condition that Joe Biden overcame as a child, but has never turned his back on.

Our dearest American friends, whom we met in Paris, had a son who stammered badly. Aaron, his dad, became involved in the American Institute for Stuttering, and we went to one of the gala dinners in New York a few years back, when Vice-President Biden (as he then was) was guest of honour. I've been to dinners like this before where the main speaker emerges from backstage, delivers his or her remarks, and promptly disappears again. Not Biden. He went table to table, speaking to the young people who've been affected by this condition.

I wasn't surprised to see that Brayden was given a prominent spot on the final evening. This has, after all, been an issue that has helped define who Biden is. And it was a brave, moving performance by the 13-year-old, as he struggled through the text of his speech, paying tribute to the help and mentoring that Biden has given him. If one of the goals of the week was to show Biden as a normal, decent, steady, empathetic, unifying man – and yes, a counterpoint to Donald Trump – then interventions like this really help.

The other aim this week has been to show that the party is united behind Joe Biden. And so a slightly uncomfortable Zoom-style video was produced with a number of the candidates that Biden had vanquished on the road to the nomination saying – with maybe slightly strained and forced smiles – what a great guy he is.

This isn't a policy heavy speech that he delivers, but clear differences on the environment, the economy, immigration and how to deal with the coronavirus outbreak are apparent. And 32 years after his first tilt at becoming a presidential candidate, Joe Biden could finally utter the words 'with great honour and humility I accept this nomination ...'

He does not mention Trump by name, but he's there alright, particularly in this key paragraph: 'Here and now I give you my word: if you entrust me with the presidency, I will draw on the best of us, not the worst. I will be an ally of the light, not the darkness. It's time for us, for we the people, to come together. And make no mistake: united, we can and will overcome this season of darkness in America.'

It is a good, carefully crafted speech. And probably is assisted by the absurdly low expectations set for it by the Trump campaign, as they continue to depict the Democratic nominee as 'Slow Joe', 'Sleepy Joe' – and with the subtext that he is more ga-ga than go-go. Biden delivered the speech well, and it left Trump acolytes on Twitter saying, 'OK, big deal, he can read a teleprompter.' I still think the Trump campaign are struggling with how to define Biden – though no doubt we will see a pretty concerted effort to pull him down when the GOP holds its convention.

Outside in the carpark-cum-cinema there is the nearest thing to audience reaction we've seen all week. People are honking their car horns and waving flags. The Bidens come out to take a curtain call and the fireworks light up the sky on this pleasantly warm Wilmington evening.

22 August

Go out with friends for dinner to my favourite little French restaurant in Georgetown. When the bill comes I am told that for ease of transactions and minimum amount of handing things backwards and forwards, the extras have been included – 18 per cent for service (steep, but normal for America), and 7 per cent for PPE. I now wish I had drunk the hand sanitiser as a *digestif*. I work out they have charged us $30 for PPE. I mean, *vraiment*!

23 August

The Republican Convention starts tomorrow, but in the White House Briefing Room this evening it felt like it had already got underway,

24 hours early. The announcement by the President of the fast-tracking of the use of convalescent plasma as a therapeutic treatment for Covid-19 had strong political overtones. Mr Trump hailed the move as a major breakthrough. It came after he'd clashed publicly with the federal Food and Drug Administration, saying there were elements of the deep state within the organisation seeking to thwart him – an incendiary accusation.

Something else the President is reportedly keen to fast-track is a vaccine being developed by Oxford University in partnership with the pharmaceutical company AstraZeneca. According to the *Financial Times*, Donald Trump would be keen to get it to Americans in October – a month before the presidential election. There is no comment from the White House. On hypothetical questions like this in the past the President has insisted that major decisions will be driven by the science. But equally, it would be naïve to ignore the tick tock of the electoral timetable.

One other thing – Mary Trump, the President's niece who wrote a deeply disobliging memoir about her uncle, has secretly recorded Donald Trump's 83-year-old sister talking about her brother. Apparently, this would be her insurance policy against any defamation action that the President might take over the book that she penned. Maryanne Trump Barry, a retired federal judge, is scathing about her brother. 'All he wants to do is appeal to his base,' she said. 'He has no principles. None. None. And his base, I mean my God, if you were a religious person, you want to help people. Not do this.'

Barry goes on to say, 'His goddamned tweet[ing] and lying, oh my God. I'm talking too freely, but you know. The change of stories. The lack of preparation. The lying. Holy shit.' You would think that the sister of the president saying this about her younger brother might be shaking the foundations. But there's barely a ripple. Liar? No principles? Lack of preparation? Yeah, whatever …

25 August

It's day one of the Republican National Committee Convention in Charlotte, and Donald Trump flies to North Carolina to thank the party after it confirms him as candidate. He is scheduled to make brief remarks – 52 minutes later, he concludes. It is a rambling speech, seemingly without a text or an argument. But the evening two-hour TV spectacular is a far better production.

It is short on detail of what a second Trump term would look like – instead it feels as though it is a procession of speakers, from diverse backgrounds – but held together by the common thread that were the Democrats to win the election it would be the end of civilisation as we know it. A Marxist hell. The American dream would be in flames. Venezuela. Looting. Mob rule. Socialism. Anarchy. Chaos.

There's a couple from St Louis who achieved fame/infamy when they went out onto their front lawn – him armed with a rifle, her with a pistol – threatening to shoot Black Lives Matter protestors if they came near their property. They were charged with threatening behaviour, but at the Republican Convention they are a star turn, talking about how only Donald Trump would save the suburbs from – well, from who exactly? Race is not mentioned, but the sub-text throughout is the 'black mob'. This speech came from their oak-panelled home replete with damask silk curtains – and a lot of mock grandeur. Their speech is not so much a dog whistle as a howl from the kennels.

But if the objective is to fire up the base, remind people about what they should feel angry about; angry enough so that they go and vote in November; fearful of what might happen to America if it votes for the Democrats – then it is probably effective. There are also the much more subtle speeches, attempting to show Donald Trump in a more sympathetic light: the hitherto unknown acts of kindness, his human warmth. And there were a number of speakers from diverse backgrounds, who dismissed the idea that Donald Trump and this administration were in some way racist.

The two most ludicrous speeches of the evening were delivered by Donald Trump Jr and his partner Kimberly Guilfoyle. They weren't on stage together. No one could share the stage with Ms Guilfoyle. Like the amplifiers in *Spinal Tap*, she was turned up to volume 11 for most of this hilariously over-the-top speech. By the end she was at 15, and I honestly thought my ears were going to start bleeding. Either that or she was going to explode. And as her speech reached its thundering, shuddering, windowpane-shattering crescendo you could see the sudden realisation on her face that she was on a stage all alone. There would be no roar of the crowd. No standing ovation. No wild cheering. Just a rather embarrassed silence and then her shiny, white teeth standing to attention as she smiled at the inanimate camera in front of her.

Her partner Donald Trump Jr just looked weird as he came on stage. He had what appeared to be a smear of grease under his eyes, and that lit social media up.

The First Lady emerged looking dressed for battle. She was in a khaki green uniform suggesting membership of some very chic military unit. After the weekend unveiling of her redesigned Rose Garden, she was on a similar mission last night – to refashion her husband's image into something more gentle. That he really does care. It was a highly effective speech. She became the first high-profile speaker to address the pain that coronavirus has brought to America. The suffering of families, the anxiety and worry. She also leaned into the most controversial issue of all tearing at the fabric of America – race: 'I urge people to come together in a civil manner so we can work and live up to our standard American ideals.' And she went on, 'I also ask people to stop the violence and looting being done in the name of justice, and never make assumptions based on the colour of a person's skin.'

Melania's speech from four years ago was the source of endless mirth, with the passages that had been clearly plagiarised from an earlier speech by Michelle Obama. But this was very much her own work. And we were told that she had not shown it to the West Wing before she delivered it. It raises an interesting question: was this the First Lady seeking to show that she has a different world view from her husband? Or was this her showing she is a player in this presidency, and can be relied upon to soften her husband's prickly edges? Either way, if the goal is to broaden Donald Trump's appeal, the speech was highly effective.

Because that does seem to be the name of the game. He needs to win back the suburbs, independent voters, and white, college-educated women – so there was a video about how well he worked with senior women, how the administration is in no way racist.

And during the course of the evening the props of reality TV and the power of the presidency are shamelessly put to partisan use. So, in the middle of the convention speeches, we cutaway to the White House for a ceremony in which the President pardons a former bank robber who's now involved in charity work; and then we dip into a naturalisation ceremony, at which the President is presiding, to welcome new American citizens from around the world – a far cry perhaps from the tough, anti-immigration policies on asylum and the granting of visas that have been the hallmark of his presidency.

A small thing about tenses and grammar. The most striking thing about the Republican Convention this evening was the way coronavirus was spoken about in the *past* tense. It has been this. It was that. If you need convincing of this, have a listen to Larry Kudlow's speech – he's the President's chief economic advisor. At a time when the average daily death toll is still around the 1,000 mark, and there are tens of thousands of new cases per day, putting it in the past tense might be a bit of a stretch. Audacious even. Or downright disingenuous. Coronavirus is an is, not a was.

26 August

I wake up to deeply troubling news from Kenosha, the city in Wisconsin where Jacob Blake was shot in the back seven times. Two protestors have been killed and one seriously injured overnight. Seems there were vigilantes guarding a petrol station and a confrontation ensued. Footage shared online shows a man with a rifle being chased by a crowd before he falls to the ground and appears to fire multiple rounds at them. Other video shows armed civilians, many dressed in military fatigues, congregating outside businesses they said they were protecting. This is not going to calm the situation.

During the day a name emerges. The alleged killer is a 17-year-old, Kyle Rittenhouse. He is white and from Illinois, which means he's travelled across the state line, armed with an AR15 assault rifle, to tackle protestors. He is also a Trump supporter, as video emerges of him at the front row of one of the President's rallies. It also seems that on the previous night he had been given bottles of water by the local Kenosha police, apparently appreciative to have an extra pair of hands – and an extra rifle – as he and other armed militia men took to the streets to protect property and if necessary tackle protestors. The kid is charged with first-degree intentional homicide.

27 August. Final day of the Republican Convention

On the South Lawn of the White House, below the Truman Balcony, the President took to the stage, with giant Trump/Pence banners at either side. If Hollywood did coronations, they would look like this. In the midst of the pandemic and economic crisis, the Trumps came sweeping down the staircase like the most sun-kissed movie stars from the golden age of cinema. Trump the frustrated TV director would have overseen the whole production – cameras on jibs to capture every move. He in navy suit with sober red-and-blue striped tie; she looking radiant in a sleeveless emerald green dress that went down to her ankles. Some on social media went for a different metaphor, saying it looked slightly fascistic – Eva Peron/Mussolini/Nuremberg were among the comparisons I saw.

The warm-up act is the golden child, Ivanka. She acknowledges that her father was not always the easiest, but look at his record at getting things done, she tells the appreciative audience.

Then came the President. Before him well over a thousand supporters, with no social distancing, and barely a mask between them. The People's House had become a party-political convention venue. And his speech was as norm defying as the setting – Donald Trump still sounding like the outsider, even though he's been in office for three and a half years. He celebrated his own achievements – I have done more for the African American community than any other president since Abraham Lincoln, he proclaimed.

But his real target throughout was his Democratic party rival, Joe Biden. There was no mention of Jacob Blake, who was shot in the back seven times in Wisconsin, but a lot about the lawlessness and the anarchy on the streets, that would get worse if Joe Biden is elected. There was no mention either of Kyle Rittenhouse or the men he's charged with having killed.

The force of the attack was that Joe Biden was a Trojan horse for the far left, who would allow mob rule to take over American cities, like Kenosha. Biden was weak, unequal to the task. And if you look at where violence had taken hold, they were all American cities controlled by Democrats.

The speech went on and on. For 70 minutes. The second longest convention speech in American history. The longest being the one he delivered four years ago. And that in a sense is the problem for Donald Trump. In that address in Cleveland in 2016, he had promised that the chaos and disorder would cease the moment he became president. And here we are, four years on, with the difference being that this time the chaos has happened on his watch. It is the same with coronavirus; the same with the economy. As the veteran US TV news titan Dan Rather put it: 'The Trump re-election strategy seems to be to argue that only Donald Trump can save America from Donald Trump's America.'

The President also said, 'At no time before have voters faced a clearer choice between two parties, two visions and two philosophies.' This might be the only thing from the evening that Democrats and Republicans can rally round and say 'absolutely'.

In the heat of a late August evening, with Washington at its most humid, the President was clearly flagging as he reached the end of his address. He was reading off the teleprompter lifelessly, like a weary marathon runner, just aching to drag his feet across the finish line and be wrapped in one of those silver-foil blankets. For the President the finish line had something rather different in store. Framed by the Washington monument, the fireworks went up and spelled out the word 'Trump' in the night sky, and then '2020'. His face may not be carved into Mount Rushmore (yet), but for a fleeting moment his name was up in lights, before disappearing into smoke, while in the background, a short distance from the White House, protestors could be heard chanting 'Black Lives Matter'.

28 August

There is a much bigger protest in Washington – thousands of people from all over America this time. The venue for the Black Lives Matter protest is the Lincoln Memorial – the place where Martin Luther King delivered his 'I Have a Dream' speech in 1963. It passes off peacefully and without incident.

30 August

The morning news brings another grim headline – another death, but this time in Portland, Oregon, where violent protests from far left and anarchist groups have been going on for months now – and the person who's been killed this time is a Trump supporter who was part of a counter-protest. Aaron 'Jay' Danielson was shot in the chest. He was wearing a hat with the insignia 'Patriot Prayer', a far right group based in the Portland area. He had been part of a 'caravan' of some 600 Trump supporting vehicles who'd gone to the city to confront the so-called Antifa (anti-fascist) protestors.

This event, however, is not met with silence by the President. Unlike the shooting in the back of Jacob Blake, where the President has not spoken his name; and unlike the two people allegedly shot dead by Rittenhouse, where the President made no mention of them, today he unleashes a barrage of 90 tweets and retweets. The Trump supporters who had gone to Portland to confront the 'Antifa' were 'GREAT PATRIOTS'. Black Lives Matter supporters are 'agitators and thugs' – and in the midst of the pandemic which has now claimed nearly 180,000 lives there was a message of condolence. Not for the dead from the pandemic, but for the far right protestors shot in Portland. 'Rest in peace Jay,' the President tweeted. It is hard not to see this as an extension of his 'fine people on both sides' comment after clashes in Charlottesville, Virginia, three years ago, when anti-fascist protestors clashed with white supremacists and neo-fascists chanting 'Jews will not replace us'.

The Democratic mayor of Portland, Ted Wheeler, lets rip at the President: 'It's you who have created the hate and the division. It's you who have not found a way to say the names of Black people killed by police officers even as people in law enforcement have. And it's you who claimed that White supremacists are good people.'

31 August, Washington to Tennessee

I am on leave for two weeks, and Linda and I are heading out of DC for a few days to try to get away from the endless and wearying noise of the campaign. The idea (big belly laugh) is that I will have a total news and Twitter detox. I will meditate, discover mindfulness, allow myself to be enveloped by the majestic beauty of the Smoky Mountains. I will catch up on sleep, eat acai bowls and drink carrot and ginger juice. I will listen to soulful music, I will eschew the news stations. I will not say the word Trump. I will not say the word Biden. Yeah, well, it's a nice idea …

And this effort is already badly compromised by an alert on my phone suggesting that the President has held a news conference where he has apparently come to the defence of Kyle Rittenhouse, the man charged with murdering two protestors in Kenosha last week. Having slated Biden for refusing to condemn the looters and rioters (in fact he has), the President then refuses to condemn *his* supporters who went to Portland and fired paintballs and mace at the Black Lives Matter protestors. But not only that, he starts to talk about Rittenhouse: 'That was an interesting situation,' he said. 'You saw the same tape as I saw.

And he was trying to get away from them. I guess it looks like he fell and then they very violently attacked him. And it was something that we're looking at right now, and it's under investigation. But I guess he was in very big trouble. He would have been – probably would have been killed, but it's under investigation.'

It's another astonishing intervention by the President. There is clearly a calculated strategy here. The Trump campaign believes the lawlessness on the streets of Kenosha and Portland will be a driver for two key groups if Trump is to win in November. First it will bring in the people from the suburbs – moderately well-to-do, educated professional middle-class, fearful that their own neighbourhood might be next; and second, maybe it will bring in even more of the white, non-college-educated men who feel marginalised and have been off the grid. Many of them rallied to Trump in 2016, but the campaign believes there are many more to be lured back into electoral politics. The President is picking up where he left off in his acceptance speech last week, making law and order the big pitch.

One effect is that it brings Joe Biden out of his basement. It was my understanding that after Labor Day (next Monday), Biden was going to start to campaign around the country. But it seems he has brought it forward. Democrats are growing uneasy that Biden hasn't done enough to distance himself from the violence and the looting; to condemn unequivocally those who have gone onto the streets to foment disorder. A party that has historically had a big bed-wetting tendency is, well, beginning to wet the bed.

The speech that he delivers in Pittsburgh is interesting – interesting, because it combines offence and defence. It makes sure that the central charge made by the President is countered, with Biden saying that people rioting and looting are not protesting, and that perpetrators should be prosecuted. He also tackles the charge that he is either a dangerous left-wing apologist or a Trojan horse for a wild-eyed socialist project. 'You know me. You know my heart. You know my story, my family's story. Ask yourself: do I look like a radical socialist with a soft spot for rioters? Really?'

But this was a speech that also took the fight directly to Donald Trump. He condemned Trump, saying the President's refusal to call on his own supporters to 'stop acting as an armed militia in this country shows how weak he is'. In Biden's convention speech he didn't mention the President by name, but it is striking just how often he does in this Pittsburgh address. 'Donald Trump has been a toxic presence in our nation for four years. Will we rid ourselves of this toxin? Or will we make it a permanent part of our nation's character?'

And one question runs through the speech as a leitmotif, whether it's on law and order, the pandemic, the economy or foreign policy: 'Do you really feel safer under Donald Trump?'

On Monday evening the President goes on Fox News, where he is given an easy ride, nice warm bath of an interview by the anchor Laura Ingraham. Discussing the shooting of Jacob Blake, the President reaches for an extraordinary metaphor to explain why the policeman may have shot him seven times in the back. Actions like that were often the result of officers 'choking' under pressure: 'Just like in a golf tournament, they miss a three-foot putt,' he said.

Anyway, where was I? Ah yes, the yoga session at the Wellness Platform ... and breathe.

1 September, Tennessee

The President has flown to Kenosha, Wisconsin – against the wishes of the local mayor and the state governor of Wisconsin. They fear his presence in the city will exacerbate an already volatile situation. There is to be no meeting with the family of Jacob Blake. The President visits burned-out buildings, and it is clear the instruction to the White House advance team is that the President wants to have the crunch of broken glass and rubble beneath his feet.

He moves to a photographic shop, which has stood on the spot for 109 years – possibly the oldest shop in the whole of Wisconsin. The owner of the store refuses to meet the President, because he doesn't want to be caught up in something that will be used for political advantage. Ever resourceful, the White House gets the previous owner of the store to meet the President – and so this slightly odd conversation takes place, with the ex-owner acting as if he still owns the place – all for the benefit of the cameras. Donald Trump asks him questions as if he is still the owner. During the visit to Kenosha, the President refuses to acknowledge that there is systemic racism in the US, and instead blames recent acts of police violence on a few 'bad apples'.

2 September, Tennessee (and polls)

The President goes to Wilmington, North Carolina. And it is one of those trips that on the schedule seems as though it will be unremarkable … but, as long experience has taught me, expect the unexpected – and just treat the phenomenon of your jaw hitting the floor as part of the normal reaction to the abnormal.

As has already been reported, we know the President has a thing about postal voting. We know he thinks – without much evidence – that it will lead to fraud. But in North Carolina he urges people to do something quite extraordinary – and actually illegal. He asks the good people of what might well be a swing state in November to vote *twice*. The phrase 'vote early, vote often' dates back to the mid-nineteenth century, and is often attributed to the son of the 8th president of the

United States, Martin van Buren. It is on the face of it an exhortation to act corruptly – but was more probably a tongue-in-cheek joke.

In 2020 the President frames his advice differently. To make sure your vote is counted, he says, try to vote by mail *and* in person – and if the system is working as well as it should, then you won't be able to. But it will be a good way to test that the system is working properly. However, voting twice is a federal crime, and in North Carolina a felony offence (in other words an offence that will result in a minimum of a year in prison). The President's tweet on the subject is censored by Twitter.

The strategy, if followed, will likely result in chaos on election night, and cast doubt on the validity of the result. The President's critics (and some within the administration) believe that this is precisely his plan if it appears that he has lost. He is accused of extreme recklessness. And his message is causing alarm among a lot of senior Republicans, who have been urging elderly supporters, fearful of Covid, to vote by mail – and who believe if these people choose to abstain instead, then the election will certainly be lost. Not for the first time the President and the Republican Party are *not* moving in lockstep.

Coincidentally, the first sets of polls since the conventions are published today. There is no great moving of the tectonic plates. The remarkable thing is the consistency. There is a little bit of tightening of the polls – but with Biden still holding a significant lead. I think what is most interesting about them is that they leave the Democrats with no room for complacency; and the Republicans with no reason to despair. The die is nowhere near cast. But if Trump was hoping for a big post-convention bump, with this laser-like focus on law and order, it doesn't seem to have materialised.

3 September, Tennessee

Another day, another candidate's visit to Kenosha. This time Joe Biden, on his first campaign stop since lockdown. His visit is very different from Donald Trump's. It is an unspoken repudiation of the Trump approach. He *does* meet with the Blake family. He *does* talk about healing and bringing communities together. The speech he made in Pittsburgh on Monday has now been edited together as a TV advertisement. During the visit Biden was far more sympathetic to issues of racial injustice and civil unrest, and the Democratic candidate insisted the focus should be on national unity.

I speak to a senior Democratic strategist with very close ties to Biden's inner circle. He lauds the deftness with which the campaign has conducted itself during the course of the last week. He goes through a whole list of ticked boxes where, tonally and substantively, Team Joe has not put a foot wrong – but then he talks to me about the greatest strategic imperative facing the Biden campaign. I am now hanging on his every word to hear what that might be – thinking it will be some nuance on messaging, or a discourse on not confusing tactics with strategy. Or remaining calm when the polls tighten, as they inevitably will. It is more prosaic than that. The single most important thing for the campaign, now that Biden has hit the road, he tells me, is to keep him Covid-free between now and 3 November.

4 September, Tennessee

It has rained heavily through the night in Tennessee, with some pretty spectacular thunder and lightning. From our window the Smoky Mountains are living up to their name. The clouds are hanging heavily in the valley, well below the mountain line, which are a blurry outline in the misty conditions. The steep hillsides are a luscious green. There is also zero phone signal. And I am off the grid for a glorious couple of hours.

After breakfast we head off back to DC on the long drive north. And I reconnect with the world. All anyone is talking about is an article written by Jeffrey Goldberg, the editor-in-chief of *The Atlantic* magazine. It is a composite of stories but with one overarching narrative: Donald Trump doesn't respect the military.

One of the central 'incidents' the article focuses on is the President's visit to France in 2018 to mark the one hundredth anniversary of the end of the First World War. He had been due to visit Aisne-Marne American Cemetery, 50 miles north of Paris, where over two thousand US soldiers are buried, nearly all killed in the Marne valley in the summer of 1918. But on the day it is pouring with rain, and the President, who is in a foul mood, doesn't go. That much is undisputed. According to the article: 'In a conversation with senior staff members on the morning of the scheduled visit, Trump said, "Why should I go to that cemetery? It's filled with losers." In a separate conversation on the same trip, Trump referred to the more than 1,800 marines who lost their lives at Belleau Wood as "suckers" for getting killed.'

According to Goldberg, one of the reasons why Trump doesn't want to go is that he thought the wet weather would mess up his hair; while the Trump version of events is that the weather was so bad the secret service said he couldn't go by helicopter, and travelling by road would cause too much disruption. I have to say, from my own experience, that US officials never seem too worried about bringing cities to a total standstill to allow a presidential motorcade to pass.

On every score, the article is terrible for the President; particularly as it is going to raise a lot of questions in the minds of veterans – who the Trump team think are firmly in their camp. The one saving grace is that all the sources reported are anonymous, and that makes it easier for Trump to deny the charges and accuse the reporter of 'fake news'.

But the language used does sound like the President. In the run-up to the 2016 election he caused astonishment when he went after Senator John McCain, who'd spent years as a POW in a North Vietnamese prison, by saying this: 'He's not a war hero ... I like people who weren't captured.' Such was the animus that Trump felt towards McCain, that when he died in 2018, and the then White House chief of staff, General John Kelly, ordered that the flag on the roof be flown at half-mast – normal protocol when a serving law-maker dies (McCain at the time of his death had been the senator for Arizona) – Trump ordered the Stars and Stripes back to the top of the flagpole. Even with McCain dead, Trump still seemed to have a score to settle.

Goldberg's article reflects badly on the President's sense of service, patriotism, heroism and sacrifice. And it is evident the White House is stung. There are furious denials. No one has done more for the military than this president, the White House insists. No one respects America's servicemen and women more. Look at what he's done for their pay.

But a bad day is made worse by a Fox News report confirming Goldberg's account. That leads to the President calling for the Fox correspondent who goes on air to say she has 'stood up' the Goldberg claims to be fired. As Air Force One returns from a Trump campaign stop in Philadelphia, the President holds an impromptu news conference under the wing of the aircraft to denounce Goldberg, and to deny the charges. Other serving and former officials do the same – but, tellingly, few Republican senators or congressmen are coming out to defend the President. Maybe they all had other pressing engagements.

He recounts being stuck in Paris, and ringing Melania back in Washington to bemoan being unable to go to the cemetery because of the weather. He tells reporters: 'I called home, I spoke to my wife and I said, "I hate this. I came here to go to that ceremony." And to the one that was the following day which I did go to. I said I feel terribly. And that was the end of it.'

Small detail: she was in Paris with him. That evening the *Atlantic* article is the headline on every network and cable channel, and splashed across the front pages.

9 September, Washington

You might get the impression that I think Donald Trump has had a torrid few days as a result of the *Atlantic* article. Well, if this was a poker game, you would have sitting across from Jeffrey Goldberg the grandest of grand fromages in the journalistic world, Bob Woodward – legend of Watergate and the downfall of Richard Nixon. Because in this poker game it is as though Goldberg is sitting with a hand of a pair of twos, while Woodward has stared him in the face, looked down at his four aces, and said, 'I raise you.'

Woodward has been working on a book (I mean, frankly, who in Washington isn't?). It has become something of a fixture of the calendar that he writes about every president. He goes about his work methodically and meticulously, speaking to anyone and everyone, building up enough knowledge to be able to recreate, almost in real time, the key meetings and events. Who said what, where they were, why they said what they said, what the consequences were of the decisions taken – and whether slanted autumn sunlight was shining in through the window at 45 degrees or 60, causing the crystal glass tumblers on the table to glint … no detail is too small for a Woodward book.

For his first book on Trump, *Fear*, the President's minders didn't let Woodward get anywhere near the principal. The President was out of bounds. But when Trump found out, he was furious – and curious. This is the great marketeer; the salesman extraordinaire. It is Donald

Trump's belief that he can charm anyone. And so for this book, *Rage*, the President went on a schmooze cruise. He would woo Woodward. Not only did he speak to the veteran journalist, he spoke to him 18 times – 18 times! Not only that, Woodward – openly – recorded every conversation. And I'm not finished yet with my incredulity: it was *mano a mano*. Other presidents who've gone down the highly dangerous Woodward route have ensured that the chief of staff, comms director and press secretary are in the room as well, in case anything needs ironing out afterwards. 'Of course when the President said x, what he really meant to say was …' Donald Trump wasn't bothering with any of that. He is his own best spokesman.

Except, of course, when he's not. The first clips to emerge air on CNN. They score a straight ten on the WTF index. It is Trump talking to Woodward in the early days of the pandemic, when the President was still touring the country doing his rallies where 20,000 of his supporters would pack themselves tight into arenas. It is when he is saying the coronavirus is really just the flu by any other name – the sniffles – and will disappear just as quickly as it arrived.

But on 7 February, when this particular interview is recorded, Donald Trump is saying something very different to Woodward – he's saying the coronavirus is five times more deadly than even your strenuous flus.

There is also the release of a March interview that the President gave to Woodward. He is speaking nine days after the White House declared the pandemic a national emergency – but in the interview, he says, 'I wanted to always play it down. I still like playing it down, because I don't want to create a panic.'

The clear suggestion from these clips is that the President just wasn't being straight with the American people. He wasn't giving them the information they needed to make sensible judgements about how to lead their lives in an age of pandemic; how best to protect themselves and their families. In private to Woodward he's saying it's really serious. To the American people he's saying it's all fine and dandy.

Biden is in Michigan today on a rare foray out of his Wilmington lair. He is there ostensibly to talk about jobs, and his 'Build Back Better' agenda. But there is only one subject that is going to cut through today, and that is the Woodward book.

And Biden happily obliges. 'He knew and purposely played it down. Worse, he lied to the American people,' Biden told his audience. 'He knowingly and willingly lied about the threat it posed to the country for months. He had the information. He knew how dangerous it was. And while this deadly disease ripped through our nation, he failed to do his job on purpose.'

The White House tries valiantly to limit the damage. Kayleigh McEnany gives a news conference seeking to defend what the President told Woodward. The easy (and default) White House narrative in these situations is that it is all fake news, media falsehoods and lies. But as McEnany tries that tactic, claiming these are just things the President is alleged to have said, reporters are firing back, 'No. It's on tape.'

14 September

Coronavirus may not yet be in the rear-view mirror – nowhere near – but the memory of what happened at the rally in Tulsa in June clearly is. Donald Trump has gone to Nevada to hold his first indoor rally since he was in Oklahoma. It is in open defiance of state regulations, which limits public gatherings to 50 because of the virus, and his own administration's pandemic health guidelines, but the President isn't bothered. He speaks to a local newspaper reporter, who asks whether the President is concerned about an event like this spreading coronavirus. 'I'm on a stage and it's very far away,' Trump said. 'And so I'm not at all concerned.'

I think the point the reporter was trying to highlight was about the thousands in the audience with no social distancing, and where only a few are wearing masks. The President's comments are seized on by the Democratic governor of the state. 'He's not concerned about all the folks who were there and who are going to go home, and their kids are going to go to school,' says Steve Sisolak. 'He's only concerned about his own health, not the health of anyone else in the state of Nevada.'

16 September

I am on supplemental pool duty, which means I am one of the 12 people in the room if there is a briefing by the press secretary or the President. And today, they are both holding a news conference. I go toe to toe with Kayleigh McEnany on the US record of dealing with coronavirus. She had told a previous questioner that America had done better than Europe and virtually everywhere else in dealing with the pandemic. I ask her how she can claim it as a success when the richest and most powerful country in the world has 4 per cent of the globe's population, but has 24 per cent of the Covid deaths. She gives alternate stats (or maybe alternative facts), preferring to concentrate on excessive deaths. I suggest that my figure is much easier to comprehend. The exchange is picked up extensively and goes viral on social media.

At his briefing the President has come with a clear purpose. It is to sell. To sell the proposition that a vaccine is around the corner, and will be available almost certainly next month – and operation 'warp speed' will ensure that most Americans will have the vaccine in next to no time.

The only problem is that this flies in the face of everything that the head of the Centers for Disease Control, Dr Robert Redfield, had earlier told Congress under oath. Poor Dr Redfield. Donald Trump has come to throw him under the bus. And then run him over with the bus, and then reverse over him for good measure. Redfield had said that even if a vaccine won approval later this year, it probably wouldn't be available to most Americans until much later in 2021 because those most in need would get the first doses. Redfield also incurred Trump's ire by saying face masks are 'more guaranteed to protect me against Covid than when I take a Covid vaccine'.

Trump said Redfield had 'made a mistake' on both counts. 'It's just incorrect information,' the non-science trained President says dismissively of the government's health expert's testimony. And he goes on and on. He couldn't explain why Dr Redfield had said what he had. Maybe he was confused or misunderstood the question, the President muses. It was brutal. I ask the President whether he still has confidence in his CDC director, given that he is so easily confused and keeps giving incorrect information. 'I do. I do. I do,' the President tells me. But that is probably little solace to poor Dr Redfield.

Inadvertently, the President has given force to the main thrust of the Democrat attack on his handling of the pandemic – namely that he doesn't listen to scientific advice, and thinks he knows best – and woe betide anyone who fails to share his Panglossian outlook. 'I trust vaccines, I trust scientists, but I don't trust Donald Trump,' Biden said in a speech from Wilmington. 'At this moment the American people can't either.'

18 September

Linda and I have gone out for a farewell dinner – she is heading back to London this weekend. My phone lights up. It is Morgan, my producer, saying I should look at a tweet from NPR (National Public Radio). But I am at dinner, and decide not to look. But one message becomes a dozen very quickly. Something's up. And, sure enough, it is a hair standing up on the back of your neck moment – in fact one of those 'where were you when you heard about …' moments. It's the announcement of the death of Ruth Bader Ginsburg, the liberal Supreme Court judge. And the ramifications are frankly colossal.

Physically diminutive at barely five feet tall, Ruth Bader Ginsburg was a giant of American justice. Her brilliance and charisma made her one of the stand-out justices in US Supreme Court history. She was a champion of equality, women's rights, minority rights, as well as healthcare, abortion and immigration. She has played perhaps the leading role in the key judgements that have helped define modern America. It is no exaggeration to say that the rights and freedoms that women enjoy – and rightly take for granted – today were largely the result of her legal brilliance, her tenacity. She was feisty and formidable.

Improbably she became a rock superstar to millennials, who dubbed her the Notorious RBG (after the late New York rapper The Notorious BIG) – a notoriety she found somewhat bewildering, but relished. If she went to talk at a university, students would queue all night to hear her. They would wear 'RBG' T-shirts. She lived near me, at the Watergate (yes, the same block made famous in a different time), and people walking along the Georgetown waterfront have been wearing masks saying something along the lines of: 'Keep your face covered. RBG lives near here'. I have just gone online, googling 'RBG face masks', to see if I can find the actual wording – I couldn't find that one in the range of RBG branded face coverings, but saw over 40 of them before I stopped counting. Yes, she became a brand as well.

To make the obvious point: can you name me one UK Supreme Court justice? Let alone one whose death has been treated as a cause for national mourning. It is partly to do with the central role the

Supreme Court plays in American public life: on all the great social issues of the day – guns, immigration, abortion, equal pay, gay rights, gay marriage, healthcare – the ultimate arbiter is the Supreme Court. But it is also about her. About RBG, only the second woman to serve on the court.

The scenes on the grand and imposing steps to the court are deeply moving. A spontaneous vigil has sprung up on this late summer's evening. Young women holding candles are crying. There is singing: from one group of people 'America the Beautiful', from another 'Amazing Grace'. People are laying flowers. Some are chanting 'R-B-G'. Rainbow flags are being waved. A shrine is taking shape. If you didn't know, you would think this is for a rock star or movie idol. Maybe a religious leader. But no, it is for an 87-year-old, owlish, opera-loving Jewish judge, who had been in ill health for some time. It is also the eve of Rosh Hashanah, the start of the Jewish new year – and some have come to recite the Kaddish, the hauntingly stirring mourner's prayer.

Hers really was a life well lived.

Reaction is coming in fast. Emails, tweets, interviews. But the person whose reaction will be critical is Donald Trump's – and he is on stage at a rally in an aircraft hangar in Bemidji, Minnesota, when news comes through of RBG's death. When he winds up he does a doorstep interview with reporters, who break the news to him. The President seems genuinely shocked by what he is told. It's all a bit incongruous, because bellowing out in the background from the venue's PA system while Trump is talking is Elton John's 'Tiny Dancer'. He keeps it simple. 'She led an amazing life, what else can you say? She was an amazing woman – whether you agreed or not – she was an amazing woman who led an amazing life.'

It's well judged. He doesn't get into any of the politics about choosing a successor, nor timetables for doing that. Tonight it is about RBG.

But you can be sure that when the sun rises tomorrow morning over the Washington Monument, that will be the hottest of hot topics.

19 September

There is a distinct autumnal chill in the air, the temperatures are way lower than normal for September. Crowds are still turning up at the court. All the TV networks – BBC included – have set up camp at the foot of the Supreme Court steps. There is a carpet of flowers, a bunch of mourners – and one conservative provocateur who is there in a suit and tie recording people on his smartphone in the most obnoxious way. Am sure his YouTube followers will lap it up.

RBG's death is the only topic of conversation and, as was utterly predictable, for all the talk of her achievements and legacy the main focus is now on who will replace her, and when, and what this will do to the presidential race. Is it good for the Dems? Is it good for the Republicans? Do the Republicans have the votes to push this through? And if they do, how many will be able to look in the mirror with a straight face?

Four years ago when Justice Antonin Scalia died, Barack Obama put forward a candidate to replace him. But the Republican controlled Senate, under the leadership of Mitch McConnell, invented a new principle. They said no Supreme Court justice should be picked by the president in an election year. Let the American people have their say, they argued, and let the new president put forward his nominee. Merrick Garland, Obama's pick, was literally not given a hearing. The Republicans refused point blank to schedule any confirmation hearings for him. But four years on, that principle which the Republican leadership set out so self-righteously, jaw jutting, chest puffed out, is gone – disappeared in a puff of smoke. That was then. This is now.

It is utterly shameless. Forget principle, this is purely about power. And whatever else Donald Trump has or hasn't done, his lasting legacy – as far as conservatives are concerned – is to have shifted the court's power balance in a rightward direction that will likely last for decades to come. It has Republicans salivating at the prospect. Liberal policies they hate that have become law, they may be able to roll back; things they fretted about from a liberal leaning court – like an assault on gun ownership rights –will never happen.

What in 2016 when Obama was president was no, no, no, has now become go, go, go.

The President tweets late morning that – no surprise – he is going to move to fill the vacancy without delay. At a rally on Saturday night in North Carolina, Trump tells the audience that he has not yet chosen a nominee, but 'It will be a woman, a very talented, very brilliant woman.' The crowd chants, 'Fill that seat!'

An election that had enough uncertainty, enough divisiveness now has a new X factor.

As she prepared for death, RBG dictated a note to her granddaughter. In it she says it is her 'fervent wish' that her replacement should not be chosen until a new president has been elected. It is a dying wish that is almost certainly not going to be granted. And, ironically, a woman known in life for her collegiality is in death going to be the spark for the most non-collegiate of scraps over who should succeed her.

21 September

The repercussions of Ruth Bader Ginsburg's death are now dominating political campaigning. At the moment it is the central issue – even though America has today passed another grim record with the announcement of the 200,000th death from Covid.

Even the two frontrunners, a Cuban American judge from Florida, Barbara Lagoa, and a 48-year-old former law professor, and now federal judge, Amy Coney Barrett, are being spoken of in terms of what they bring to the campaign in November – much less what sort of justice they would be for the decades to come. Lagoa's big attraction – according to this decidedly short-termist analysis – is that she will do wonders for Trump's vote in the always crucial Florida. It would be a move that will delight the huge Hispanic population there. But social conservatives believe that Coney Barrett's observant Roman Catholic background will help enthuse evangelical groups and other social conservatives whose prime concern is the reversal of America's abortion laws.

The other preoccupation at the moment is vote counting: where are we with the Republicans having enough support to drive this measure through? Everyone has been waiting on Mitt Romney, the former presidential candidate from Utah. You'll remember he was the only Republican senator to vote for Donald Trump's impeachment – and the animus between the two is profound. But today he announces that he is not going to block Donald Trump's nominee.

The disappointment among Democrats is palpable. They were convinced that Romney would *not* side with the President. But they shouldn't have been. Romney is a Mormon. He is a social conservative. He might loathe Donald Trump, and abhor the way he conducts himself, but Romney's goal is, and always has been, a Supreme Court with a clear conservative majority that can deliver on the priorities of religious groups like the Mormons. And this is a really important wider point about American politics. Millions will have voted for Trump in 2016 not because they loved him or his values, but because they saw him as a vehicle to deliver a more conservative judicial system. And if, as now seems likely, the President is going to notch up three Supreme Court appointments in four years – then, happy days. Trump has done everything religious groups wanted and more. You have to go back to the 1950s and Dwight Eisenhower to find a president who has had the opportunity to appoint three justices in his first term.

In Pennsylvania, where Trump is holding a rally, they have a new chant. If the top two hits from 2016 were 'Lock her up' and 'Build the wall' – 2020 now has 'Fill that seat'.

22 September

I wake to polling data from *ABC News* and the *Washington Post* suggesting the race is tightening; they say Trump is 4 points up in Florida, and 1 point up in Arizona. These are the best figures that Trump has had in an age. It also comes as I sense there is growing disquiet in some Democratic circles that Biden is being out-muscled in the 'ground' game. Because his campaign is being so fastidious about social distancing, he is leaving the arena free to Trump, whose campaign has thousands of people in the key swing states knocking on doors.

Now Trump has tweeted an aerial photo boasting about the rally he held last night in Pennsylvania – the picture shows thousands of people packed tight into an arena, with zero social distancing and hardly anyone wearing masks.

I am meant to be cutting a piece for the *Ten O'Clock News* on RBG lying in repose. It is an amazing scene on the steps leading up to the Supreme Court. Four hundred of her former clerks, dressed in black, with face masks to match, have formed up in socially distanced rows to watch her Stars and Stripes draped casket being carried up to the Great Hall of the court, where a short service will be conducted. There is something slightly austere about the way it looks; almost like a scene from *The Handmaid's Tale*.

But there is nothing chilly about the service, conducted by a rabbi. Her singing of the 23rd Psalm in Hebrew is beautiful; and the address from the chief justice, John Roberts, is perfectly judged – this was the woman, he said, who had dreamed of becoming an operatic virtuoso, but had ended up becoming a rock star. A lot of the grizzled TV anchors and commentators are clearly deeply moved by what they are witnessing, their voices faltering with emotion as they salute the prodigious achievements of this daughter of a bookkeeper from Brooklyn.

As it turns out, such are the vagaries of television, my piece is dropped from the running order because of unfolding news from Louisville, Kentucky. There, back in March – predating the death of George Floyd – 26-year-old Breonna Taylor was killed by three police officers. She was in her apartment when police, executing a 'no-knock' search warrant, burst in. Taylor's boyfriend, Kenneth Walker, thinking the intruders were burglars, opened fire with a handgun. He, along with 11 other witnesses, said the police did not announce themselves. The police then fired over 20 rounds, hitting Breonna five times. She would die of her injuries.

The case only really came to prominence *after* the death of George Floyd in Minneapolis, as it was seized on as another example of police using excessive force against black people. Today the grand jury made its recommendations: legal action is only to be taken against one of the policemen, and even then for the comparatively minor offence of 'wanton endangerment' – not of Breonna Taylor, but the other people who were in the apartment block, because of stray police rounds ricocheting around the building, through windows and doors. It is a long way short of the murder charges that Breonna Taylor's family had been demanding, and is another occasion when the criminal justice system seems long on 'criminal' but way short on 'justice'. As I am writing this just before bed, reports are coming out of Louisville that two policemen have been shot by protestors/agitators. It is going to be a long, tense night in Louisville, and I suspect other cities around the US.

One other thing in this febrile atmosphere: the President is asked at a White House briefing whether, given the unrest, he would commit to a peaceful transfer of power post-election – a question to which in normal circumstances the only possible answer would be 'yes'. But the President equivocates. 'Well, we're going to have to see what happens,' he says.

I have earlier had dinner with a seasoned political operative in Washington, and we discuss Donald Trump's comments. 'One thing you have to understand,' he tells me; 'the President is never going to concede defeat.'

23 September

The President's equivocation on the peaceful transfer of power is reverberating. This morning he went to pay his respects to RBG (although his respect didn't extend to taking any notice of her dying wish that the appointment of her replacement should wait until after the election). He and Melania, both wearing masks, stood by her coffin at the top of the steps to the court. Across the piazza below, in front of the court, the boos were unmistakable. The vast crowds of ordinary people lining up to pay *their* respects started chanting 'Vote him out'. Not quite a Ceausescu moment, but for a man used to the adoration of the crowds this will have been uncomfortable. Just how uncomfortable became clear this evening at his rally in Jacksonville when, a propos of nothing, he declared that he had barely heard the booing. Am left wondering why, if he really hadn't heard much, did he mention it then?

More politely, but no less firmly, senior Republicans are pushing back at the President's remarks. Sure, they are not mentioning Donald Trump by name – but the message is clear: there will be a peaceful transfer of power. Mitch McConnell, the Senate majority leader, tweets: 'The winner of the November 3rd election will be inaugurated on January 20th. There will be an orderly transition just as there has been every four years since 1792.' Mitt Romney, the former presidential candidate – and this week supporter of the President over the Supreme Court replacement – is blunter. He says, 'Fundamental to democracy is the peaceful transition of power; without that, there is Belarus. Any suggestion that a president might not respect this Constitutional guarantee is both unthinkable and unacceptable.' Others pile in too.

Tomorrow I am appearing on the BBC News Channel programme *Newswatch*, and I need to discuss the likely questions I will be asked about BBC reporting on the US. So I have a conversation with our foreign editor, Andrew Roy, in London about the teams that will be coming out to help cover the election, and how the numbers will be way down on four years ago. I suggest, only half-jokingly, that maybe they should be sent out on 4 November. Yes, the election is on 3 November – but increasingly I am coming round to the view that the *real* campaign begins after the election. That is when legal battle will be joined. A battle that will go all the way to the Supreme Court. Andrew reminds me that he was bureau chief in Washington in 2000, when they had to wait 36 days before, eventually, George W. Bush was declared the winner after the wrangle over those hanging chads in Florida. My suspicion – which I hope to God I am proved wrong over – is that this will be a thousand times worse. Every ballot in every county in every swing state will be the subject of legal action.

There is a whole series of nightmare scenarios and what ifs. What if, on 3 November, Donald Trump looks like he's won – only to discover a few days later, when all the postal votes have been counted, that he's lost? Will his supporters accept that? Will he accept that? What if he orders Republican state legislatures to declare the electoral college votes before all the postal ballots have been tallied? And darker

– much, much darker – what if he tells his supporters to come out and resist any attempt to 'steal' the election from him? There are a lot of serious, grown-up people I know who are deeply fearful about post-election unrest.

As a counterpoint, there is a fascinating article I've just read about a section of the White House that is making meticulous preparations for a totally conventional handover of power. It's led by a New Zealander and former tech executive, Chris Liddell, who is one of the very few people to have served in a senior capacity in the White House since the outset. According to the Politico report he's filed two different transition reports in May and August, fulfilling congressional mandates. Meanwhile the Justice Department has already agreed to start processing security clearances for key Biden personnel in case he wins. It's all a far cry from the 'no surrender' rhetoric of the President.

I'm in touch with a senior European diplomat who fears that it is Donald Trump's refusal to accept a smooth handover that preoccupies foreign embassies, and that is being endlessly war-gamed. What if, on election night, the Associated Press calls it for Biden and other senior Republicans concede? Do they issue a statement congratulating the new Democrat president? Or do they have to wait until Donald Trump admits defeat? And what do they do if he doesn't? You don't want to be the foreign power to congratulate Biden only to find that Trump somehow manages to cling on. Or vice versa.

As I say, I hope I'm wrong, but this feels as though it could be a presidential election in two acts: Act 1, the people speak; Act 2, the lawyers decide. And a Supreme Court with a decisive conservative majority might be just the thing for the President.

26 September, the White House

RBG is to be replaced by ACB. Amy Coney Barratt is Donald Trump's choice to replace Justice Ginsburg. I receive an email from the White House protocol office to say that I have been given clearance to attend the ceremony where the President will introduce her. Unfortunately, I have to go live onto the evening news, and although I will be live at the White House, I will be on the North Lawn – on what they call Pebble Beach, the row of broadcast tents lined up on the western edge of the perimeter from which we do all our live broadcasts. And the main event is taking place in the Rose Garden, on the South Lawn. And there is no way I can move between the two. So close and yet so far. It sounds as though there is the atmosphere of a garden party. An army band plays pleasant, jaunty tunes, and people mill around before the hundred or so guests take their seats. These include close personal friends, Republican congressional leaders, who will help steer her nomination, key White House personnel, and the vice-president is there – an ideological soul-mate of Judge Barrett.

This morning she was in Indiana, at home with her seven children, almost completely anonymous. By the end of today, after being introduced by the President, she will become a new lightning rod in this country's divided politics. The reshaping of America's judicial system in a much more conservative direction will undoubtedly be one of Donald Trump's lasting legacies for years to come. But there's something else, much more short term. If the election result is contested – and it's hard to see that it won't be; if Donald Trump is refusing to accept defeat – and he's said as much – where does this get resolved? It will be up to the Supreme Court, with perhaps by November a 6–3 conservative majority. Amy Coney Barrett's first act might be to decide the direction of American democracy.

The 48-year-old mother of seven is a Roman Catholic, and she follows the same 'originalist' interpretation of the law as her mentor, the late Antonin Scalia. She is well known in conservative legal circles, and is undoubtedly extremely well qualified. Just how shrewd a choice she is becomes clear in her extremely well-judged remarks at the White House. One of the extraordinary things about the fiercely conservative and combative Antonin Scalia was his close relationship with Ruth Bader Ginsburg. They disagreed vehemently on matters of law, but remained the closest of colleagues, often attending the opera together. Today ACB (as we haven't yet got used to calling her) pays tribute to that relationship and also is lavish in her praise for Ruth Bader Ginsburg.

27 September

It has been the pot of gold at the end of the rainbow for financial and political journalism these last four years: the search for Donald Trump's tax returns. In 2016 he became the first president in nearly half a century not to disclose his financial affairs. The reason he gave was that he was under audit by the IRS. But experts scoffed: being under audit doesn't mean you can't release your returns. Bits and pieces have dribbled out – a tantalising glimpse into the complex web of companies that he runs. His niece leaked a lot of detail about how the family structured its money. But they weren't the returns themselves. Tonight the little fissures in the dam became a giant hole. The *New York Times* seems to have the whole bloody lot: a pot overflowing with doubloons, ingots and gold bars – and the data to prove it … and it is astonishing.

In the year Donald Trump became president he paid a total of $750 in income tax. The same in 2017, his first year in office. In ten of the preceding 15 years, he paid no income tax at all. One person on social media points out that in 2016 he paid the porn star, Stormy Daniels, $130 thousand, and the IRS just $750 – maybe, the commentator writes, if the IRS wants more money it should do to him what she allegedly did. I resist the career limiting urge to retweet it. Another speculates that if that was all the tax due, the President probably received one of the stimulus cheques of $1,200 that were sent out to all low earners in America to help with the Covid economic shutdown – and signed by Donald Trump.

There are other eye-popping features in this treasure trove. Trump has managed to offset $70,000 against tax for hairdressing for television appearances – that is quite a sum. And then there are the more serious numbers. The President apparently has personal debts totalling $400 million – which begs two simple, but hugely uncomfortable, questions: to whom is he in debt, and is there a national security implication to it? The detail we don't know, because the President won't release his tax returns. Going through the various details reported by the *New York Times*, it is hard to avoid this conclusion: either Donald Trump is a really lousy businessman – he reported such massive losses, that were only obviated by the fortune he earned from endorsements as a result of presenting *The Apprentice* on NBC; or he has cut an awful lot of corners in his tax returns. You could see why he wouldn't want detail like this to be released to the public. Or, as this scathing line in the *New York Times* puts it: 'Trump has been more successful playing a business mogul than being one in real life.'

The President holds a news conference at the White House where he rails against the newspaper. 'It's totally fake news. Made up. Fake.'

But the Democrats are going to town – T-shirts are being produced with 'I paid more income tax than Donald Trump' – and asking people to retweet if they paid more federal income tax than $750. They also have an ad with what the average teacher, nurse or firefighter pays in income tax compared to the President.

Whether or not this punches through in a way that other issues haven't (I suspect it will, but I have been wrong often before), in the week of the first presidential debate, surely this will put him on the defensive.

They talk in US elections about the October surprise – the event that comes out of nowhere to upend the rhythm of the political campaign. This time it's come four days early.

28 September, Cleveland, Ohio

We have tepid coffee, donuts and trail mix. Yes! We are on the road again. John, Morgan and I are in the crew car heading 350 miles north to Cleveland, Ohio, for the first presidential debate. It's a stunning drive. The trees which line the interstate are starting to turn – oranges, yellows, browns – not yet burning red, but a few with hints of purple. Still the only subject is the President's tax returns. On the journey I get an alert that he has tweeted: 'The Fake News Media, just like Election time 2016, is bringing up my Taxes & all sorts of other nonsense with illegally obtained information & only bad intent.'

Hang on a minute. Last night it was 'totally fake news. Made up. Fake'. Today it is 'illegally obtained information'. Er … which one is it?

29 September, Cleveland, Ohio

The stage is set for the first presidential debate. Donald Trump comes out like a raging bull – he wants to destabilise Biden with constant interruptions, disparage his opponent with *ad hominem* insults, and whether by accident or design demean the whole debate process. For all the tumult of the past few months, for all the upset and the crises that have blown in and out, the polls have remained remarkably steady. Biden is well ahead. So it seems that Trump is the boxer going into the 12th round, knowing that he is massively down on points, and that the only way he can win is by delivering a knock-out punch to the chin. And he is swinging. It is really ugly. I've seen more elegant bundles in a school playground, and it made the food fights in *St Trinian's* look positively genteel and demure by comparison. But for all the blows raining down on him, Biden doesn't go down.

It is car-crash TV, with the host, Fox's Chris Wallace, increasingly powerless to rein in the President. Biden had a strategy that he just wanted to talk directly to the American people, and would try to ignore Trump as much as possible. I bet he had written on his hand 'Look straight to camera, address the people, don't engage.' Some of the time it works effectively, but it is clear his exasperation levels are growing – and so it becomes the drunken street brawl he'd hoped to avoid. He calls the President 'a clown', tells him to 'shut up', says he is the worst president in American history. And Donald Trump rips into him for his mask-wearing habits, saying he is dumb and a Trojan horse for the left.

The President is so over the top, so boorish and rude that I think an adequate, not particularly great Biden performance is made to look much better than it was.

The most notable part of the debate is when Trump is asked to condemn the behaviour of white supremacists and militias who've gone onto the streets, heavily armed, to confront rival protestors. The President havers. He just won't do it. When asked about one of the groups, the Proud Boys – a group that promotes violence, is misogynistic, Islamophobic and racist – he tells them to 'stand back and stand by'. The group is so delighted that by the time I get back to my hotel in Cleveland they have changed their motto to that, and are flogging T-shirts and all manner of swag with the President's comments on them. The group is saying it is getting a flood of enquiries and new recruits.

I am really struggling to work out the Trump strategy. If the goal is to reach out to the undecideds, the wavering, the people needing reassurance about his temperament, it is hard to see how he has advanced his cause at all. Frank Luntz, the Republican pollster, conducts a focus group with those people immediately after the debate. He puts up a word cloud where his floating voters describe the President in one word – most popular are crackhead, unhinged, bully, horrid, chaotic, unpolished, an ass, arrogant, un-American. Well, maybe they are unrepresentative, but it doesn't sound like he's won this group over.

At the end of the debate the two wives come on stage to congratulate their men. It is a telling split-screen moment. Melania comes up – without a mask – and stands by her husband. They don't embrace. They look out at the non-audience with fixed, slightly uncomfortable smiles. Jill Biden comes up on stage – with mask – only removing it to give her husband a big kiss and a tight embrace which they hold for a few seconds. The difference between the two couples could really not be more marked.

CBS declares Biden the winner in the snap poll they've conducted. But winner? Loser? I don't want to sound too pompous, but it feels as though American democracy is the loser of this fracas.

2 October, Washington

I have known tumultuous days – but in my 35-plus years in journalism I am not sure I have ever seen a day like this. We're going to do it chronologically.

At 01.45 my mobile phone, which I always keep by my bed, goes off. It is Paul Danahar, the Washington bureau chief. I haven't learned much in my many years as a foreign correspondent, but I know when the phone goes off in the middle of the night, it is not going to be for the delivery of good news. Paul tells me the President and First Lady have both tested positive for coronavirus. Holy crap. The *Today* programme wants me live at 08.10 – so 03.10 my time

– *Breakfast* want me before that, and the Radio 4 bulletins want a piece. My heart is racing.

But though my mind is a bit of a fog, one thing – seemingly paradoxical – is crystal clear to me. This is simultaneously astonishing, unbelievable and jaw-dropping – after all Donald Trump is the most protected man in the world, and is tested for Covid on a daily basis – and not in the teeniest bit surprising. Whether born of arrogance or a belief that you can will coronavirus away, there is a lax, lackadaisical, blasé attitude in the White House. I have written before about how few staff members wear masks – and that is because of a culture that comes down from the top. The President has always been ambivalent about their use, and so if you are a young staffer, you probably think it is career limiting to wear one. I remember that a day or two earlier one of the news outlets had got hold of an internal White House memo telling staff that face masks were optional, but 'not a good look'.

And lately the President has been hurtling around the country again as if Covid-19 has gone away. There are rallies where he's not wearing a mask, and neither is most of the audience. His key staff saunter out to Marine One chatting amiably, close together, maskless. This may be harsh – but this feels as though it was an accident waiting to happen.

The broadcasts go well – much better than my attempts to get back to sleep after them. It is hard for the mind not to perform somersaults, and play any number of 'what if' scenarios.

Kayleigh McEnany, the President's press secretary has released the memo from the White House physician, Sean Conley, confirming the diagnosis. But Conley's memo says something else that catches my eye. 'Rest assured,' he writes, 'I expect the President to continue carrying out his duties without disruption while recovering.' I have to say that sounds more spin than substance. The President has only just been diagnosed. And as we know he is male, 74 years old, and clinically obese according to his last medical. How can Conley say he expects the President to be able to carry on 'without disruption'? How can he possibly know?

Having not slept a wink, I turn on *Fox & Friends*, the President's favourite breakfast show. One of the anchors is, I think somewhat tastelessly, thinking out loud how this could help the President electorally. If he gets over it quickly, then he will be the exemplar of there being no need to be afraid of Covid, that the Democrats have exaggerated the dangers etc. I can't help thinking that from now until polling day the focus is going to remain stubbornly fixed on the pandemic – and that is not where Donald Trump wants or needs the conversation to be. And anyway, the guy's just been diagnosed – who knows how this plays out medically, let alone politically.

Late morning there is a 'gaggle' with the White House chief of staff, Mark Meadows, on the driveway – he confirms that the President has mild symptoms, but is otherwise fine. He is working as normal. The First Lady has apparently got mild flu symptoms, but is also OK.

I go down to the White House to do a live for the *Six O'Clock News*. Just like after a thunderstorm, the atmosphere has changed. The place feels on edge. Staff are suddenly being much more assiduous about wearing their masks. Maybe I am projecting my own feelings, but the place seems a bit panicky. I notice there is no marine guarding the entrance to the West Wing. Just as the Royal Standard flying above Buckingham Palace tells you whether the Queen is at home; so the presence of the marine guard tells you whether the President is there. He is, according to the latest medical bulletin issued by Commander Conley, convalescing in the East Wing residence, where he will stay until he recovers.

I go back home to cut a fresh piece for the *Ten O'Clock News*. A new medical bulletin reports that the White House has administered an antibody cocktail to the President successfully. I see that Paul is calling me again. I suspect it is to tell me that this or that word will need changing in my script, or to discuss coverage plans for the coming days. It is not that. Nothing like.

Paul is the most no-nonsense, no-fuss, old-school journalist you could imagine. He's been and done and seen it all. He was on the roof of the Palestine Hotel in Baghdad when 'shock and awe' heralded the start of the 2003 invasion of Iraq; he has rescued journalists being held hostage in Libya; he's been kidnapped at gunpoint in Africa. It is fair to say his conversation can be profanity laced. But I can tell immediately there is something about his tone that is urgent. 'You can't breathe a word of this to anyone,' he tells me sotto voce – a sure way to get the attention of another hack. 'But we've had a highly confidential tip that preparations are in place for the President to be moved to the Walter Reed Medical Center [the famous military hospital on the northern outskirts of Washington] later today.' Paul must know this is 100 per cent kosher. It is being kept hush-hush because the President doesn't want a word of this to leak until after the financial markets have closed.

This is startling. At 01.00 this morning the President tweets that he has tested positive. Mid-morning he has mild symptoms. Mid-afternoon he has had a successful treatment. Now it's late afternoon and he's being admitted to hospital. Events are moving at helter-skelter speed. My mind goes back to Boris Johnson's admission to hospital – but there is one critical difference. Unlike Downing Street, the White House has a team of doctors and nurses working round the clock. There is a fully equipped surgery and sick bay. If the President is only presenting with mild symptoms, the White House Medical Office is fully able to look after him.

We alert the editor of the *Ten O'Clock News* just before the bulletin starts, to warn him of what might happen. Just before we go on air I can hear the helicopter coming in to land on the South Lawn. But when I go live I am unable to make mention of it – there is still no confirmation. Moments after I finish, the news breaks. And so I go back on air to reveal that the President is being admitted to hospital – 'out of an abundance of caution', according to the White House spokeswoman.

This would be epic news at any time, but just a month out from the most divisive presidential election? We are entering uncharted territory. On air I make clear my scepticism about him being fine, and it just being a precautionary move – but if the President's health has declined from the diagnosis early on Friday morning, it's been bloody quick.

I stay at the White House and do lives for *Newsnight* and for *BBC World* – I am live on air as the helicopter takes off to move him to Walter Reed. An election campaign that needed no more shocks, no more agitation, has now been totally upended. Will there be any more debates? Does campaigning get halted? And on and on the questions rattle around my head, with no clever answers.

As we wrap the series of lives with my White House cameraman, Ron Skeans, I just say 'Wow'.

My long day is not over. I have to pre-record a *Today Programme* interview at just gone midnight, and I am flagging a bit. But just when you think the day can't get any madder, it is fast becoming clear that last Saturday's event in the Rose Garden when the President introduced Amy Coney Barrett to the world has become a 'super-spreader' event. Through the course of the evening more and more people who were there are issuing statements to say they have contracted coronavirus. Three Republican senators who were due to have played a crucial role in getting her confirmed onto the court have gone down; so too the President's former aide, Kellyanne Conway; the head of the Republican Party, Ronna McDaniel; and the Trump campaign manager, Bill Stepien; and Chris Christie, the former governor of New Jersey who's been with the President all week, has it – along with three

of my colleagues in the White House Correspondents Association –
and there are many others awaiting test results.

And having last weekend felt totally bummed that broadcast
commitments meant I couldn't attend the Rose Garden event – even
though I had received clearance for it – I am now feeling total relief.
Elated almost. I have clearly dodged a bullet.

You could not make this stuff up. If we're going to talk the politics
of this for a minute, this has happened in the White House, not some
overcrowded meat packing plant in South Dakota. If the President
wanted a good advert for his handling of the coronavirus outbreak,
today is not it.

I see one comment that makes me laugh over the super-spreader
event, because remember, the Democrats are seething that the President
and the Republicans want to railroad this confirmation through. 'It's
made Democrats believe in God, and Republicans believe in Science.'

Right, just need to stay awake for another two hours …

3 October

I have slept, and see that the President's physician is going to give a
press briefing at 11. Commander Conley, your first proper appearance
before the cameras is going to have a global audience. The world is
waiting to hear what you've got to say. After a career in the shadows,
you now have to be ready for primetime.

About 40 minutes after the due time, the doors of the Walter Reed
Medical Center open, and about ten men in white coats emerge and
walk purposefully towards the microphone. Conley is the first to
speak, and he starts by saying, 'The President is doing very well,' and
that they are 'extremely pleased' with the progress he's made since the
diagnosis 72 hours ago.

A loud, clanging alarm goes off in my head. The President tweeted at 01.00 on Friday morning that he'd contracted coronavirus. It is now Saturday morning. But 72 hours ago? Conley is suggesting the President was diagnosed two days earlier. Two days in which he gave a press briefing – without a mask; flew to Minnesota to address a rally – without a mask; and on Thursday went to a private fundraiser at his New Jersey golf course, Bedminster – again without a mask. This is incredible.

The doctor is asked about whether the President has had to be given oxygen. It is immediately noticeable that he answers like a lawyer, not a doctor. 'He isn't receiving any supplemental oxygen now,' Conley says, using the present tense. Yes, but that's not what the reporter asked. He asked whether he had been given oxygen. Conley slips and slides in his responses. 'Thursday no oxygen. None at this moment. And yesterday with the team, while we were all here, he was not on oxygen,' he says when pressed. Yeah, so if that's the case what about Friday morning at the White House, when the team hadn't been assembled … but he evades.

Here's the problem, if you're going to dissemble over something like this, why should anyone believe anything else you say? The *New York Times*, CBS and the AP news agency later report from multiple sources that the President did indeed need oxygen before he left the White House yesterday morning. So, as I surmised, the move to Walter Reed was not just an abundance of caution. The President really wasn't well.

I am convinced of something else too. The President has told Dr Conley what he can and can't say. And that is all part of a piece. There is an extraordinary letter from 2015, when Donald Trump was running for the Republican nomination, and people were demanding to see health reports. He produced an appallingly typed letter from his then physician Harold Bornstein. Do look it up. It is priceless because it is so clearly written by Donald Trump himself. There are lines like

'His lab test results were astonishingly excellent. If elected Mr Trump, I can state unequivocally, will be the healthiest individual ever elected to the presidency.'

And with the first White House physician, Ronny Jackson, who came to the Briefing Room to give a news conference on the President's health, you felt it was the same. He too, in a slightly more formal manner, said all the things that the President wanted to hear: that he would live to 200 with his fantastic genes, if only he'd eaten better! You don't go in front of camera without having it impressed upon you exactly what it is the President wants to hear.

Conley wraps and goes back inside, but White House chief of staff Mark Meadows hangs around, and he calls the pool reporters together for what he hopes will be an off-the-record chat. The problem is that what he says seems to contradict totally what Conley has just reported on the President's condition. He says there was great concern over Trump's vitals on Friday morning. And that the next 48 hours would be critical. What makes this comically worse is that he brings the pool reporters together into a gaggle while there are still a mass of TV cameras around from the news conference. Moments after he speaks to them, news reports come out on the wires and on social media describing how a senior White House source said this, someone close to the President said that … The cameras are still filming, so it really doesn't take an Inspector Morse to put two and two together about the mystery WH source. Sergeant Lewis could easily figure this one out by himself.

It is shambolic. Totally dysfunctional. The way this has been handled is as though this was just another policy wrangle – a budget row on the hill, a controversy over immigration, a bit of a spat with the chairman of the Federal Reserve. Guys, no, this is sort of life or death – and it's the President's life we are discussing here.

4 October

Donald Trump has always believed that his best communications director is himself. And after that day of evasion, contradiction, muddle and corrections, the President decides he'd better take charge. From his suite at the Walter Reed hospital he releases a video on Twitter and Facebook.

He is sitting at the end of what looks like a boardroom table, sort of sub-*Apprentice*. You'll probably think this is really sad, but I am more fascinated by the mechanics than the content. For a start, there is not a hair out of place on that carefully coiffed head. So, who did that? His hair is a confection. It doesn't just happen. Has some poor hairdresser had to don full PPE, visor, N95 etc and bring out the curling tongs and hairspray to get the President ready? Also, who is filming it? Who has adjusted the lights? Who put the mic on him? The President is not wearing a mask. So how many people are in the room – and did they have a choice?

The only concession to him being in hospital is that he's not wearing a tie. He looks pale – but that could be due to the absence of the orange foundation and powder that he is normally caked in when he appears in public – and which you would probably need a hammer and chisel to remove.

He also sounds hoarse. And he won't like that. This is a president who's always equated sickness with weakness – but his usual bullishness is replaced with a little more hesitancy about his health. 'I think I'm doing fine,' he says.

Look at how he went after Hillary Clinton in 2016 when she collapsed with pneumonia after a 9/11 service in New York. He derided her as being weak. He has regularly gone after people on Twitter for weakness, for crying like a baby. There is reporting now that the President sought to resist being moved to hospital for precisely that reason. And according to the reports there was a furious row, with the clincher in the argument being his doctor telling him on Friday morning that he could either walk to the helicopter now or be filmed being taken out on a gurney in two days' time.

Outside the hospital, there is a noisy vigil of Trump supporters (among them the founder of the Proud Boys). The President said he had a choice – he could have hidden away (a not so subtle dig at Joe Biden), or carried on meeting the public. Actually he was always careful not to get too close to the general public at his rallies for fear of contracting coronavirus.

During the course of the day there is another medical bulletin from Dr Sean Conley – and an attempt to clear up the misinformation mess from yesterday. Conley, who is good looking in a slightly bland sort of way, seems to me too young to be the President's physician, and it feels as though his smile is being held in place by rivets. Again he talks about how pleased the doctors are by his progress. And finally he answers the question that he so artlessly avoided the day before about whether the President had been given supplemental oxygen. He had.

So eventually he is asked this question – why hadn't he been straight from the off? His answer, for a serving military officer and the physician to the President, is really one for the ages: 'I was trying to reflect the upbeat attitude that the team, the President, that his course of illness has had. I didn't want to give any information that might steer the course of illness in another direction. And in doing so, you know, it came off that we're trying to hide something, which wasn't necessarily true.'

It wasn't necessarily true? Those sound like the words of a spin doctor, not a real doctor – they also sound as though Commander Conley was not addressing the American people, he was speaking to an audience of one: Donald Trump. Just like the day before, he is saying what the President wants to hear.

And there is another important statement. All being well the President will be going home tomorrow. This is so interesting – the logic that is given is that the White House can provide any treatment he needs. Well, if that is the case why did they ever move him to Walter Reed in the first place? This is such an exercise in obfuscation and deflection. They also refuse to answer the question point blank when was the last time the President had tested negative for coronavirus. It is an important and pertinent question. If the answer is before last Tuesday's debate with Joe Biden, then it is perfectly possible the President went on stage already infectious with coronavirus.

These are details – let's stand back for a minute and reflect on what exceptional times these are. I end my report on the Sunday evening news thus: 'All elections feel uncertain, but there has never been a president hospitalised in the final stages of a campaign, let alone in the midst of a pandemic. If anyone tells you they know what is going to happen next, don't believe them.'

I am outside the Walter Reed hospital to do a live after my report with Mishal Husain. It is noisy and raucous on the street. But am vaguely aware just before she cues over to me that it has become quieter. The police are moving in and clearing traffic from the six-lane highway that runs outside the medical centre. It is obvious that something is going on, but what seems uncertain. But then rolling up towards us comes the unmistakable sight of the presidential motorcade, moving at about three miles an hour. Surely not? Surely not a Covid joy ride? But yes, it is. The world's most impatient patient, with a mask on his face, diagnosed with coronavirus only three days earlier and still infectious, is waving to his supporters. He passes within about six feet of where I am standing. With cameraman Sam Beattie I do a 'stand-up' – which you only get one go at. Luckily, I make it up and words fall out of my mouth in just about the right order and it sounds vaguely intelligible. Sam does a great job pulling off a tight shot of Trump in the car to find me at the roadside.

The spin is that this is the President thanking his supporters by coming out to salute them. The alternative is that this is the President needing the cheers and adulation of the crowd.

Much later a darker thought occurs to me. Was this a fearful President thinking he is about to die, waving a mournful farewell to the adoring fans who've kept him and held him aloft? Maybe I am overthinking the situation. But we are only three days into his diagnosis, and as I said in my live with Mishal, Covid can come roaring back, just when you think you are over the worst. Whatever, there was something decidedly odd about this bizarre event.

Not to say dangerous. The drive-by hasn't just involved the full motorcade – what about the secret service personnel who are in 'the Beast' with him? And the driver? Just so the President can go up and down Wisconsin Avenue waving from a hermetically sealed car – completely airtight because it's been designed to withstand a chemical weapons attack – aren't they being put in absurd danger?

5 October

Now we are just awaiting the confirmation that the President is coming back to the White House. He will still need a final treatment of the anti-viral drug remdesivir, and he's still on the powerful steroid, dexamethasone – but this morning you'd say it was his Twitter feed that's on amphetamines. After a brief hiatus, it looks as though the campaign for next month's presidential election is all systems go as he goes full caps lock on a whole variety of policy issues. They are coming in rapid fire.

I am working from home, and am about to do *PM* with Evan Davis, one of those reassuringly intelligent and perceptive voices on radio. It has just been announced from the White House that the President's press secretary, Kayleigh McEnany, has tested positive for coronavirus. She's been speaking to reporters over the weekend, carefully taking off her mask to discuss the President's health following his diagnosis, probably brought about by not wearing a mask. I was at a 'gaggle' she gave two days earlier on the White House driveway.

I suddenly feel a wave of stress come over me. It is part tiredness from lack of sleep, part anxiety that I may have been exposed to it – and I guess part rage at the utter recklessness of this White House; that rules the administration have set for the country have not been followed in the seat of power. The Q & A with Evan goes well, but I mention that I was at the gaggle with Kayleigh on Friday. He asks on air if I am going to get tested, and I recall really mumbling my answer. I am thinking out loud on Radio 4 about what I need to do.

I later see a tweet from someone who said that though Jon Sopel said nothing critical, you could tell there was a cold fury in his voice about the situation he and other White House journalists had been put in. Spot on.

After *PM* I go back to the White House to do a live for the *Six O'Clock News*. The place is strangely silent. Like a Sunday. Some are quarantining, others are working from home. And it is clear there is deep unease among many staff. What are the safety protocols? What should staff be doing? They have had little information. And what about the maids, the butlers, the cleaners, the valets, the flower arrangers, those who work in the laundry in the residence? Not everyone who works in the grounds is a political appointee. These are people in modestly paid jobs with few privileges.

The President's helicopter is to take off from Walter Reed at 6.30. Before he became President, Donald Trump was a reality TV star, and he has a brilliant eye for the visual. His departure from hospital is a made for television spectacular, timed to coincide with all the network bulletins being on air. It is also the only time we could all get together to record our podcast – just after Emily Maitlis had come off air after doing *Newsnight*. Trump walks out of the famous gold doors of the Walter Reed Medical Center, a mask on his face, but fists pumping. He returns by helicopter, barely a ten-minute journey. We are recording the latest *Americast* as all this unfolds. After about five minutes, Marine One passes over my riverside apartment, and I commentate as it flies low, hugging the contours of the Potomac and banks right to fly by the Watergate, the Kennedy Arts Center and over the Lincoln Memorial. As it comes in to land, in the background there is the Jefferson Memorial, in the foreground the White House as Marine One touches down on the South Lawn. A White House video with stirring music is released soon after. The strategy: to show the American people he was the man who'd fought coronavirus – and won. The warrior president who's seen off the hidden enemy.

He marches up the steps to the South Portico, and the first thing he does is rip off his mask. All the cameras trained on him from below look up to find the President standing to attention, saluting. There is no one out there that he is saluting to, but the salute goes on. There is something just a touch South American military junta about it. On a grainy long lens, we capture him doing take after take of a campaign video that the White House will release later. He is not wearing a mask as he interacts with a photographer, cameraman, sound operator, lighting person. In the video he says: 'I stood out front, I led. Nobody that's a leader would not do what I did. I know there's a risk, there's a danger, but that's OK.'

He said that people should not be afraid of Covid; that it should not dominate them – this despite the virus having claimed 210,000 American lives to date. But his doctors have warned that he is not out of the woods, and as he reached the top of the steps to the residence and removed his mask he was clearly gasping for breath. His chest was heaving, his shoulders moving up and down. To me, as someone who has suffered from asthma, it all looked very familiar.

It seems very much that there's a gap between the image he wants to project and a more fragile reality.

6 October

I was due to be on a plane to Salt Lake City this evening ahead of the vice-presidential debate tomorrow, but London has taken the view – wisely – that until we are clear about the real state of the President's health, it is better that I stay put in Washington.

It is now about 9pm and I am sitting at the table trying to write up the day, but every 30 seconds my phone is lighting up with a new Donald Trump tweet (like many of us in this city, I get an alert every time his thumbs get active). I am trying not to allow myself to get distracted – a good Californian Cabernet Sauvignon and the fourth game of the NBA play-offs between the LA Lakers and Miami Heat are the background music to my writing. But I succumb to temptation and start reading the Trump tweets. There is no thread to them. Just the President firing off in random directions. A pot-shot at Hillary Clinton, who still seems to live rent-free in the President's head; the battle for the Supreme Court; a pretty gratuitous attack on the Fox News anchor, Chris Wallace, who officiated the first debate; the towering nature of the economy before coronavirus, etc. There is a slightly manic quality to them.

I receive an email from a GP in the UK. It is not someone I know. The email is wittily headed 'roid rage'. And this is what the doctor writes: 'Donald was given Dexamethasone (a potent steroid) for his covid infection. This drug is well known to have significant side effects and is therefore only usually given in an intensive care setting. One of the most serious effects is "steroid psychosis" characterised by confusion, mania and acute psychotic states.'

The President has been confined to quarters now for nearly a week, since when the polls from the first presidential debate have come out and they all point in one direction: it was an unmitigated disaster for the President. Who knows what side effects the drugs are having? Who knows what the lingering effects of the illness are?

But while we are in the ending sentences with question marks mode, here are a couple more that really do need answering urgently if there is to be any trust. The central question which the White House is ducking, and is so critical: when did the President last test negative for Covid? An addendum to that is: did the President comply with the rules of the Presidential Debates Commission, which require a negative test within 72 hours of the debate?

The more the White House refuses to answer these questions, the greater the suspicion that the President went onto the debate stage with Joe Biden while Covid positive. The administration is always keen to share information when it shows Donald Trump in a good light, so it is hard to avoid the conclusion that the reason for this coyness over where and when he was last tested for coronavirus is because, pure and simple, it will be a political embarrassment.

The President has tweeted that he wants next week's debate to go ahead in person in Miami as scheduled. But if you're the Biden camp, and you don't know the answers about the state of the President's health when he debated in Cleveland, Ohio, a week earlier, are you going to agree to that while he might still be infectious?

There was a strange day a month or two back when Kayleigh McEnany claimed that the President was tested at least once a day, only for Donald Trump to contradict her later on in the afternoon. He apparently hates the tests – and doesn't see why he needs to take them, particularly when no one is meant to be allowed to enter his orbit unless and until they themselves have been tested, and tested negative. There is speculation that it is weeks since he was last tested. It is a rumour that the White House could easily quash at a stroke by one public statement from the President's physician – but they are staying schtoom. Not a word.

This might also explain something else that doesn't quite compute. If you look at the trajectory of the President's illness, it bears no relation to what is the normal course of the disease. Often after diagnosis you feel OK or moderately lousy for the first week, and then worryingly after a week to ten days it comes roaring back – and that is when people are knocked sideways. With Donald Trump we get confirmation that he has tested positive last Friday at 01.00, and by six o'clock that evening he is on his way to Walter Reed, having, we now know, required oxygen twice.

Maybe what happened last Friday was the seven to ten-day second wind of coronavirus – and that he had been shedding the virus for a whole week before that. If it's true, leave aside the magnitude of the political scandal that that could have happened (and it is pretty astonishing), what about the public health aspect to it? Surely it would be a matter of urgency to contact and trace everyone who has been in contact with the President over that period – and they should all be self-quarantining.

One of those in that boat is the Vice-President, Mike Pence. He has been in regular contact with Donald Trump. They were together the previous weekend at the Amy Coney Barrett super-spreader event. Yet tomorrow he will be in Utah for the vice-presidential debate with Kamala Harris– the head of the coronavirus task force, going against the advice he has given to the American people.

And the extent to which the White House is behaving with a wanton insouciance is highlighted by astounding news coming out of the Pentagon. The weekend of the Coney Barrett garden party there was another event at the White House – indoors! It was for 'gold star' families – military families who've lost loved ones in the service of the nation. The Vice-Commandant of the Coast Guard, Admiral Charles Ray, was there and he has tested positive. As a result America's top brass – the Joint Chiefs – led by the Chairman of the Joint Chiefs (America's top military commander), General Mark Milley, are *all* self-isolating. The Pentagon feels it necessary to state publicly that none of this will affect the nation's military preparedness to respond in case of an attack. But how extraordinary. And what a contrast: a White House behaving as though nothing has happened, and the top echelon of the US military playing it by the book.

I am just about to finish, but we now have confirmation that the President's closest aide and speech writer, Stephen Miller, has tested positive. Oh, and so too has the senior military officer who is always at the President's side carrying the 'nuclear football' – the suitcase which carries the codes to launch an all-out nuclear war. I can't decide whether this last piece of news gives me cause to sleep more soundly, or cause to feel more anxious. The latter, I think. Everything is making me feel more anxious at the moment.

7 October

Debate day for the vice-presidential candidates – but the President is chomping at the bit to show he's back. A video is released in which he says it is a blessing from God that he caught coronavirus. It taught him that it can be survived and that it's not a big deal. Kind of hard to imagine that those who have lost loved ones would use a phrase like that. It often feels as though his remarks could do with being put through an empathy strainer. He promises to make the antibody cocktail, Regeneron, that he received at Walter Reed available to everyone who becomes sick with coronavirus. But he doesn't explain how this will happen. He hails it as a cure for the disease – a claim that not even the manufacturers of the drug make for it. A therapeutic, yes, maybe – but a cure?

Just need to say one other thing, and it is about the President's colour. No, it is not that he is looking pale and drawn. Anything but. I don't know who is doing his *maquillage*, but the foundation base? Honestly, one shade darker and he'd be in the same trouble that Justin Trudeau got into for wearing black-face. Years and years ago, I was in Blackpool to present our live coverage of the party conferences (something we did then). It was me, Huw Edwards and Sheena McDonald. There was this dear old lady whom the BBC had hired to do the make-up for us. She only had one colour foundation base, and it was for the palest, most lilywhite English complexion – which broadly speaking is not my skin tone. She finished making me up and I looked as though I had seen several ghosts, while suffering from severe anaemia. Donald Trump in this video looks as though someone has held him by his feet and dipped him in toffee.

Whoever wins in November will be the oldest president ever to hold office. That means this debate between Kamala Harris and Mike Pence has generated more interest than any televised vice-presidential debate in history. The old line about the VP being a heartbeat away from the Oval Office has never seemed more pertinent. All the more surprising that both of them were allowed to escape scrutiny. I mean, sometimes not even the most cursory nod in the direction of the question that the moderator – who is decidedly moderate – has posed. This is incredibly frustrating to watch. Why doesn't the presenter, Susan Page, the Washington bureau chief from the newspaper *USA Today* get in there and say, 'Yeah, very interesting – but that wasn't what I asked you.' It's frankly hopeless. Pence doesn't attempt to answer the question about why the death rate in the US is so much higher than most countries; Harris does a total body swerve around the issue of packing the Supreme Court to restore the balance if Amy Coney Barrett is confirmed.

I can't help thinking this might come back to bite the Democrats. Why can't you give an answer to that question? Remember millions voted for Donald Trump in 2016 for his promise to appoint conservative justices. If Dems leave an impression they might 'fix' the courts, isn't that going to galvanise many of these people to come out once again to vote for Donald Trump to stop that happening? I wouldn't be surprised if the Trump campaign seize on this.

Both circle each other warily. They are respectful, and when Pence does overstep the mark, and tries to talk over Kamala Harris, she very firmly says, 'I am speaking.' She is a brilliant prosecutor, but what is noticeable this evening is that she is pulling her punches. There is plenty that Pence says that you feel she wants to pick apart. But she doesn't. This is the dilemma for smart women in public life and that ghastly word 'likeability'. She's all too aware that on social media, and then the wider media, they will start picking over her performance and ponder whether she was too aggressive; too shrill; too bossy. All words that would never attach to a male politician. So it looks like her MO tonight is to deliver good soundbites attacking the President and his record, without getting into a brawl. She smiles a lot, but you sense there is an inner rage at what she is having to let go. But it feels as though Pence is occupying similar territory.

On the Covid crisis, Kamala Harris delivers a perfect soundbite when she says this is the greatest failure in American history; Pence retorts that from day one all the President has cared about is the well-being of the American people. Both make their points and move on. That is the tenor of the next 90 minutes. This has none of the fireworks and histrionics of last week's presidential debate.

Harris, the product of Asian and Jamaican parents, looked like a cricketer who'd walked onto the pitch with instructions from the captain not to flash wildly at balls outside the off stump – and don't try to knock the ball out of the ground, just play a straight bat and nudge the odd single here and there. Be more Boycott than Botham.

Both sides will claim their person won. More likely (to change my laboured sporting metaphors) it was a nil-nil draw. This was at least a more serious, policy-focused debate – the kind that's been notably absent from the campaign so far. Almost a throwback to a bygone age when civility and politics could walk alongside each other.

I could imagine that in a Covid-free time both of them might have repaired to the green-room afterwards and had a big glass of wine, agreeing that that went OK. She held her end up; he held his. And then, seeing as Kamala Harris and Mike Pence might be the standard bearers for their parties in 2024, agreeing that they will do it all again in four years' time – but then without the kid gloves on. A scoreless draw is probably a result both will settle for. But it's hard to see that this debate will in any way change the dynamics of the presidential race. And if it doesn't change the dynamics of anything, then it's a win for Joe Biden, who is already ahead in the polls.

And how many vice-presidential debates have changed a race? The most memorable intervention ever in a VP debate was when the experienced Democratic senator, Lloyd Benson, gave the young Republican, Dan Quayle, a right thrashing. Quayle says he has all the experience that John F. Kennedy had when he became president. Benson is lying in wait with a brilliantly honed putdown. Addressing the younger man he retorts: 'Senator, I served with Jack Kennedy. I knew Jack Kennedy. Jack Kennedy was a friend of mine. Senator, you're no Jack Kennedy.' Boom!

It is rolled out every time debate season comes around as one of the best put-downs of all time. It was. But did it have any impact on the 1988 race between the Democrat Michael Dukakis and his Republican rival George H.W. Bush? None whatsoever. Bush totally crushed Dukakis.

Anyway, the highpoint of the debate tonight has without doubt been the arrival of a very black fly in Mike Pence's very white hair. For two minutes it is impossible to listen to a word he says as the fly sits there quite happily. Social media comes out of the somnambulant slumber it has drifted into as the two have droned on purposefully. Of all the tweets one of my favourites was this is the only black friend that Mike Pence has. And another, given the Vice-President's views on abortion, has the fly saying, 'I've laid eggs, but you're going to have to let them go full term – your rules not mine.' No, I don't retweet either.

8 October

Astonishing news coming out of Michigan. The FBI has arrested 13 men who were part of a right-wing militia, and who've apparently been under surveillance after hatching a plot to kidnap and put on 'trial' the Democratic state governor, Gretchen Whitmer. She has clashed publicly with the President over the restrictions she introduced to keep people safe. Early on in the outbreak it led to Donald Trump urging his supporters on Twitter to 'liberate the states'. The states that needed liberating are those, it should be said, run by Democrats. And a group of bearded and heavily armed men, called the Wolverine Watchmen, duly turned up at the Michigan state house. It seemed a terrifying foretaste of how violence could very easily erupt.

According to prosecutors the conspirators discussed recruiting a force of 200 to storm the state capital building in Lansing and take hostages, but later switched to a plan to kidnap Whitmer at her vacation home. At a news conference, Whitmer accused Trump of fomenting political extremism, citing his comments in last week's debate with Joe Biden when he told members of the Proud Boys to 'stand back and stand by'. She said, 'When our leaders meet with, encourage and fraternise with domestic terrorists they legitimise their actions, and they are complicit.'

And the President's first response to news that the FBI has foiled an attempt by domestic terrorists to kidnap a democratically elected official? He says she is a terrible governor.

There is one other area where the President has been characteristically blunt. At 07.30 an email drops into my inbox from the non-partisan Commission on Presidential Debates announcing that next Thursday's debate – which had been due to be held in Miami – will instead be virtual, not in person, as a result of the President's illness. The Biden camp responds immediately that it will accept the new arrangements. The President is due on Fox Business, where he will give his reaction. And it is to the point – both about the format and the chosen moderator. 'No, I'm not gonna waste my time on a personal debate. Sit behind a computer, ridiculous. They cut you off. He's a never Trumper. I'm not doing a virtual debate. They didn't even tell us about the debate.'

This would make total sense if Donald Trump was sitting on a handsome winning margin over Joe Biden, and just wanted to pursue a risk-free glide path towards polling day. But this looks as though he is cutting off his nose to spite his face. Does he think that this is going to force the Commission to go back and revert to the original in-person format? I am left wondering whether the campaign might strike a more conciliatory tone – after all everyone recognises that, yes, there are still three weeks to go, but if Donald Trump is going to force a reset in this race, then a TV debate, with maybe 80 million people tuning in, is the way to do that. Conciliatory? Forget it. Here is the official statement from the campaign manager:

President Trump won the first debate despite a terrible and biased moderator in Chris Wallace, and everybody knows it. For the swamp creatures at the Presidential Debate Commission to now rush to Joe Biden's defence by unilaterally cancelling an in-person debate is pathetic. That's not what debates are about or how they're done. Here are the facts: President Trump will have posted multiple negative tests prior to the debate, so there is no need for this unilateral declaration. The safety of all involved can easily be achieved without cancelling a chance for voters to see both candidates go head to head. We'll pass on this sad excuse to bail out Joe Biden and do a rally instead.

This needs a bit of unpacking. Now let's begin with the opening statement that the President won the first debate. The polls following the first debate show Biden widening his margin over Trump considerably. Indeed, show me any polling that says Trump won the first debate. Secondly why re-litigate the referee, Chris Wallace, as though he makes any difference or made any difference to what unfolded? I could continue to go through this statement, deconstructing it point by point – but that would be to ignore the more important truth; to fail to separate the wheat from the chaff.

Bill Stepien, Trump's campaign manager, has not drafted this to persuade the organising body to change its mind; he hasn't written it for Donald Trump's supporters; it is not designed for wider public consumption. No, this is written for Donald Trump himself, in what Stepien thinks will be suitably Trumpian language and phraseology that the President will approve of. Though not quite as exaggerated, this is what we saw a week earlier from the White House physician at Walter Reed – when he said he'd wanted to keep the tone upbeat and didn't want to concede that the President needed oxygen. That was for Donald Trump.

There used to be talk of the 'grown ups' who would tell the President in plain language what they thought. Now it looks as though he is surrounded by 'yes men' who will echo back to the Commander in Chief exactly what he wants to hear – whether it is smart or stupid, whether it helps him or not.

Biden on hearing this seems bemused – but his campaign quickly goes from throwing hands up in horror at the latest move from the Trump campaign to a blasé shrug of the shoulders. Fine – if you don't want this, we will go our own way and go ahead with a town hall style conversation with one of the TV networks instead next Thursday. At which point, the Trump campaign seems to want to engage and come up with a workable alternative, and demands an additional debate. Team Biden has moved on.

By behaving the way it has, all the Trump campaign has achieved is to ensure that there won't be a second TV debate – in any form. They must be high fiving in Wilmington, Delaware. Another trip hazard has been removed from Joe Biden's path.

There are some pretty rare words of criticism from the Senate majority leader, Mitch McConnell, who in appearance is rather tortoise like. He says he hasn't been to the White House for months because of their lax and cavalier attitude towards wearing masks and maintaining social distancing. And he says some people have 'got what they deserved'.

This is a man who weighs his words carefully, and is extremely deliberative. He is also normally excruciatingly loyal to the President. Some are applying the rats/sinking ship metaphor to these comments. I'm not sure that characterisation is correct. More likely it is the majority leader giving licence to other Republican senators to break with the President if they want to.

Worth remembering that Mitch McConnell's prime concern is not the re-election of Donald Trump; his focus is to keep Republican control of the Senate – and latest polls suggest that may be slipping away. If Trump has to be the victim to keep his caucus intact, so be it.

10 October

Donald Trump is making his first appearance in front of an audience since his illness. He is going to speak to black and Latino voters. He will be on the White House balcony; they will be on the grass in front of him. The President speaks for a relatively short period of time, for him – around 15–20 minutes. But he seems raring to go, and again makes light of the disease.

11 October, Orlando, Florida

Very exciting. Today am heading to Florida, ahead of Donald Trump's first post-Covid rally. I get out of the wardrobe my wheel-on roller bag, and there in the suitcase is my press pass and lanyard from early March and Bernie Sanders's Super Tuesday event in New Hampshire. I realise I haven't been on a US internal flight since the beginning of March. Seven months. Incredible. When I moved into my apartment I thought I would barely spend a night there. The reality? I have barely left it.

Some important polling from CBS – because these are the first to be conducted since Trump's Covid diagnosis. Leave aside the headline number, it's the qualitative stuff that interests me. In three key states – Michigan, Nevada and Iowa – voters feel President Trump set a bad example during his illness, handling things in a way they call 'irresponsible'.

These people tell the pollsters his behaviour made them feel 'angry' rather than 'confident', and many even say they were *offended*.

Most voters in Michigan think the Trump administration's policies are making the outbreak worse. And another toxic finding for the President: large majorities feel that he received better medical treatment than they would have done if they became sick.

Meanwhile Joe Biden holds a large advantage over Mr Trump on being seen as someone who cares about others, and he draws more favourable ratings for how he handles himself personally. And, in line with other recent polls, they say he would be better on handling the outbreak.

The United Airlines flight to Orlando is rammed. Dulles is heaving. I feel I am not in the least bit mentally equipped to cope with so many people in such a confined space. Panic attack would be overstating it, but I am not comfortable having so many people around me. We are flying first class, which will afford us a bit more space. On the plane I find I am sitting next to my friend and rival, Robert Moore from ITN. It feels good to be travelling again, and we swap gossip of the strange goings on in his organisation, and I entertain him with the latest intrigues from mine. We both roll our eyes at the hopelessness of both. Camaraderie combined with the competition is one of the great things about being on the road; about being a journalist.

And first class on United is really living up to the billing. Dinner consists of a little clear goodie bag. And in the bag is a small bottle of water, a packet of pretzels that came runners-up in the 'smallest packet of pretzels ever made' category – and a dry biscuit. A feast for a king. Morgan had messaged John and me earlier in the day asking whether we wanted her to pick up a sandwich for us. We both said no and, having seen the teeny-weeny pretzel packet and dry biscuit, are now regretting it.

It takes us 45 minutes to find the car-hire location, as the one in the terminal we have arrived in has closed because of Covid – but without any signposting to say so. Then when we get to Avis they have no record of our booking. We queue, and eventually get an SUV that is big enough to take all our kit. And clearly the previous occupant had chain-smoked his way across Florida in what must have been a pretty dense fog in the car. It reeks.

The hotel is lovely, and one I have stayed in before, and we check in tired and hungry. The receptionist hands us a leaflet and charmingly and slowly takes us through the options: what we can get from room service, the restaurant and bar options, where breakfast is served, before giving us our room keys. 'So what's available now?' we ask. 'Oh, nothing,' he says nonchalantly, 'everything is now just closed. But there's a takeaway pizza place a couple of blocks from here.'

It's great to be back on the road. I think.

12 October, The Villages, Sumter County, Florida

This is America's largest retirement community. And when I say big, I mean humungous. Let me just dazzle you with stats, because I am sure you are thinking a glorified old people's home. No, you're not even close. The Villages has a population of 130,000 people. It covers 35 square miles – which is bigger than the city of Southampton – and it sprawls over five zip codes. It is manicured to within an inch of its life. There are activities galore. You could live out your days here and never see a black face, and the only Latinos you'll come across will be mowing your lawn or cleaning your houses. It is Disneyworld for the elderly. In the main town square and on the esplanade you cannot escape the piped, ersatz music. Golf leisurewear seems *de rigueur*. I'm sorry, but it seems utterly soul-sapping.

Nearly everyone moves around in golf carts – and not just generic golf carts, often highly branded ones. Some looking like they are vintage cars, others like tuk-tuks, and some even wannabe sports cars. And many of them are bedecked with Trump/Pence paraphernalia, others with Biden/Harris logos. In 2016 Sumter County voted massively for Donald Trump. He won overwhelmingly. But in 2020? Even the Republicans I speak to are not exactly exuding confidence. One old boy – a staunch Republican – tells me a lot of his friends are refusing to look him in the eye over which way they're going to vote. He's convinced they're going to vote Democrat. Even the head of the Republican Party association in the Villages sounds as though he is going through the motions.

The latest polls suggest there has been a massive turnaround in the grey vote. The over-65s seem to have had enough, and one survey I read had Biden leading the President by 2:1. If the old people in Florida are moving in that direction, then Donald Trump will lose this state. And if he loses the sunshine state it is hard to see any path to the 270 electoral college votes that he must secure to win a second term. It is as blunt as that. For Donald Trump it is MUST win.

And that will explain why you can't turn on a television in Florida without being assailed by Trump or Biden TV ads. So far – and we are still three weeks from polling day – the two campaigns have spent around $200 million in Florida alone on commercials. That is probably four times what Labour and Tories spent combined in the whole UK general election campaign in 2019. And what the Dems and Republicans are spending is just in one state.

It is an hour and a half drive across the citrus groves of Florida to get to where Trump is holding his event. His rally at Sanford International Airport (I wonder what international destinations Sanford Airport serves) gives no sign that he is under pressure – or, more importantly, that he has just emerged from hospital with ill effects having needed a mass of drugs to restore his health. His energy levels are formidable. And the thing that people forget is that he is an entertainer. The thousands who've queued for hours to listen to him haven't done so because they want to listen to some treatise on health policy for the twenty-first century. They've come because he is entertaining and funny. And he doesn't disappoint with his promise to come into the audience and give everyone a big kiss. Just as well hardly anyone is wearing a mask.

And you can see how much he loves being in front of a cheering crowd. This does for him what spinach does for Popeye.

He promises even to kiss all the men. And he comes on stage to 'Macho, Macho Man'. And leaves dancing to 'YMCA', hopefully giving the band members of Village People an unexpected pre-election boost. Maybe the campaign feels it needs to do more to lock in the gay vote.

I fall into conversation with one of the vendors who is flogging Trump-branded tat. He is a general contractor on a dairy farm. But he thought about a year ago he'd see if he could sell the odd T-shirt and hat. He now has three stalls, and reckons he's now making a profit of around $20,000 a week. The presidential election can't come late enough for him.

We set up to do our live report for the *Ten O'Clock News* adjacent to these stalls – it makes a vibrant backdrop, with Trump flags fluttering. A tall thin guy comes up to us with a look of disgust on his face. 'Have you noticed how it's only you guys in the media who are wearing masks?' he says. We are too close to transmission for me to get into verbal fisticuffs with him, though I want to. We just smile and ignore him. How can us wearing masks cause so much upset and distress to him? Why has he gone out of his way to upbraid us about it?

Like so much to do with Donald Trump, much of it feels totally normal, when it is all totally frigging nuts. Crowds are pouring into a roped-off area of the airfield. Cranes have been brought in, from which hang gigantic US flags. Dusk is falling. It feels like an evening kick-off football match. But of course in the UK and the rest of the US crowds aren't pouring in anywhere for anything. Our countries are flocking-free zones. They're not allowed. Yet the man whose prime responsibility is to keep Americans safe, something he swore an oath on the bible to do at his inauguration, is going against all CDC advice and bringing thousands together without social distancing and with few masks. If you stop and think about it for more than a nano-second you realise how crazy this is.

13 October, Miami

We drive to Miami – it's about three hours from Orlando – and record Americast when we arrive. Biden is also in the area. He speaks to a drive-in event in Broward County, where the audience are socially distanced in their cars. And Biden went on a familiar attack: Trump had been reckless in dismissing the threat Covid had posed to this at-risk population. 'To Donald Trump, you're expendable. You're forgettable. You're virtually nobody. That's how he sees seniors. That's how he sees you.' And Biden said the only senior Trump cares about is himself.

There is an odd social media post from Donald Trump – it is the 'Biden for President' logo, but with the 'P' crossed out – and it contains a bunch of gaga-looking old people. In other words, Biden should be a resident in an old people's home. Am sure the creative team thought it was clever. But is it smart? If you want to win in Florida, surely you don't make the elderly the punchline of a joke.

Trump is at a rally in Pennsylvania tonight. I know his book was *The Art of the Deal*, and that he sells himself as the super-clever businessman who always keeps the other side guessing – but I think he would make a terrible poker player. Donald Trump can't help telling you what he thinks. He wears his heart on his sleeve. If he's frustrated, you know it. He is the most transparent politician I have ever reported on. And tonight in PA it's clear he's been given a detailed presentation on the state of the polls, and where he is most vulnerable in this state that he carried in 2016. As I've written previously, the migration of white, college-educated women away from him has been one of the most notable trends since 2016. And so he makes this not ever so subtle pitch. 'So can I ask you to do me a favour? Suburban women, will you please like me? I saved your damn neighbourhood, OK?'

I'm not sure it's the best chat-up line I have ever heard.

15 October, Miami

Looks like the Trump campaign has an October Surprise to unleash on Joe Biden. Or let me put that another way: the Rupert Murdoch-owned *New York Post* has an October Surprise. Seeing the banner headline 'BIDEN SECRET E-MAILS', I feel I am being transported back to the 2016 election, but these aren't Joe Biden's emails, they are – allegedly – from a laptop belonging to Joe Biden's son, Hunter. He's the one who became a director of the Ukrainian energy company, Burisma – a position that he has since said would probably not have been offered to him had he not been Joe Biden's son.

There is a lot about it which makes me rather uneasy. For a start there is the 'so what' element to the story. Last time I looked, Hunter Biden's name is not on the ballot. The newspaper alleges that he took his laptop into a repair shop in Delaware, and forgot all about it. Then the owner of the shop had a peek at what was on it. And when he saw the list of emails he alerts the FBI. But they weren't interested, and then somewhere along the line it ends up in the hands of Steve Bannon (who as I have noted is facing federal charges over misuse of border wall funds) and Rudy Giuliani, the President's personal lawyer. Hmm.

There is more. The *Washington Post* reports that the CIA has briefed the President about its concerns that when Giuliani was investigating

Hunter Biden in Ukraine he was being played by a Russian agent. So the provenance of the story looks decidedly dodgy. The nearest thing to a 'smoking gun' is apparently an exchange between father and son in which Joe Biden agrees to meet a Burisma executive – but there is no proof that the meeting ever took place, and certainly no allegation that US policy changed towards Ukraine in any way. And all the *Post* offers are screengrab photos, which could easily have been doctored. There is enough to cause concern that this is genuine fake news – if that is not an oxymoron.

The question we ask in situations like this is 'Does the story stand up?' This one doesn't seem to, so we give it a wide berth, to the fury of Trump supporters who assail me on Twitter. It looks like the social media companies regard it similarly – but they go one step further and ban retweeting of it, and take the drastic measure of briefly shutting down the *New York Post*'s official account. The story then morphs into one not about Hunter Biden, but about Twitter and Facebook behaving like 'big brother'.

This evening we have the 'duelling town halls'. Tonight we should have had the second presidential debate between Joe Biden and Donald Trump, but after the President pulled the plug on plans for it to be held virtually we have, instead, two rival networks holding their own separate town halls with the two presidential candidates.

Inevitably most eyes are on Donald Trump, who is up the road from where we are staying in Miami. And the first thing that strikes me is that he makes not a single mention of the Hunter Biden 'bombshell', the hold-the-front-page scandal. Not that he is given much opportunity.

The President is kept on a tight leash by the NBC presenter, Savannah Guthrie – who does a brilliant job. Never aggressive or hectoring, she is just very persistent in a conversational way. Broadcast journalism students should watch it, as it is an exemplar of how to do tough without the need to be a Rottweiler. Her best line comes when she is asking Trump why he retweeted a conspiracy theory that Seal Team 6 didn't really 'get' Osama Bin Laden (that, of course, happened on Obama's watch). When he says: 'That was a retweet, that was an opinion of somebody, and that was a retweet. I'll put it out there, people can decide for themselves, I don't take a position,' Guthrie responds: 'I don't get that. You're the president – you're not like someone's crazy uncle who can just retweet whatever.' Within a very short time the hashtag 'CrazyUncleDonald' is trending. He also refuses to disavow the far right QAnon conspiracy theorists, saying he knows nothing about them, though adds they are strongly opposed to paedophilia – unlike the rest of us, of course.

There are a few other notable moments. The President cannot – or will not – say whether he was tested for Covid on the day of the first presidential debate. Given the salience of this question, and given the repeated demands for this information, I can't help thinking that if – if – the President had tested negative on that day of the debate in Cleveland, you bet he would have said so.

Another striking moment is when he seems to confirm the *New York Times* report on his taxes. Yes, he does owe $400 million – but he won't say to whom – and says it is just like us having a mortgage of $100,000 – it represents a small proportion of his wealth.

The Biden town hall has fewer highs, and fewer lows. To be honest it is rather dull. Biden's most awkward moment is when he refuses to answer the question about whether he will try to pack the Supreme Court if Amy Coney Barrett is confirmed. It seems a very inadequate response.

Anyway I know you'll want to know how we spent the day. It has been studying the Latino vote. And what better opportunity than today, when one of the most prominent Trump supporters, Carlos Gavidia, has organised a boat parade for the President along Miami's famous inland waterway. And because we want to have autonomy over what we film, when we join the parade and when we leave it, we have to charter our own vessel. I know: work, work, work.

It turns out that Eric Trump is on the lead vessel, so we then have a rather comedic moment where the skipper of our boat is trying to manoeuvre to the prow of the vessel where Eric Trump is standing. It is the first time I have done a 'doorstep' interview between boats, which I fear could easily result in us both ending up in the drink.

This is Donald Trump's Hispanic armada, making a splash against Miami's famous skyline. Around 200 boats – it is chaotic, noisy and exuberant. If every election throws up a new way of campaigning, this is 2020's innovation – the boat parade. Both Republicans and Democrats are pouring millions into ads for the Hispanic TV market. Even on Spanish language stations there's no escape from the election.

Florida is where the election could be won and lost, and Joe Biden was here earlier in the week. And though he has a spring in his step as he comes out on stage, polls suggest he is doing way worse among Latino voters than Hillary Clinton did four years ago. But why? The number two in the Democratic party for the crucial Miami Dade district is Maria Lopez. She gives a brutally candid answer, saying that the Trump playbook has been nothing short of genius. She says for the past three and a half years the President has been characterising the Dems as a socialist party. A party of the hard left. And what Lopez says the average migrant from the Cuban, Venezuelan and Honduran diaspora hears is a message that what they fled from as refugees might be coming to the United States if Biden wins the election.

I ask her if this is hurting the Democrats. She says it is. I ask her does she believe the polls suggesting the Dems are ahead in Florida. She says she doesn't. When I ask what would she say if Bernie Sanders, or the New York firebrand Alexandria Ocasio-Cortez offered to come and canvas in Miami Dade, she says she would say no, thank you very much. Her body language and her words are not offering the same confidence that the campaign is trying to project. Nothing like. This is one of those rare interviews you do during an election campaign where you get something much more valuable than pre-packaged soundbites – you get a brutally candid assessment.

After about an hour at sea, the skies blacken and the rain lashes down. As these Trump boater voters discovered today, the climate in Florida changes fast. Predicting whether it will be sunshine or heavy rain come 3 November is decidedly risky. For both parties.

16 October, Miami

Looks like the President has not overly impressed the Republican senator for Nebraska, Ben Sasse. He's been on a call and said this about Trump: 'The way he kisses dictators' butts. I mean, the way he ignores that the Uighurs are in literal concentration camps in Xinjiang. Right now, he hasn't lifted a finger on behalf of the Hong-Kongers,' he said. 'The United States now regularly sells out our allies under his leadership, the way he treats women, spends like a drunken sailor. The ways I criticise President Obama for that kind of spending, I've criticised President Trump for as well. He mocks evangelicals behind closed doors. His family has treated the presidency like a business opportunity. He's flirted with white supremacists.'

18 October, Rehobeth, Delaware

I have come away for 24 hours to stay with very well-connected, Democrat-supporting friends. Rehobeth is on the ocean – all broadwalks and candy stores. Our friends live a little to the north in a beautiful enclave. It is stunning. We talk politics and families pretty much non-stop. He is super-smart and has worked in previous admin-istrations at a very senior level. He's optimistic about Biden's chances, but not overly.

I am starting to feel vindicated in deciding to give the Hunter Biden/laptop story a wide berth. The *New York Times* is reporting that there is deep unease at the *New York Post* over its publication, and the two journalists whose byline appeared on the article didn't want their names included. Also it's emerged that Rudy Giuliani tried to give the story to Fox News, but they wanted more details about the provenance of the story and the authenticity of the hard drive before they would run it. So Giuliani took it to a Murdoch-owned newspaper, instead of a Murdoch-owned TV network. It all feels very murky, dodgy as hell. Though that isn't preventing Republicans claiming it is the smoking gun that incriminates Joe Biden.

Stories like this are a nightmare for credible news organisations. If you don't cover the story you are accused of censorship, of suppressing the news – and when it becomes the single issue of conversation for Republicans, then you are, sort of, failing to cover their campaign. But if you do cover it, then no matter how many caveats you insert, no matter how many eyebrows you raise, by airing it on primetime TV you are giving the story a degree of credibility as 'a thing'.

By way of comparison, four years ago when the FBI reopened the email investigation into Hillary Clinton just a couple of weeks before the election, that was huge. Epic. Whether it was fair or not didn't matter; whether it showed anything – in the end it didn't – didn't matter either. The fact that the FBI had done this was just a massive event – and arguably *the* event in the 2016 election. But this isn't that.

19 October, Rehobeth, Delaware

Donald Trump is holding a call with campaign staff which we journalists have been allowed to join. It is a chance for the President to
tell the teams on the ground, who are straining every sinew, that the
promised land of election victory is still within sight. The President is
suitably upbeat. He says things are turning around, and though early
voting might favour the Democrats, there will be a red wave on election day itself, when Republicans will turn out in their millions to
vote him back.

But then he starts talking about coronavirus and he launches into
a full-frontal assault on Dr Anthony Fauci, deriding him as 'a disaster'
and claiming 'people are tired of hearing Fauci and all these idiots'.

It seems what has triggered the President is Dr Fauci's appearance
on CBS's *60 Minutes* the night before, in which the country's leading
infectious disease expert said he was 'absolutely not' surprised Trump
had contracted the coronavirus himself. The 79-year-old pointed to
the 'super-spreader' event that had taken place at the White House at
the end of September, when next to no one was wearing a mask.

Fauci also told CBS the White House had been controlling and
limiting his media appearances. This too clearly riled the President,
who tweeted that he 'seems to get more airtime than anybody since
the late, great Bob Hope. All I ask of Tony is that he make better decisions. He said "no masks & let China in".'

This is all very puzzling. A week ago, the Trump campaign was
trying to leverage Fauci's popularity and trustworthiness by including him in an advertisement (to the doctor's absolute fury); now the
President is piling into someone who enjoys much higher approval
ratings than he does. It also does one other thing. It puts the focus back
on the President's handling of coronavirus, at a time when new cases
are spiralling again and the death toll in the US has topped 220,000.

The debates commission has come back with new rules for Thursday's final presidential showdown in Nashville, Tennessee. After the Cleveland food-fight, the rules will change. When one candidate has their two minutes to give an answer, the microphone of the other person will be cut. The unenviable task of keeping order will fall to Kristen Welker, an NBC White House correspondent and weekend anchor, who has been chosen as the moderator. She is a lovely and smart woman. But the new rules bring much snarling from the Trump campaign. Donald Trump is on the attack. She's a radical Democrat, she's always screaming questions at me, she's no good, he tweets. All of which is odd, because when she was made an anchor at the beginning of the year he said the network had made 'a very wise decision'.

The campaign is also going after the neutral body which runs the debates. 'President Trump is committed to debating Joe Biden regardless of last-minute rule changes from the biased commission in their latest attempt to provide advantage to their favoured candidate,' reads the opening paragraph of the Trump campaign response.

The President is also ramping up his language against Joe Biden. He is demanding that his Attorney General, Bill Barr, charge him with corruption over the emails between him and his son Hunter. 'We've got to get the AG to act, and act fast,' he tells Fox News. 'This is major corruption,' he declares, without saying what is corrupt.

Joe Biden, though, has been nowhere to be seen. And according to the draft schedule we get – sent on a 'not for broadcast' basis – he's not doing any campaigning on Tuesday, or Wednesday either. He's staying in Wilmington, prepping for Thursday's debate. Again, the contrast between him and Donald Trump could not be more stark. The President is speaking at multiple rallies per day; he is stopping to give press interviews; the crowds he's attracting are huge, and the tweets incessant. But Biden is sticking to his socially distanced and time distanced public events, happy for the distinction to be drawn. Seems a big gamble to me to leave so much of the stage to Donald Trump.

20 October, Nashville, Tennessee

Two weeks to go. Just two bloody weeks! It seemed at the outset that the campaign would stretch with infinite elasticity into the future. But now we are getting to the end – what Sir Alex Ferguson would call squeaky bum time. Am writing this on the United flight into Nashville, with the world's smallest packet of pretzels and a dry biscuit for dinner again, and all washed down with a small bottle of water. Yum, you really can't beat air travel within the US.

Nashville is such a cool city – the music city. We film at a place called the Nashville Palace. It is not on the main drag, Broadway, in the centre of the city, where most of the country-and-western bars are clustered. This is a few miles out on a strip mall. It is unprepossessing. Untouristy. Basic. And the music is just phenomenal. There seems to be a revolving cast of characterful cowboys who wander up on stage, pick up a guitar, nod an acknowledgement to a musician who is already there, and then make a harmonised sound that suggests they've been in rehearsal for weeks. Confession: when I was 19, I went busking in Paris – so I can play the guitar a little bit. These guys are out of this world.

The manageress of the bar forces me to drink a shot of 'moonshine'. I am rendered dumb for the next five minutes. My mouth is opening and closing, but no sound is coming out. There is a fire at the back of my throat that needs extinguishing.

A new New York Times/Siena College poll has Biden at 50 per cent and Trump at 41 per cent – so no big shifts. And while I am recovering from my brush with moonshine, I am reading about Donald Trump's rally in Erie, Pennsylvania. Sometimes you can't believe a word he says. Sometimes he is disarmingly honest. Tonight it is the latter. He tells his audience that he is only there because the pandemic has upended everything, and seen his poll position decline.

'I wasn't coming to Erie. I mean, I have to be honest. There was no way I was coming,' Trump told his audience. 'I didn't have to.' But then he went on: 'I would have called you and said, "Hey, Erie, you know, if you have a chance, get out and vote." We had this thing won … and then we got hit with the plague, and I had to go back to work. Hello, Erie, may I please have your vote?'

21 October, Nashville, Tennessee

I want to describe what I think is a genuine and unconscionable moral outrage. The Trump administration as part of its zero-tolerance policy on immigration decided that it would separate mothers and their children when they reached the border. Cages had been built to 'house' the illegal immigrants. My purpose here is not to criticise the policy – people can make up their own minds on whether it is ever justified to separate mothers from their babies.

No, the unimaginable, horrifying part of this is that the policy was enacted without the bureaucratic preparation necessary to implement it. And so, two years on from the policy being abandoned and a court ordering the administration to reunite families who'd been separated at the US–Mexico border, the parents of 545 children still can't be found. That's according to a court document filed on Tuesday by the US Justice Department and the American Civil Liberties Union. So 545 youngsters have been made orphans by the American state. It is a terrible stain on a country famously built by immigrants.

To get access to the campus where tomorrow's debate will be held I have to undergo a Covid test. A testing facility has been set up near one of Nashville's famous landmarks – a life-size recreation of the Parthenon, built at the end of the nineteenth century for the Nashville exposition. The testing clinic is being run by a local healthcare company, HCA. It is so unbelievably efficient that it gives a glimpse of what life could be like pre-vaccine. I arrive, fill in various forms, am tested, and come out with a result – negative – in half an hour. They are processing hundreds of people a day. Henry Ford would be proud of the production line they have established.

By coincidence, our daughter Anna is undergoing something similar in London. She has had a bad headache and a bit of a dry cough, so is going to get tested as well. She's told her result will take 2–5 days.

22 October, Nashville, Tennessee

There is always so much drama with Donald Trump. It's emerged that he walked out of his big set-piece interview with *60 Minutes* that will air on Sunday, taking exception to the line of questioning being pursued by the veteran anchor, Lesley Stahl. Not only does he stomp off, he gets the White House to release its own video of the interview to justify his decision. It shows the President as prickly and defensive, and aggrieved that he is treated so much more harshly than Joe Biden.

When he arrives in Nashville, Donald Trump comes to the hotel where we are staying. I have friends in the city who know someone who is attending. Lunch at the Marriott with the President has a price-tag of $250,000 per person. Let no one question my $12 expense claim for my chicken Caesar.

The debate is being chaired this time by Kristen Welker, whom I know from the White House – she is part of the brilliant NBC team.

I send her an email wishing her luck, and I say I hope she will enjoy the experience. In terms of presentation she is very inexperienced, and Trump has been doing his best to undermine her before the debate, saying she is a crazy Democrat and always screaming questions. In my experience she is always carefully modulated and scrupulously polite. I cannot imagine how nerve-shredding a moment like this is going to be, particularly given what happened in the first debate. But as she introduces the two candidates there is no sign of unease. She is poised and in command.

Joe Biden emerges onto the stage masked; the President maskless. That's identical to the first debate, but this is altogether more restrained – and all the better for it. Yes, the shouting is replaced by a series of emoji faces – eye rolls, mock indignation, derisive laughter – but the exchanges are still sharp. The President claims coronavirus is turning a corner, and that Americans are learning to live with it. Quick as a flash Biden counters that Americans are dying with it.

The President goes after the Biden family, taking aim at the former vice-president's son Hunter and the money he had made abroad; the money the family had made. Before the debate got underway the Trump campaign announced that Hunter Biden's disgruntled former business partner would be a guest of the President at the debate. A repeat tactic from four years ago – when Donald Trump invited a group of women who'd accused Bill Clinton of sexual assault to be a destabilising force for Hillary Clinton. During this debate the President said the American people demanded answers as he repeated a slew of allegations about money that Hunter Biden had pocketed.

But Biden wasn't going to take any lectures from the President about transparency, when Donald Trump still hasn't produced his tax returns. 'What have you got to hide?' Biden demanded of his rival. And went through a list of questions the President doesn't want to answer about his own financial affairs.

Joe Biden is chugging along effectively, but then the subject turns to climate change, an issue that Democrats love to talk about. But the Democratic candidate says that under his administration there would be a 'transition from the oil industry' to combat climate change.

Trump is lethal. He pounces on this. The Democrats want to kill off the oil industry, he charges. He asks the people of Texas, Oklahoma and Pennsylvania (where there is a sizeable fracking industry) whether they are listening. Immediately after the debate, Biden aides are into damage limitation mode. What their candidate had meant was that he wanted to transition away from oil subsidies, not away from oil itself. Before boarding the plane to return to Delaware, Biden makes comments to reporters. Trump has scored a bullseye, and I bet his campaign team are going into overdrive working out how to make the most of this.

Joe Biden has sought to portray himself as the healer and unifier; while Donald Trump sees himself as the outsider who is there to fix America's broken politics. I go to a bar in Nashville where Trump supporters have gathered. Most striking is how empty it is. Three weeks ago for the first debate it was rammed, with a few hundred people there. Tonight there are around a dozen. But it is interesting talking to those who are there. They think Trump has done well, that he was infinitely better than he'd been three weeks ago. But I didn't speak to one person who thought it would change anyone's mind, or make any difference to the outcome of the election.

23 October, Nashville, Tennessee

We have just recorded the podcast in my room, which is a good deconstruct of the debate. I am just about to finish the edit for my TV news piece when I get a message from Linda that Anna has tested positive, and is really upset. Nashville is feeling a long way away from North London right now. And it feeds into anxiety that Linda is feeling: she had met Anna for a sandwich on Monday, and then went to visit her 93-year-old mother on Wednesday. All very fraught. Aaarrghh, I am so done with this wretched disease.

24 October, Washington

Donald Trump is maintaining a punishing schedule of rally after rally. Starting the day in the Florida heat, and ending the night in the frigid cold of Wisconsin. His energy levels are unbelievable. The Trump campaign is trying to argue that this is 2016 all over again: behind in the polls, a late surge, the stage set for an improbable victory. And certainly Trump seems to have the bit between his teeth. He is campaigning hard. He is on form and on fire. But …

But there are bits of data which point in the opposite direction. And there is a gobsmacking chart I have seen on young people voting early. The assumption is that among 18–29-year-olds the likely split is possibly 4:1 Democrat to Republican. Let's just take Michigan.

In 2016, Trump won the 16 electoral college votes in Michigan by just over ten thousand votes – on a turnout of nearly five million electors. That is a cigarette paper's width of margin of victory. In that election around seven thousand 18–29-year-olds voted early. Today, ten days out, that number already stands at around 140,000. That is an increase of 2,000 per cent – so far. If most of those people are Democrats, already that has more than erased the margin of Trump's victory four years ago.

The President is railing against the media's coverage of coronavirus at a rally he's giving in North Carolina, insisting the corner is being turned. But this is a classic example of the rhetoric flying in the face

of the reality. Yesterday the US hit a new one-day record for new cases
– 84,000. There are currently 41,000 hospitalised. And more than 900
people died yesterday. And if you look at the trends, the arrows are
pointing upwards.

On one of the Sunday shows, the President's chief of staff, Mark
Meadows, commits the unusual offence of saying exactly what is on his
mind. Pressed about the rising numbers of new infections and what
the administration is going to do about it, Meadows blurts out, 'We're
not going to control the pandemic.' He tells the CNN interviewer,
'We are going to control the fact that we get vaccines, therapeutics and
other mitigations.' In other words, we're gearing up for the next stage
– but we're not going to do anything right now.

Am about to go to bed when I read that a whole slew of the VP's
officials has just tested positive, including his chief of staff, Mark Short,
and his body man – both of whom have been in close contact with
Mike Pence. As head of the White House coronavirus task force, Pence
won't need reminding that the recommendations he drew up are that
he should self-isolate for the next 14 days – in other words, miss the
rest of the campaign. But he has declared himself an essential worker,
obviating the necessity for that.

25 October

CBS polls are out in some of the key swing states, suggesting the race is
tightening. But they are in North Carolina, Florida and Georgia. Aside
from Florida, hardly top Democratic 'must win' states. More interesting
are other polls suggesting that Biden is widening his lead. But then I
go to fivethirtyeight.com, the best numbers and geek website – and the
astonishing thing is how static the polls are. Nothing has really changed.

Linda has tested negative, mercifully. One less thing to fret about.

27 October, Warm Springs, Georgia

One week to go and I am on an early morning flight to Atlanta. I am in first class and it is 07.30, and there is a young woman sitting in front of me on the Delta flight. She is late twenties or early thirties, smartly dressed, professional. Her long brown hair is scraped back in a makeshift bun. She asks one of the cabin crew for a coffee. And I think, great, that's exactly what I want as well. But the stewardess says that because of coronavirus they are not serving hot drinks. 'OK,' the young woman says without missing a beat, 'I'll have a red wine instead.' I have to stop myself from laughing out loud.

When I studied microeconomics at university there was the whole concept of 'substitute goods'. There were three conditions that had to be met. First, products had to have the same or similar performance characteristics, the products had to have the same or similar occasion for use, and products would be sold in the same geographic area. The classic is butter and margarine. Or a Big Mac and a Whopper. Or Pepsi and Coke. I had never thought of red wine and coffee as substitute goods. It is 07.30! And she drained a very large plastic tumbler of Cab before it was 08.00. Respect.

The reason that I am on my way to Georgia is that Joe Biden is heading here today. The thing about US elections is that although the country is huge, there are around 40 states that neither candidate bothers with because they are all either safely in the Democrat or Republican column. For over a quarter of a century Georgia has been a state that Democrats have not gone anywhere near because it has been safe-as-houses Republican. But in a sign of growing Biden campaign confidence their man is spending the day – with one week to go until polling day – stirring things up in this Southern state. The polls are incredibly encouraging, and his team believe it is there for the taking.

If Biden can win here, then we are looking at a really big Democratic Party victory next week. His first stop is in this two-horse town called Warm Springs. It is a place that time forgot. The hotel on Main Street looks like it hasn't been modernised in 50 years; the sign offering fudge, ice-cream and hand dipped cones is ancient, likewise the restaurant across the street where we had lunch. There is a stall near the gas station offering vine tomatoes and 'hot boiled peanuts', a local speciality. They are a treat I have tried once before – and, after one mouthful, vowed never again. And Joe Biden's reason for being here in the hills of rural Georgia is wrapped in the sepia tones of history and nothing to do with likely voting intentions in a week's time.

Warm Springs, about 60 miles due south of Atlanta, is where the great Democratic president of the New Deal, Franklin Delano Roosevelt, would come every year after he contracted polio. The springs were found to offer therapeutic relief from the pain and discomfort of the disease. He was diagnosed with this terrible condition in 1921, leaving him paralysed from the waist down. (My late mother was left disabled by polio a decade or so later when she was a girl.) Warm Springs gave him the belief to resume his political career. He would come here every year from 1924 (except 1942 when he might have been busy with America's involvement in the Second World War) until his death in 1945, to stay in what became known as the Little White House – a modest white, clapboard house on the edge of the town. And he established in Warm Springs the first sanatorium to help young children with polio.

And Joe Biden's message was also about healing – but this time America's divisions and broken politics. From here he went into Atlanta – a city that is really driving the Democrats' comeback in the state, and where the white, college-educated women in the suburbs seem to be abandoning Donald Trump.

It is that group that the President seems intent on wooing back at his rally in Lansing, Michigan, this evening. And it seems nostalgia for the 1940s is infectious. The President addresses the women in the audience saying, 'Your husbands, they want to get back to work,' before going on, 'We're getting your husbands back to work. And everybody wants it.'

Have to say that if you're trying to win back college-educated, savvy, twenty-first-century women, I'm not entirely convinced that this is tonally quite right, tbh (as they say in the twenty-first century).

29 October, Atlanta, Georgia

Donald Trump Jr has been on Fox News to talk about his sifting of the evidence on coronavirus, and to back up his father's argument that it is a problem that is going away. On *The Ingraham Angle* he says to the anchor, Laura Ingraham, that the number of deaths from the disease have now declined to 'almost nothing'. Around a thousand deaths a day? Almost nothing? That is, over the course of a week, more than the number of American servicemen who died over the whole period of the Afghanistan War, which started in 2001, and the war in Iraq. Rightly, the death of all those servicemen and women is a source of great pain for the US. So how do you dismiss – with a sweep of the arm – the death toll from Covid as almost nothing?

October 30, Washington

Four days to go and Donald Trump is in Michigan, and who is in the audience but Laura Ingraham, who did the interview with Don junior the night before. 'I do believe Laura Ingraham is here some place. Where is Laura? Where is she?' said the President as he cast his eyes across the crowd in search of the Fox News host. 'I can't recognise you. Is that a mask?' Trump said, seemingly amused. 'No way. Are you wearing a mask? I've never seen her in a mask,' he tells his appreciative audience. He then adds, 'She's being very politically correct.' Cases are surging, but wearing a mask has become the punchline of a joke. Is it any wonder few in his audience wear a face covering?

Much as Donald Trump would like to see the Covid outbreak shrinking and disappearing in the rear-view mirror, it is still front and centre. At this most critical moment in the election campaign, new cases are hitting record highs, deaths are ticking upwards to more than a thousand per day, ditto the numbers being admitted to hospital. And some of the areas worst hit are in swing states – like Wisconsin – where this election will be decided. But he's determined not to change course, holding mass rallies where there's no social distancing. This morning the President, leaving the White House ahead of another busy day of campaigning, tried to put a much more positive gloss on the situation, by again insisting a corner is being turned, that a vaccine has nearly arrived.

But that is not the view of his White House Coronavirus Task Force Coordinator, medical advisor Dr Deborah Birx. She has warned there is a 'broad surge' of the pandemic across the country as the weather cools, flatly contradicting President Trump's claim that the US is 'rounding the turn'. She said on a call with state governors that nearly one-third of the nation is in a Covid-19 hot spot, and things aren't getting any better as people turn to indoor activities.

Joe Biden is making a virtue, almost a comparison point, of holding socially distanced events, with masks obligatory. The polls still show the Democratic challenger holding comfortable or narrow leads in all the key swing states. And there are signs of growing frustration from the President about the state of the race. This morning he started tweeting at just before 3am that if he loses next week it will be down to the Supreme Court and some decisions they've made. Perhaps the greatest frustration is that the coronavirus is stubbornly refusing to bend to his will – or the electoral timetable.

31 October, Falls Church, Virginia

Happy Halloween. Though it doesn't feel much like Halloween. The houses and streets of Georgetown aren't filled as usual with skeletons, ghouls, giant spider's webs, giant spiders and coffins. Kids are not wandering the streets in crazy costumes, knocking on doors and coming away with a mountain of tooth-rotting candy.

I have spent the afternoon watching events in London, waiting for Boris Johnson to give a news conference on Shutdown 2. What a dismal day. Hard to accept that we (in Britain) are back where we were seven months ago. Awful. Also seemed very much that the scientists flanking the Prime Minister are not seeking to disabuse my colleague Laura Kuenssberg when she suggests the PM ignored advice from his experts for a 'circuit breaker' a few weeks earlier.

That said, the situation – as Deborah Birx sketched out yesterday – is pretty dire here too. Yesterday we had nearly 100,000 new infections. Yep, another record for the US. Daily deaths are creeping upwards – and the overall death toll has passed 230,000. In 47 states cases are rising. But this is resulting in *no* new action here. The line from the administration is that we are rounding the turn.

That is so obviously alarming his medical experts. Now Dr Fauci has weighed in. 'We're in for a whole lot of hurt. It's not a good situation,' the country's leading expert on infectious diseases is telling the *Washington Post*. 'All the stars are aligned in the wrong place as you go into the fall and winter season, with people congregating at home indoors. You could not possibly be positioned more poorly.'

And I see research from Stanford University showing that the Trump rallies may be responsible for up to 30,000 additional corona-virus cases and 700 deaths. Remember the only mass audience events taking place in the US at the moment are Trump rallies. There are not thousands attending baseball, football, basketball or ice-hockey.

CNN is reporting tonight that at a Trump rally in Pennsylvania the thousands of supporters who'd been ferried out to the venue by shuttle buses were left abandoned in frigid temperatures at the end – because the buses didn't turn up – and had to walk the three or so miles to where their cars were parked. CNN is also reporting its last set of polls from some of the key swing states – and in each of North Carolina, Arizona, Michigan and Wisconsin, Biden is on 50 per cent or above. These are numbers you dream of three days out.

And in Biden-land, the Democratic candidate is holding a drive-in event with Barack Obama. I'm afraid to say, the more you see of Obama and Biden together, the more obvious it becomes why Biden was his number two. America's first African American president has 1,000-megawatt star-power compared to Biden. His speech rips into the President's obsession with crowd size. And as he leaves the arena, the secret service detail walks Obama through a high school gym. The former president, who is wearing a bomber-jacket, is thrown a basketball. From the edge of the court he dinks an elegant jump shot and – swish – he drains a three-pointer. Too cool for school. Obama is articulate. He is funny. He is clever. And he just seems a dude. Trump, you get the impression repeatedly, is consumed by his antipathy, jeal-ousy even, of his predecessor. Almost as though Barack Obama is the Mozart to Donald Trump's Antonio Salieri.

Morgan, John and I spend this morning at a polling station in Virginia, and there are long lines of people availing themselves of the opportunity to vote early. Call me a saddo, but I love days spent reporting from polling stations – and it is something I have done around the world. What greater celebration of democracy is there than when 'we the people' decide whether we kick our rulers out, or give them another go. It is the very definition of empowerment; the reminder that they are our servants, and they answer to us. But that is not the mood this morning at the Thomas Jefferson Library in Falls Church.

I am sure the 'founding father' of the fledgeling republic, after which the library is named, would be thrilled to see that, over two hundred years on, the passion about voting is undimmed. But I suspect he would have been deeply troubled by what he heard these voters saying. They are fretful. Anxious. There is a deep-seated worry that this election, far from ending the bitter divisions that cleave at US society, will instead exacerbate them. One woman with her two kids wells up as she talks to me. She fears for the soul of the nation, for the country her children are growing up in.

I drive back into DC, and how is the nation's capital preparing to see in the joyous moment of election day on Tuesday? Everywhere you look you see pick-up trucks and teams of workmen with power saws, chipboard and plywood, boarding up shops, boarding up offices, boarding up any building that could be vandalised. Something similar in the Deep South happens every time the meteorologists tell residents that a hurricane is barrelling towards them. An act of God. But on Tuesday America seems to be bracing itself for a very different type of storm, and one that is entirely man-made.

1 November, Scranton, Pennsylvania

So we're finally nearing the end. That bit in an Olympic marathon where the runners enter the stadium for the last 400 metres on the track, straining aching muscles and tired bodies to sprint to the finish.

And as I sit here contemplating what has been an extraordinary, sometimes unsettling, certainly unimaginable (who had global pandemic
on their bingo card?) election campaign and trying to figure out what
happens next, it is all crystal clear to me.

There are three possible scenarios, and I realise I wouldn't be in
the least bit surprised if any one of them came to pass (actually there's
a fourth scenario, but I'll get to that later).

Having reported on this president's effort to buy Greenland, and
when the Danes refused to sell to the former property developer,
watched as Trump cancelled a state visit in revenge; having learned
that he paid off a porn-star just before the last election; having
been in Helsinki and listened to him saying he preferred to believe
Vladimir Putin, who was standing next to him, rather than his
own intelligence agencies; having seen him investigated, impeached
and then cleared; having watched him drive past me outside the
Walter Reed Hospital when he was infectious with coronavirus;
having been called 'another beauty', just for saying I was from the
BBC – I really have come to realise that anything can happen, and
frequently does.

So, to the three possible scenarios. The first is that the polls are right
and Joe Biden gains a comfortable victory on Tuesday night. Listen –
being a pollster in this election season has had all the excitement of
being a Saudi Arabian TV weather forecaster: 'Today will be hot and
sunny, and looking forward tomorrow will be hot and sunny too.' For
all the turmoil and tumult of this campaign – and very unlike four
years ago – the national polls and crucial state polls have been unbelievably consistent. Nothing has happened. Nothing has moved. Biden
has enjoyed a big lead nationally, a smaller lead in the sunbelt states
– Florida, Arizona and North Carolina; and a similar margin in the
northern industrial ones – Wisconsin, Michigan and Pennsylvania. If
you go onto fivethirtyeight.com, where they keep a running average

of all the mainstream polls, they say there has been a tightening in the race of 0.1 per cent.

When we report polls we normally say there is a 3 per cent +/- margin of error. Only a 0.1 per cent change over several weeks is incalculable. So if on Tuesday night this turns out to be the result, I won't be in the least bit surprised

Which brings me to the second possible outcome. It is that, as in 2016, the polls are wrong and Donald Trump wins a second term. Key to his success is what happens in Pennsylvania and Florida. No one believes polls showing Biden 3 or 4 points ahead in the Sunshine State – it is far tighter than that. And in 2020 Trump is doing far better with Latinos than he was in 2016. Likewise Pennsylvania where, in the west of the state, the white working-class vote could be what pushes the President over the line.

In this Covid-restricted election I have been in Florida, Ohio, Tennessee, Pennsylvania, North Carolina, Georgia and Virginia. And wherever you go you find Trump supporters that don't just like the man, they adore the 45th president. And the Trump campaign calculation is that just as in 2016, when they brought many people out to vote who were 'off the grid' – beyond the pollsters' slightly dodgy radar screens – they will do the same again.

Also, I want to say a word about these rallies the President has been holding. Democrats have piled in saying how irresponsible he is to bring thousands of people together when there is no social distancing at a time of pandemic. I don't want to get into that argument. But you'd better believe there is smart calculation in doing this. To attend these rallies you have to sign up on line, there then follows a sophisticated data-mining operation to see whether you are on the electoral register – and if you're not, they will sign you up. Thousands and thousands of people have been enrolled as a result of these multiple rallies – and in a tight election, that might make all the difference. The

Trump campaign has built a formidable database of mobile phone numbers, and all these people will be nudged on polling day to make sure they go and vote.

The one other reason that a Trump victory would not surprise me in the least is that Joe Biden is hardly an inspiring campaigner. If ever anyone represented an old guard, it is him. The ageing process is cruel to everyone, but Donald Trump seems so much more vibrant and vigorous than Biden, even though they are only three years apart. And maybe the Democrats' uber-cautious approach to physically knocking on doors – laudable though it might be during a pandemic – will give an advantage to Trump, whose own team have shown no such restraint. It is not as if Biden is 'hope', to borrow the Obama 2008 slogan. All he offers is 'nope' – he's not Donald Trump.

But 'nope' in 2020 is hugely powerful. There is a surging 'negative partisanship' which looks as though it might be a decisive factor in this election. It's not that people want Biden, it's that they've had enough of this noisy presidency which has seen America become so bitterly divided.

Which bring us to the third scenario. And it is the same as the second – the polls are wrong. Except this time the polls are wrong in the opposite direction. And this is the possibility that not only does Biden win, he wins big; it is a blow-out election, akin to Ronald Reagan's victory over Jimmy Carter in 1980. Or George H.W. Bush's victory over Michael Dukakis in 1988.

In the final week of the campaign the President has seen coronavirus cases surge to all-time highs, with hospitalisations rising, deaths ticking upwards to a thousand per day. He's also seen the stock market having its worst week since March – a barometer of economic health this president cares passionately about. Unlike 2016, when Donald Trump had a very clear message to the American people – he wanted to build a wall, he wanted to keep Muslims out, he wanted to renegotiate trade deals, he wanted to bring back manufacturing – in 2020 he's struggled to articulate what a second term would be about.

So if the 'blow-out' came to pass, Biden doesn't only win the states I've listed in the first scenario, he takes Texas (Texas!), Ohio, Iowa, Georgia, possibly even South Carolina. Unlikely maybe, but if you follow the money, and look at the polls, look at the patterns of early voting, look at where the Democrats have intensified campaigning, look at the extraordinary number of new voters, it is not impossible.

I mentioned at the outset there is – conceivably – a fourth scenario. And don't ask me to go into the mechanics or the consequences, but … because of the way Nebraska splits its electoral college votes, it is conceivable that in the race for 270 electoral college votes – the magic number that secures you the presidency – you could finish with Biden on 269 and Trump on 269. And after billions of dollars spent, you end up in total, gridlocked, legal quagmire, America divided hell.

It's never happened before, but impossible? This is 2020. How 2020 would that outcome be?

2 November, Scranton, Pennsylvania

Scranton is a scrappy, working-class town in north-eastern Pennsylvania. It is Joe Biden's own backyard, where he spent a good chunk of his childhood, and which he claims as his spiritual home. He's repeatedly sought to distinguish himself as the kid from Scranton, while Donald Trump is the rich kid from Park Avenue. If you're thinking of this as a Monopoly set, Biden is Old Kent Road, Trump is Mayfair. Oh, and while we are on cultural comparisons, Scranton is where the American version of the toe-curling sitcom, *The Office*, is set. So think Slough, too, if you like.

Scranton is also known as the Electric City, a tag given to the city in the 1930s and 1940s because of its role in serving the demand for coal and textiles during the Second World War. Now it finds itself being fought over by Trump and Biden supporters. The President is due to hold a rally at the airport down the road at lunchtime. We arrived late last night, having driven up from Washington.

I open the curtains to find that the city has had a dusting of snow overnight. And there is a bone-chilling wind blowing. We go out to the airport, where the President is holding his second rally of the day. His day started at Miami. He gave a speech in North Carolina, is coming here to Scranton – and then will fly on to Michigan, Wisconsin, then Michigan again before flying back to DC. It's five rallies in four states, and he'll be clocking up 2,500 miles in one day.

And with temperatures hovering around freezing – though feeling a good deal colder with the wind chill – thousands are pouring into a makeshift open-air arena at the airport. It's easy to characterise his supporters as uneducated white men, but his audience is way wider than that. We park next to a people carrier, and notice that the parents have brought their small children along – an act of cruelty, I'd say – there are still two hours to go before he's going to be on stage.

I see a bunch of young Hasidic Jews wearing Trump 2020 flags as Superman capes, mixed with their tzitzit tassels hanging from the waistband of their trousers. And there are gun owners for Trump, gays for Trump, farmers for Trump, and Uncle Tom Cobley and all for Trump. They are dressed up in Trump costumes. And my favourite? A golden Labrador called Stanley, whose owner has dressed him in a long red tie and a blond wig. A Labradonald.

His supporters look at you with sheer incredulity when you ask if he is going to win. They have no doubt. Zero. None. Look at the numbers turning up at his rallies, they tell me. Look at the enthusiasm. Look at the thousands who are turning out in the cold – and in the midst of a pandemic. They have a point.

After cutting our piece it is a long drive back to DC, ahead of what is going to be an exceptionally long day tomorrow

3 November, Washington. Polling Day

I was aiming to sleep in, because I know I will be working pretty solidly for the next 36 hours, but my mind is whirring, so instead I have come to sit at the kitchen table and write. I suspect I am going to regret this later on. Just as a scene set, I am in my PJs, dawn is breaking, and it is a beautiful, clear, crisp autumn morning. I know that the thing I will miss most about America when I move back to the UK (an odd thing to be reflecting on as I gird myself for possibly the most important day of my broadcasting career) is sunlight. I have no idea what the statistics are, but it is bright and blue and clear so much more often here than it is in cloudy, overcast Britain.

The President is on his favourite TV show, *Fox & Friends*. He sounds hoarse and tired – not surprising given his punishing schedule from the day before. He has given it his all. In spite of all the speculation that the President would claim victory long before the final votes are counted, he is much more circumspect, saying he will play no games. He will wait.

Later in the morning he goes to his campaign headquarters in Rosslyn, Virginia, just across the river from where I live. He is there to thank campaign workers for their efforts. 'I think we're going to have a great night,' he tells them. 'But it's politics and it's elections and you never know,' Trump said. He claimed all is going well in Florida, Arizona and Texas. He notes the importance of winning Pennsylvania. And then he says something revealing: 'Winning is easy. Losing is never easy,' he said. 'Not for me it's not.' I wonder whether that is a quote we will be playing back in the coming days.

Biden is still out on the road, and is campaigning in Scranton, where we were yesterday. He returns to the house where he grew up, and does a bit of old-fashioned rabble rousing as he speaks to people with a bullhorn in his hand and – naturally – a mask over his face. It is not a winning combination – the pictures are fine, but we can barely make out a word that Biden says.

After lunch I get a request from the editor of the *Ten O'Clock News* to hurry out to a polling station to get 'some colour' from there for the piece that will air in a couple of hours' time. It would be a mad dash, and it is exactly what we did over the weekend. And uncharacteristically (I think!) I go from nought to tantrum in about three seconds. I shout that I am not going. It is purely cosmetic. What a waste of time. Forget it.

Am now thinking that getting up early this morning was not such a good idea after all. I am tired and tense. But sort of feel a bit better for letting off some steam; having a good vent. It's not an election campaign if you don't have one proper strop and throw your toys out of the pram.

Fittingly for a presidency like no other, this campaign has drawn to a close like no other: the President hospitalised with coronavirus a month ago before coming roaring back with extraordinary energy and determination, as if he'd never had the disease – as if America wasn't in the grip of a pandemic – and holding rallies with no social distancing and few wearing masks – to the exasperation of his public health experts. He's hoping, praying he will enjoy a similar electoral recovery tonight. For throughout, the polls have had him behind Joe Biden in all the key swing states.

The Democratic challenger has fought a careful-as-you-go campaign, wanting the focus to stay fixed on the President's handling of the pandemic. The stakes couldn't be higher and the nation couldn't be more divided. In major cities across the land today's celebration of democracy is marked by anxiety and unease. But the Biden camp seems bullish, talking everything up. They 'feel good'. Florida is a true toss-up, they tell us, but everywhere else – Michigan, Wisconsin, North Carolina, Georgia, Philadelphia and Arizona – they claim they are not seeing the 'red tide of low-propensity voters' that President Trump is usually successful in turning out. 'There is not a crush' of Election Day voters.

Our live position is on the roof of the Chamber of Commerce building, which directly overlooks the White House. It is the most magnificent view across Lafayette Park to 1600 Pennsylvania Avenue. As I go live on the *Ten O'Clock News* my earlier grouchiness is replaced by a sense of excitement; a wondering about what is to come. It is also the most beautiful evening. The clocks have just gone back and the sun is going down, the trees are in their late autumn colours and the White House is seemingly aglow. Though tempted, I resist the 'is this also the sun going down on the Trump presidency?' line – but only just.

I go home to collect a few bits and pieces and then drive to the hotel near the White House where we are going to base ourselves for the night, and it seems that every shopfront and office is covered in plywood. Washington is entirely boarded up, and workers are being told not to come to work tomorrow for fear of social unrest. And it is perfectly possible that the result of this election won't be known for several days, adding to the tensions. Lawyers are standing by to fight this out for both campaigns; but a much greater worry are the militia groups who will need little provocation to fight this out on the streets.

As the polls close in the first states on the East coast I am juggling the competing demands of the TV and radio special programmes, and keeping an eye on exit polls – and in particular Florida.

It is nine in the evening, and I am getting a distinct sense of *déjà vu*. The polling data emerging from Florida looks catastrophic for Biden. He is ahead in Miami Dade – where two or three weeks ago the Democratic Party leader warned us how well Trump was doing with Latinos – but by nothing like the same margin Hillary Clinton was four years ago. And unless he is going to build up a big lead here, then surely these 29 electoral college votes are going to Trump – the first important step towards securing a second term. The *New York Times* says it is 95 per cent certain that Trump is going to hold Florida – that will be a big blow to the Biden camp, though there are still many paths by which he gets to 270. Exit polling says that Trump is performing better this year with Latino, non-white and white female college graduate voters than he did four years ago.

Four years ago I sat in the Javits Center in New York, expecting like much of the rest of the world to be reporting on a Hillary Clinton win, in line with all predictions – and this was where her victory party would be. This building made of glass, the perfect setting for the symbolic shattering of that last ceiling to women's political ambitions. The realisation that while the roof might sustain a few cracks, it wasn't going to shatter came as we watched the votes coming in from Florida and the upper Midwest. There was no shattered ceiling, just a lot of tearful, shattered dreams as Hillary Clinton supporters disappeared into the New York night disconsolate and despairing at what had unfolded.

And so there are echoes of that tonight. Boy, is there going to be an inquest into the failing of the polling companies if this continues on the current trajectory. And it is making the bullish, almost braggadocious Biden briefing from earlier in the evening look misguided and foolish – unless they know something we don't. In the Trumpland corner of Twitter it is clear their tails are up. They are smelling something on the wind, and it's an aroma they are liking very much.

4 November

Good morning. It has just gone midnight, and I am in a hotel room on Black Lives Matter Plaza – previously known as 16th and H Street. We are recording an *Americast* of what we know so far. As we are recording we get word that Biden is going to the Chase Centre in Wilmington to make a statement. Surely not a concession? Things not looking good, but it's surely premature to throw in the towel.

He is surprisingly upbeat. 'We feel good about where we are. We really do. I'm here to tell you tonight that we believe we're on track to win this election.' He stresses that mail-in ballots when they are counted will make the difference.

So, he clearly doesn't believe this is 2016 mark 2. Maybe I am wrong, but this looks deeply tactical. The Democratic Party has serious PTSD from the 2000 election, where there is now a view that during the wait for the Florida results to come in, Al Gore allowed George W. Bush to dictate the narrative. Bush always gave the impression that it was just a matter of time before he would be confirmed as president. And eventually Gore graciously conceded. I have spoken to many Dems involved in this campaign who have vowed not to make the same mistake. So this is Biden trying to frame the debate – it may not look good now, but you wait … it'll come good when postal votes are counted.

The party can't be that great over in the East Room of the White House, because it is clear that Donald Trump was glued to the TV as Biden made that statement. And his hitherto inactive Twitter thumbs are set in motion. The Democratic challenger has barely got his face mask back on, before Donald Trump tweets this: 'We are up BIG, but they are trying to STEAL the election. We will never let them do it. Votes cannot be cast after the Poles [sic] have closed.'

Now let's leave aside the slur on the Polish people – this feels like it is the start of the war. The accusation that the Democrats are trying to 'steal' the election is based on what? Votes are being counted. That's what happens in elections. And they are legally cast ballots.

I am going over now to the live position to appear on the radio and TV special. I am wearing my face mask as I cross Black Lives Matter Plaza – it might protect me from coronavirus, but if I spend too long here, it is not going to stop me getting high. The smell of weed is overpowering.

I make the point on air that the polls look like they are way off-beam. For all that the pollsters declared that they knew how to find the shy Trump voters, the result in Florida suggests they failed dismally. And what is unfolding in other key swing states looks much the same.

Word is now coming that Donald Trump is to make a statement. At around 02.15 he walks into the East Room, with a backdrop of Stars and Stripes flags. An election night that had been simmering now explodes as the President is in attack, attack, attack mode. 'This is a fraud on the American public. This is an embarrassment to our country. We were getting ready to win this election, frankly, we did win this election. So our goal now is to ensure the integrity – for the good of this nation – this is a very big moment. This is a major fraud on our nation.' He says this will go to the Supreme Court and – on the basis of nothing – says that he has won the election.

Morgan and I return from our rooftop live position. It is the middle of the night now, but there are thousands on the streets, and a big group has broken away, intent on marching on the White House – 'Burn down the plantation!' they shout. The White House was built by black slaves. At the entrance to our hotel, the security people have unscrewed the door handles – so you can't open the door and have to ring to be let in.

I get to bed at about 04.00 and sleep fitfully until 07.30. Morgan arrives from her apartment with coffee from a café near where she lives, and I think it's a quadruple shot flat white. Well, that has got my pulse going and heart racing.

In the dawn light, nothing seems any clearer. There are still millions of ballots to be counted. There is still a fragile unease. This could get bumpy, and Americans will need to show patience, trust and fortitude – all things in desperately short supply.

The banner on Joe Biden's website now reads: 'When all of the votes are counted, Joe Biden will be the next President of the United States.' Maybe. It's a message he reiterates as he comes out to make a statement. He also makes a plea for a lowering of the political temperature and a coming together. Fat chance of that right now.

But maybe things are shifting – the networks are calling Wisconsin for Biden, one of the states that Trump improbably won in 2016. That's the first 'gain' in the Dem column. And now Michigan is looking good.

And sure enough, at just after 4pm, Michigan is called for Biden too. Another big gain. Does one dare use the word unassailable? The state of play is that Biden is now on 253 electoral college votes, 17 short of the magic number; Trump is on 213. And Joe Biden is ahead in Arizona (which, controversially, and to Donald Trump's absolute fury, Fox has called for Biden – though none of the other networks has) and ahead in Nevada too. And if you look elsewhere, the Dems are sniffing they might pull something off in Georgia, and Pennsylvania as well, even though Trump at the moment is hundreds of thousands of votes in front.

Although exhausted, we are all too wired just to go home, so I invite Morgan and John to come to my apartment to celebrate our coverage – it has been a fantastic few weeks, and I feel really proud about what we've done as a small, tight team. I stop and buy a couple of bottles of fizz. And John Landy, cameraman extraordinaire, picture editor supreme, engineer when he needs to be, tells me he used to work in a champagne bar in his native Australia. So while I go and change out of my suit, I leave it to him to remove the cork from the bottle. Frankly, Lewis Hamilton after winning a grand prix would have done a better job of keeping it under control. Champagne goes everywhere, except in a glass – on the ceiling, on the walls, all over the floor. John is so irritatingly competent and together all the time that this is a glorious moment. What a lovely way to unwind.

5 November

Another beautiful morning. I have had a little sleep, and feel better. But having gone to bed thinking this was more or less done, and that Biden was on course to become the 46th president, I'm now not so sure. Biden now just needs to pick up Arizona and Nevada, and he's up there … but this morning as I turn on the TV it is all looking much tighter. Trump is closing the lead on Biden in Arizona, as a result of the latest batch of votes coming in from Maricopa County.

This next bit is hilarious. Yesterday in Detroit, Michigan, Trump supporters were chanting 'Stop the count, stop the count,' as Donald Trump's lead started to dwindle. They were demanding that no more votes should be counted. But out west, in Arizona, it's the reverse. Overnight, Donald Trump supporters gathered at the counting centre in Phoenix, where Donald Trump is trailing Joe Biden – but where the President is closing the lead. And so the chant from the Trump loyalists here is 'Count those votes, count those votes …' It's all about principle!

As things stand we are waiting for counting to finish in Arizona and Nevada, states where Joe Biden holds narrow leads, in Pennsylvania in the North-East, where the President had enjoyed a massive lead, and Georgia in the South, where the President is just about ahead. Maybe MAGA should become Make America Wait Again.

Donald Trump hasn't spoken publicly since he made his statement on election night, but his campaign has launched multiple lawsuits since then, demanding a recount in Wisconsin, calling for counting to be stopped in other states, with allegations of fraud. A news conference is given by Ric Grenell in Nevada, where the campaign is claiming there's been voter fraud. Grenell is Donald Trump's former Director of National Intelligence. After the presser he is chased by a reporter from MSNBC, who is demanding to know what evidence there is of fraud. Grenell has nothing to say, and looks shifty. It is road-crash TV.

Donald Trump meantime is taking to Twitter: 'All of the recent Biden claimed states will be legally challenged by us for voter fraud and state election fraud. Plenty of proof – just check out the media. WE WILL WIN. America first'. The tweet is flagged by Twitter for being misleading. Actually, look at his Twitter feed and around a third of his recent missives have been flagged by the social media organisation for being disputed. This is the President of the United States, repeatedly falling foul of a social media company that really doesn't want to be playing the role of policeman.

The Democrats are watching all of this warily – and have an army of lawyers ready to go into battle if that's what this election comes down to. But just as he did yesterday, Biden comes in front of the microphones in Wilmington to ask his supporters to remain calm, assuring them that he is on course for victory, that all will be fine. He is determined to keep control of this.

Neither side is giving an inch. Neither side is giving up. There is defiance from the Trump camp; determination from Biden. Who's going to prevail? Watch this space.

I am cycling home from my live on the *Ten O'Clock News* and I am now within a block of the apartment, but the police have sealed off all the roads that lead to it. Seems there is someone 'armed and dangerous' on the street where I live. I am told I am not allowed to cross the tape they have strung over the sidewalks. But, I argue with the police sergeant, Donald Trump is about to give a news conference and make his first public statement since that election night statement from the East Room. I think the word to describe his reaction to my remonstrations is unimpressed. And when I tell him I am from the media, he is even less interested.

The one phrase I am sure Donald Trump will not use as we wait for his presser is 'I concede'. For months, as I have previously said, the President only sees two conceivable outcomes. One is that he wins; the other is that the election is stolen from him. And that is exactly the approach Trump takes as he walks into the Briefing Room, sounding downbeat.

'If you count the legal votes, I easily win. If you count the illegal votes, they can easily steal the election from me,' the President claims. Again, he offers no evidence for his assertions. Who knows how this plays out – and I have been wrong so many times about Donald Trump, let me be wrong again. He sounded a little forlorn, slightly as though he was going through the motions. There is a long list of grievances. The media are against him. Silicon Valley has it in for him. Wall Street sought to fund his demise. The pollsters are intent on destroying him. And all these groups are in cahoots with the Democrats. And on it went. At the end he didn't hang around to answer questions, just stomped off.

But, astonishingly, some of the US networks didn't stay with his address to the nation until the end. When the President started making his unfounded allegations, they cut away – and said, in terms, the President is making allegations without foundation, so we're pulling away. Remember there is normally much more reverence for the president than there is for a prime minister. The President is the head of state. There is deference to the office. Well, not to the holder of the office at this moment, it seems.

I turn to Fox News. He is not getting full-throated support here either. They are not being as vicious as CNN, but it is not the reaction the President would have wanted or expected. And now I see this from Larry Hogan. Who he? Well he's the Republican governor of Maryland. 'There is no defence for the President's comments tonight undermining our Democratic process. America is counting the votes, and we must respect the results as we always have before. No election or person is more important than our Democracy.'

And maybe much more significant than that is the coverage in the *New York Post*, the Rupert Murdoch-owned newspaper, which a few weeks ago had been the conduit for the Hunter Biden laptop story. Tonight its headline is that 'Downcast Trump makes baseless election fraud claims in White House address.' That is hardly a ringing endorsement.

Is he being cut adrift? Rupert Murdoch is utterly ruthless. If he thinks someone is done, there is no room for sentiment. Maybe he thinks it's all over. And Murdoch is a brilliant businessman. Maybe he's thinking it's time to cultivate Biden and leave Trump behind. Look at the way he abandoned John Major in the 1990s and got behind Tony Blair. Maybe I am reading too much into it.

But there is clearly frustration within the President's inner circle over the lack of support he's getting from the Republican Party. Rudy Giuliani, the President's lawyer, enters the fray – even if the former mayor of New York and most recently bit-part star of the new Borat film, in which he is filmed lying on his back, apparently undoing his trousers while awaiting the ministrations of Sacha Baron Cohen's sidekick, might not bring the reputational heft the President would like. 'Where is the GOP,' he wails. 'Our voters will never forget.' At which Eric Trump weighs in with 'NO THEY WON'T.'

I am back at home this evening and I have resolved that it will be alcohol free and election free. And what is the scene right now? Well,

I am doing exactly what I vowed not to do. One, I have a glass of wine sitting beside my laptop (a nice New Zealand pinot, seeing as you ask), and two, I am watching CNN. It is mesmerising. Whatever they pay their veteran number cruncher, John King, it is not enough. He is a brilliant communicator, and he has a fabulous story to tell. The numbers are astonishing. In Pennsylvania Donald Trump was ahead by more than half a million votes on election night, but with every new set of postal votes counted, the Trump lead shrinks and shrinks and shrivels. And at this rate Biden is going to win Pennsylvania – and with it the presidency.

It is the same story in Georgia. It is now 9.35pm and Biden has statistically drawn level with the President. But in Arizona, it is going in the opposite direction. Here Trump is closing the gap on Biden's lead. So, as you can tell, my evening of Zen calm, soothing music and political detox has gone to shit.

6 November

Am awake at 05.30 and looking at my phone. Seems that since I went to bed Biden has pulled ahead in Georgia. It's a thousand votes here, a few hundred votes there – although in terms of the popular vote Biden is 4 million votes ahead. Each time I try to get out of bed, something else happens. Now going on a Zoom call with the *Americast* team to figure out when we can record, given all our different broadcast commitments. Dino Sofos, the genius podcast editor, asks me to record a mini-episode by myself as a holding update. Which I do once I get out of the shower.

But by the time I've made a cup of tea, everything has changed. The Donald Trump lead of 600,000 votes in Pennsylvania has now become a Biden lead of 5,500. It's hair standing up on the back of your neck time. This feels like 'the moment'. The fat lady sings. The ref blows the final whistle. Or, as they say here, 'And that's the ballgame.'

So I record another mini-episode. Biden is going to become president-elect. Now it's just a question of time. Of waiting a little longer. He's now ahead in Pennsylvania, Arizona, Nevada and Georgia. There is no way back for Donald Trump.

There's a statement from the counsel to the Trump campaign saying, in essence, the fight goes on. 'This election is not over. The false projection of Joe Biden as the winner is based on results in four states that are far from final ... Biden is relying on these states for his phony claim on the White House, but once the election is final, President Trump will be re-elected.'

But it feels like a mealy-mouthed statement. It's a quibble here and quibble there. If Biden runs the table in Pennsylvania, Nevada, Arizona and Georgia – you are going to need some pretty solid evidence to overturn the results of these four states.

Meanwhile the opposition to the President's legal blunderbuss seems to be growing. Senator Mitt Romney piles in. The President is wrong to say that the election was rigged, corrupt and stolen, he says. And he accuses Donald Trump of recklessly inflaming 'destructive and dangerous passions'. Another Republican senator, Pat Toomey, from Pennsylvania – the state at the epicentre of this election – says he finds the President's comments very disturbing. 'There is simply no evidence that anybody has shown me – or anyone else I'm aware of – of any kind of widespread corruption or fraud.'

More expected, and more entertaining is the attack from the Democrat mayor of Philadelphia. Mayor Jim Kenney tells President Trump, to 'put his big boy pants on' and 'acknowledge the fact that he lost.' Sometimes you just can't beat the inventive invective of American politics.

But the day is dragging on, and we are still no further on in electoral college votes. Biden is still on 253 votes – 17 short of victory; Trump is on 213. In Georgia, the peach state, all is not peachy. The election authorities announce that they are going to order a recount because it is so close. And it seems there are problems with the Pennsylvania vote, which might hold things up for a few days. How many times can I go on the TV and say Biden is within touching distance …? I suspect several.

The bureau chief Paul Danahar brings me and Nick Bryant together on a call to talk about the problems there are with the count in Nevada and Pennsylvania. Our partners at CBS warn this could go on for days yet.

But undoubtedly the most interesting thing emerging this evening are the noises coming out of the White House. It doesn't sound a happy place. A lot of aides haven't turned up for work. The mood is sombre. President Trump is restlessly moving between the residence and the West Wing, spending a lot of time on the phone. He's raging at the Republican Party grandees for not defending him, and he's venting at his son-in-law Jared that there isn't a crack legal team ready to go into battle. There is no shortage of writs flying. But what there isn't is a legal strategy. Is this sustainable?

7 November

What a day. Tumultuous and astonishing don't begin to describe it. It is a day that unfolds in multiple locations at different times. So forgive me if I borrow from the TV drama, 24, and go all Kiefer Sutherland, with split screens as events unfold in different places, before going full screen as we concentrate on one part of it.

08.00 Georgetown

Sleep, it is good to be re-acquainted with you. We've been apart too long. It is the most beautiful autumn morning, cool, crisp, not a cloud in the sky, and Alexa tells me it could get up to 22 degrees today. The plan is that – assuming nothing changes – I will only be required to do a 'live' for the late bulletin, and someone else will do the packaging. I go out for a long walk along the canal. It is beautiful out. And I come back and cook myself scrambled eggs on toast for breakfast with a big mug of tea.

09.30 The White House

Donald Trump is off to play golf, by the sound of things, but he has tweeted that his crack legal team, led by Rudy Giuliani, will be holding a news conference at the Four Seasons in Philadelphia. I wonder what evidence they've turned up. It will take place at 11.30am. But not long after this tweet comes another, but this time from the Four Seasons Hotel itself, in what looks like an epic piece of trolling of the President by the luxury hotel chain. It is one for the ages: 'To clarify, President Trump's press conference will NOT be held at Four Seasons Hotel Philadelphia. It will be held at Four Seasons Total Landscaping – no relation with the hotel.'

To say that Four Seasons Total Landscaping is not the same as the Four Seasons Hotel is the understatement of the century. It is like saying the Taj Mahal curry house on the Bayswater Road is not the same as the Taj Mahal in Agra.

On his way to golf, the President is tweeting in the car – and he is in full caps lock mode: 'I WON THIS ELECTION, BY A LOT!' he declares, with what sounds like a good deal of petulance. One of many, many tweets that Twitter flags as potentially containing inaccurate information.

11.00 Georgetown

Biden's lead is creeping up in Pennsylvania, and we've had a tip that when the Democratic challenger's margin goes above 30,000, it's possible that the networks will call it for him – and once they do, the 20 electoral college votes from PA will put him over the 270 mark that ensures victory. Paul Danahar calls and asks me to write a 40-second summaries piece that can run as soon as any announcement comes. I tell him that I need to jump in the shower and clean up. He tells me (I am convinced not joking) to take my phone into the shower with me in case anything changes. I don't. But I wash quickly and scribble a quick 'He's done it' so that the moment the race is called – if it is called – I can file this into London.

11.15 CNN studios, Washington

John King is reporting that a new 'vote dump' is imminent and that the latest batch of ballots have now been counted. For my family in London – and I think across much of the UK – King, a handsome silver fox CNN veteran, has become crack cocaine. You get one fix of him, but it quickly wears off and you need another. What are the latest numbers? Let's drill down into this or that district. This is all playing out as lockdown 2 is kicking in – so millions in Britain are at home and seemingly taking a ludicrously unhealthy interest in the US elections. I have friends in London who've never been to Pennsylvania asking me what I think will happen in Allegheny County, and what should they read into the high turnout in Erie County. Maitlis tells me on the podcast that she knows of people planning post-Covid road trips to the key contested counties of the 2020 election. Insane, but wonderful.

Anyway, back to John King's big board – and Biden has moved beyond a 30,000 lead over Trump, and then with much whooshing and whizzbangery the BIG announcement is made: Wolf Blitzer (their version of David Dimbleby) makes the historic statement that Joseph R. Biden Jr is the president-elect of the United States. They really do 'the moment' well. Other networks follow suit.

Van Jones, a black commentator, author and lawyer who is in the studio as the result is declared, provides the viral moment of the day with his emotional and heartfelt reaction to the result. 'It's easier to be a dad, it's easier to tell your kids character matters – it matters,' he said. 'This is vindication for a lot of people who have really suffered. "I can't breathe" – that wasn't just George Floyd. A lot of people felt like they couldn't breathe,' he said, choking back the tears, and wiping his eyes with a handkerchief. 'This is a big deal for us, just to get some peace and have a chance for a reset. The character of the country matters. Being a good man matters. I just want my sons to look at this, look at this, it's easy to do it the cheap way and get away with stuff.'

11.30 Four Seasons Total Landscaping, Philadelphia

The news conference venue is in the car park of a run-down shopping centre in a slightly crumbly neighbourhood. And Four Seasons Total Landscaping is next to Fantasy Island Adult Books and Novelties, and just across the street from the Delaware Valley Cremation Center. The company, which is more used to providing mulching, weed control, shrub pruning and leaf removal – among other services – is now letting out its parking lot at the back for the most bizarre news conference ever. Trump/Pence posters are plastered to the small garage door, and a lectern is put up in front.

This is where the counter-revolution shall begin. Let history record that the story which began with Donald Trump descending the gold elevator in his ritzy Manhattan apartment block on 5th Avenue to launch his presidential bid, ends here in a scruffy suburb of Philly, five years later. And with social media almost wetting itself laughing. It's as though we're watching a particularly ridiculous episode of *Veep* that has never been screened before because the writers thought it was too far-fetched.

So much of what Donald Trump did with the endless procession of rallies was slick. But the fact that they could book a garden centre by mistake speaks to the utter unprepared shambles of these final moments of the Trump campaign, whose confidence from Wednesday has become angry incredulity today. Rudy Giuliani, whose credibility just seems to diminish every time he opens his mouth, snorts derisively at the news that the networks have called Pennsylvania. 'The networks,' he screeches; 'the networks!' he says again, his voice rising in an untenable crescendo; the intention being to ladle on the sarcasm. They don't decide elections, he tells reporters – the courts do.

You just wonder whether at this moment a little 'oh shit, what have I just said' alarm might have been triggered in his head. It doesn't seem to have done. No, Rudy, it's not the courts who decide, it's the people who decide – a notion that he probably thinks is hopelessly naïve and innocent.

Insult is added to injury, because as the reporters see the alerts about all the networks calling the race, they all wander off, not staying to listen to the rest of what the Trump lawyers have to say. And all anyone remembers are the jokes: 'The press conference that the White House announced would be held "at the Ritz" will actually take place next to the Ritz Crackers endcap-display in the snack food aisle of the Wawa at 7912 Roosevelt Boulevard,' one person tweets. And then there are the garden centre jokes. Make America Rake Again. Lawn and Order.

11.30 Trump National Golf Course, Sterling, Virginia

The pool report has it that the President left the White House at just after ten, the on-duty pooler noting: 'The president left the White House residence and walked alone to his vehicle. He wore a black windbreaker, dark pants and a white MAGA hat. It is a lovely day with blue skies and only a light breeze, but he leaned forward as he made his way towards the vehicle, as if he were heading into a stiff wind.'

A stiff wind indeed. Trump must be on the third or fourth hole of his round by the time the networks have called it. You just wonder whether any official has dared interrupt the round to tell him the news. Or whether they get to the 18th and someone says, 'I know what, Mr President, why don't we play 36 holes ... such a lovely day.' No word comes from the golf course. We get one shot fed back to us of him playing. He is on the green, with a long putt to the pin. He strikes the ball firmly, but it comes up four feet short of the hole. What a glorious picture to write to in television terms: the President just coming up short.

11.30 My Georgetown apartment

From this moment my quiet Saturday morning goes helter-skeltering out of control. I write a script for a piece for the teatime news bulletin, while trying to get dressed, while trying to stay across the TV networks and Twitter, while trying to answer phone calls, and I then cycle to the White House to be live at the top of the news. There is a slightly festive atmosphere in Georgetown – there are car horns honking and a few people waving. It is much the same as I lock up my bike on the corner of 17th Street and Pennsylvania Avenue – as close as my bike can get to the White House. In the live bit that I do from inside the White House grounds I say that Donald Trump is off playing golf –

something I point out that he will soon have a lot more time for. The bulletin is excellent – it captures the drama of the moment and the historic nature of what is unfolding.

12.45 *The area around the White House*

In the half-hour that I have been inside the White House grounds the world has changed outside. Now it is not just the odd car horn honking. It is a traffic jam of cars, all converging on the blocks that surround the White House; the occupants waving flags and shouting. Now, instead of one or two people wandering around, it is thousands of Americans homing in on the people's house. Washington is a liberal, Democrat voting city. And it is the most perfect autumn day. At lunchtime it is 21°C, there is not a cloud in the sky. People are in shorts and T-shirts. A last blast of summer temperatures before winter's unwelcome embrace. It is Saturday. The Biden victory is producing its own soundtrack – it is car horns, whistles, maracas (who knew so many Washingtonians had maracas?) and bells. And human whoops of delight. Great big, unrestrained dollops of human delight. This is not just around the White House, it is across Washington. And it is not just across Washington, it is across the big cities of America.

I call Linda and Anna on FaceTime to show them the scene. It is joyous, exuberant, vibrant, noisy. There is such a release – an explosion, if you like – of emotion after a tense few days. There really is an unrestrained outpouring – I so wish they'd been there to share this moment with me instead of being stuck in lockdown London. I run into our bureau chief, Paul Danahar – he too is here sharing the scene with his family. Paul, whom I have already described as an old school, tough as boots, no nonsense hack, will probably sue me for defamation for writing this. But we have a handshake and a bit of a hug. It has been the joy of a lifetime to have been able to cover this amazing period of history – from Donald Trump's victory night in New York to this moment, with all the highs and lows in between. All journalists want a fantastic story to cover. The Trump presidency has been this. If Hillary Clinton had won four years ago – and I am talking purely journalistically – it would have been nothing like as interesting. Danahar has been a great friend and a brilliant editor throughout all this. What a wild ride we've been on together.

As I wander about in this crazy, noisy scene there is something else that strikes me about the crowd. There is something visceral.

In 2008, when Barack Obama was elected, I was in the US. I had been reporting from Culpeper, Virginia, a town which the BBC had adopted for the campaign. As I drove back into DC in the small hours of that Wednesday morning, every traffic light you stopped at, people would get out and hug each other and weep. There was a fuzzy feeling of warmth that after America's long, painful history – from slavery, through Jim Crow, through segregation, through the civil rights struggle – it had taken the giant leap and elected this charismatic young African American as its 44th president.

The emotion that night was such a positive one for Obama. The sentiment in DC now is, yes, of course pleasure that Biden has won, but it is also of hatred and loathing and detestation of Donald Trump. And among those who felt marginalised by Donald Trump there is relief that the man who they see as having poked them in the eye, is now getting a taste of his own medicine. There are people holding rainbow flags. There are immigrant groups. There are people with strong political affiliations and people with none. They are dancing on the streets of Pennsylvania and 17th – but the real pleasure is they think they are also dancing on Donald Trump's political grave. And across Lafayette Park on 16th Street – now Black Lives Matter Plaza – it is a wild party. A Fox News reporter says that there is a celebration but also a very strong smell of marijuana – as if the causal relationship is self-evident: people are partying because they've smoked weed, not because Donald Trump has been defeated.

12.45 Trump Campaign HQ, Rosslyn, Virginia

The President may be out playing golf, but the machine is whirring. A statement is released:

> We all know why Joe Biden is rushing to falsely pose as the winner, and why his media allies are trying so hard to help him: they don't want the truth to be exposed. The simple fact is this election is far from over. Joe Biden has not been certified as the winner of any states, let alone any of the highly contested states headed for mandatory recounts, or states where our campaign has valid and legitimate legal challenges that could determine the ultimate victor.

That is the defiant message we received – but you should see the fund-raising email that was sent to Trump supporters – yes, supporters. One was sent to my colleague from the *Daily Telegraph*, Ben Riley-Smith:

> Ben,
>
> This is your FINAL NOTICE.
>
> So far, you've ignored all our emails asking you to join us in DEFENDING THE ELECTION. You've ignored Team Trump, Eric, Lara, Don, the Vice President AND you've even ignored the President of the United States.
>
> TENS OF THOUSANDS of Patriots have stepped up for the VERY FIRST TIME in the last 48 hours – *why haven't you?*

OK, fair's fair. It doesn't say, 'I know where you live, and where your children go to school.' Nor does it say, 'It would be awful if you stepped out into the road and a car ran you over' – but I have never seen an election communication like it. It is positively menacing. You're not a proper patriot if you're not throwing money at us for the legal fight, seems to be the barely disguised sub-text.

14.30 *Presidential motorcade from Trump National, Sterling, Virginia*

It is just after 2.30 when the President gets into 'the Beast' for the journey back into DC. As he drives out of the gates, large crowds have gathered. Some are cheering him on; others booing and jeering. One holds up a placard saying 'You're fired'. Another reads 'Pack your shit and go'. Some cars are driving up and down with Trump flags. But as the journey progresses, and the convoy nears the White House, so the mix of pro- and anti-Trump supporters perceptibly changes. It is those who are celebrating his defeat that are now lining the roads as he gets near the White House. He looks gloomy as he emerges from his vehicle and enters the building.

17.00 *Phoenix, Arizona*

My colleague on the West Coast, Sophie Long, has been sent to cover a pro-Trump gathering at the statehouse in downtown Phoenix. From afar, it looks like a party; a celebration. People are wearing red, white and blue, waving huge flags in the bright sunshine, a repurposed fire engine blaring John Denver, hot girls in hot pants and cowboy hats wearing Trump flags as capes, horns tooting as cars go by. But as you get closer you hear the now familiar chants: 'Stop the Steal', 'Fox News Sucks' (Fox is reviled by Trump supporters for being the first to call Arizona for Biden), 'Count the Votes'. Sprinkled among the crowd are heavily armed men with rifles, ammunition belts and revolvers strapped across their bodies. They say they are there to protect the crowd from 'Antifa' and the far left – and are doing this as a visual display of their Second Amendment rights: the right to bear arms. And they make clear they have zero intention of giving up.

The atmosphere is edgy. Some people our crew choose not to speak to. Others, who appear friendlier, are approached. Sophie asks them if they accept the result. They look at her as if she has lost her senses. There has been no result, they tell her. The votes are still being counted. The election was corrupt. This isn't over – about that they are emphatic. It's a scene that is being played out in other locations across the United States, where angry Trump supporters are gathering. An America believing, clinging to two entirely different realities.

And Trump supporters are right in one critical respect. This hasn't been a total rejection of their man. He may have lost, but he has won more votes than he did in 2016. Though Democrats might wish it were so, this is not a repudiation of Trump and Trumpism; 2016 was not an aberration. It wasn't just a crazy, misguided holiday romance that they have now thought better of. Tens of millions of Americans watched what he did over the four years he was president, and were happy to renew the contract for another term. And that has another big knock-on for politics in Washington. Republican lawmakers will know that Trump is still wearing the sheriff's badge, and this will make them decidedly queasy about telling him he needs to accept defeat, when millions of his supporters don't and won't. He may be on the cusp of losing power, but you'd better believe he is still powerful.

17.00 The White House

I have come back to do my report for the main evening news. Just alongside our live position is the chief political correspondent for Fox

News, John Roberts, who is supremely well-connected to this administration – and a Trump favourite – and he is reporting that for all the outward defiance, some advisors, and maybe even Donald Trump himself, are beginning to accept that the President has no legal avenue, that it is done – and they need to find a way to manage this.

If Donald Trump were to open his bedroom window he would be all too aware of what is happening outside. Now even inside the White House grounds the sounds of the car horns and the celebrations can be heard clearly coming from 17th Street, H Street and Black Lives Matter Plaza. The ring of steel that's been erected around a wider than normal perimeter will keep the party goers out – but their noise and joy is infiltrating the most secure building on earth.

20.00 Wilmington, Delaware

Have the eyes of the whole world ever been on Wilmington, Delaware, before? They are tonight. Joe Biden and Kamala Harris are addressing the nation as president-elect and vice-president-elect. And after a presidency of continuous turmoil, upheaval and division this is a clear resetting of the compass. With Joe Biden at the helm, the ship of state will be steered into calmer waters. Even the setting for the speech – a car park in Wilmington, Delaware – seems to speak to the change of direction for the country.

Kamala Harris – the first woman to be VP, the first person of colour to hold the position – gives a brilliantly pitched speech. 'While I may be the first woman in this office, I will not be the last – because every little girl watching tonight sees that this is a country of possibilities.' And she continues to address the next generation: '... to the children of our country, regardless of your gender, our country has sent you a clear message: Dream with ambition, lead with conviction and see yourself in a way that others might not see you, simply because they've never seen it before. And we will applaud you every step of the way.'

The president-elect, who is a practising Roman Catholic, peppered his speech with biblical references. There was a time to build, a time to reap and a time to sow – but now was a time to heal, he told his audience – who honked their car horns appreciatively. Unity, coming together, putting aside differences, cooperation, no more demonisation, were the themes of this speech; will be the themes of his presidency. His only mention of Donald Trump is to say how disappointed his supporters must feel, and that he would be a president for *all* Americans.

But much of the speech is an implied rebuke to the current occupant of the White House. His most immediate priority would be to form a working party to deal with the coronavirus pandemic that would be driven by the science. He would fight racial injustice. Tackle climate change. He would be inclusive. Whether he'll succeed or not is another question. But there's no mistaking that he wants to chart a very different course for the – still – most powerful country in the world.

That said, how easy will it be for him to govern? The Democrats didn't do anything like as well in the Senate and House races as they had hoped and predicted. And that is going to make it much easier for Republicans to stymy Biden initiatives. There will have to be an inquest into why the Democratic Party didn't do so well in the so-called down-ballot races. But that is for another day.

There is a spectacular fireworks display at the conclusion – even eclipsing the Trump pyrotechnics at the end of the Republican Convention. The excitement is palpable among the crowd, and it's clear to see on the faces of Kamala Harris and Joe Biden.

He may be old, he may make the odd verbal slip, he may not have been the most inspiring candidate, this might have been his third attempt to win the presidency, after the best part of half a century in public life, but as I watch the scene unfold I am left with one powerful thought: whatever his shortcomings, could anyone else have beaten Donald Trump? Almost certainly not. Barack Obama argues that in politics you don't choose the moment, the moment chooses you. This is Joe Biden's moment. As Tony Blair said in 1997, it is a new dawn, is it not?

23.00 Johns Hopkins University, Baltimore

But some of the contours of this new dawn look just the same. At this famous academic institution, just an hour down the road from Wilmington, they've been compiling the most reliable coronavirus statistics for America; for the rest of the world. On 7 November over 120,000 Americans tested positive, a new and grim record.

2020 hasn't been a normal election. 2020 hasn't been a normal year.

Index

JS indicates Jon Sopel.